POINT TAKEN

POINT TAKEN

How to Write Like the World's Best Judges

Ross Guberman

OXFORD
UNIVERSITY PRESS

OXFORD
UNIVERSITY PRESS

Oxford University Press is a department of the University of Oxford. It furthers the University's objective of excellence in research, scholarship, and education by publishing worldwide.

Oxford   New York

Auckland   Cape Town   Dar es Salaam   Hong Kong   Karachi   Kuala Lumpur   Madrid
Melbourne   Mexico City   Nairobi   New Delhi   Shanghai   Taipei   Toronto

With offices in

Argentina   Austria   Brazil   Chile   Czech Republic   France   Greece   Guatemala
Hungary   Italy   Japan   Poland   Portugal   Singapore   South Korea   Switzerland
Thailand   Turkey   Ukraine   Vietnam

Oxford is a registered trademark of Oxford University Press in the UK and certain other countries.

Published in the United States of America by
Oxford University Press
198 Madison Avenue, New York, NY 10016

Library of Congress Cataloging-in-Publication Data
Guberman, Ross, author.
  Point taken : how to write like the world's best judges / Ross Guberman. — 1st edition.
      pages cm
  Includes bibliographical references and index.
  ISBN 978-0-19-026858-9 ((pbk.) : alk. paper)
  1. Legal briefs—United States. 2. Legal composition. I. Title.
  KF251.G83 2015
  808.06'634—dc23
                                                              2015004449

9 8 7 6 5 4 3 2

Printed in the United States of America on acid-free paper

Note to Readers

To Heidi, Sean, and Meghan

Contents

Introduction | xxi

PART ONE Set the Stage: The Opening | 1

Teaser Opener: Succinct and Unresolved | 3
    Jed Rakoff, *Garcia v. Bloomberg* | 4
    Lady Hale, *Dunhill v. Burgin* | 5
    Antonin Scalia, *Smith v. United States* | 6
    Michael Ponsor, *Thomas v. Consolidated Rail Corp.* | 7
    Roger Traynor, *Drennan v. Star Paving Co.* | 8
    Lord Denning, *Cummings v. Granger* | 8
    Alex Kozinski, *Flowers v. Carville* | 9
    John Roberts, *Blueford v. Arkansas* | 9
Teaser Practice Pointers | 11
Trailer Opener: Detailed and Unresolved | 12
    Richard Posner, *Cecaj v. Gonzalez* | 12
    Alex Kozinski, *Mattel v. MCA Records* | 15
    Michael Musmanno, *Schwartz v. Warwick-Phila Corp.* | 17
    Michael Kirby, *Green v. the Queen*, dissenting | 18
    D.P. Marshall, *Little Rock School Dist. v. North Little Rock School Dist.* | 19
    Learned Hand, *Cheney Bros. v. Doris Silk Corp.* | 20
    Diane Wood, *JCW Investments v. Novelty* | 21

Trailer Practice Pointers | 23

Sound Bite Opener: Succinct and Resolved | 24

    Patricia Wald, *Hubbard v. EPA* | 24

    Marsha Berzon, *Reed v. Massanari* | 25

    Benjamin Goldgar, *In re Earley* | 25

    Elena Kagan, *Florida v. Harris* | 26

    Ruth Bader Ginsburg, *United States v. Virginia* | 27

    Shira Scheindlin, *New York Magazine v. Metropolitan Transit Authority* | 28

Sound Bite Practice Pointers | 29

Op-Ed Opener: Detailed and Resolved | 30

    Beverly McLachlin, *Seaboyer v. H.M. the Queen* | 30

    John Roberts, *Attorney General's Office v. Osborne* | 32

    Ruth Bader Ginsburg, *Astrue v. Capato* | 33

    Marsha Berzon, *United States v. Trimble* | 34

    Benjamin Goldgar, *In Re Brent* | 35

    Michael Ponsor, *United States v. Watts* | 37

Op-Ed Practice Pointers | 39

PART TWO The Tale: The Facts | 41

    Robert Megarry, *In re Vandervell's Trusts (No 2)* | 42

    Lord Denning, *In re Vandervell's Trusts (No 2)* | 43

The Signal and the Noise: Cut Clutter | 44

    Benjamin Cardozo, *Palsgraf v. Long Island Rail Road* | 44

    Patricia Wald, *United States v. Morris* | 45

    Benjamin Goldgar, *In re Brent* | 48

    Jan Paulsson, *Pantechniki S.A. Contractors & Engineers (Greece) v. Republic of Albania* | 48

    Richard Posner, *University of Notre Dame v. Sebelius* | 49

    Roger Traynor, *Drennan v. Star Paving Co.* | 50

    Oliver Wendell Holmes Jr., *Baltimore & Ohio R.R. v. Goodman* | 51

    Patricia Wald, *Hubbard v. EPA* | 52

Michael Ponsor, *United States v. Binette* | 52
Brett Kavanaugh, *Belize Social Development Ltd. v. Government of Belize*, dissenting | 54
Edward Carnes, *Ash v. Tyson* | 54
Alex Kozinski, *Mattel, Inc. v. MCA Records, Inc.* | 55
D.P. Marshall, Jr., *Little Rock School Dist. v. North Little Rock School Dist.* | 56
Big Picture: Add Background | 57
Shine a Light: Emphasize Key Facts | 59
Michael McHugh, *Green v. The Queen* | 61
Michael Kirby, *Green v. The Queen*, dissenting | 62
Do You See What I See: Adopt a Narrative Voice | 67
Diane Wood, *JCW Investments v. Novelty, Inc.* | 67
Richard Posner (sitting by designation), *Apple v. Motorola* | 68
Lord Denning, *Cummings v. Granger* | 69
Clean-Up: Enhance Visual Appeal | 73
Frank Easterbrook, *FTC v. QT, Inc.* | 73
Benjamin Goldgar, *In Re Brent* | 74
Michael Ponsor, *Angiodynamics, Inc. v. Biolitec, Inc.* | 76
Michael Kirby, *Green v. The Queen* | 76
Practice Pointers for Fact Statements | 77

PART THREE The Meat: The Legal Analysis | 79

Overview: The Skeleton | 81
Overview: In the Flesh | 83
Example: *Snyder v. Phelps* | 83
John Roberts, *Snyder v. Phelps* (Section II) | 84
With You in Spirit: Paragraphs as Dialogues | 97
Shira Scheindlin, *United States v. Awadallah* | 99
Beverly McLachlin, *Schmeiser v. Monsanto* | 101
Marsha Berzon, *Minasyan v. Mukasey* | 102

Michael Ponsor, *United States v. Watts* | 105

Frank Easterbrook, *Matter of Sinclair* | 106

Antonin Scalia, *Scott v. Harris* | 108

Order out of Chaos: Internal Organizational Devices | 108

A. Headings | 108

Shira Scheindlin, *New York Magazine v. Metropolitan Transit Authority* | 109

Beverly McLachlin, *Schmeiser v. Monsanto Canada Inc.* | 110

Lord Sumption, *Cox v. Ergo Versicherung AG* | 111

B. "Umbrella" Introductions | 111

Benjamin Goldgar, *In re Earley* | 111

Beverly McLachlin, *Seaboyer v. The Queen* | 112

Roger Traynor, *Drennan v. Star Paving Co.* | 113

C. Bulleted and Numbered Lists | 114

Antonin Scalia, *Scott v. Harris* | 114

D.P. Marshall, *Little Rock School Dist. v. North Little Rock School Dist.* | 116

Benjamin Goldgar, *In Re Brent* | 117

Patrick Schiltz, *Shiraz Hookah, LLC v. City of Minneapolis* | 118

Lord Sumption, *Prest v. Petrodel Resources Ltd.* | 119

O. Rogeriee Thompson, *United States v. Seng Tan* | 120

Me, Too: Analogizing | 121

Jed Rakoff, *Garcia v. Bloomberg* | 121

Benjamin Goldgar, *In re Brent* | 122

D.P. Marshall, *Tucker v. Southwestern Energy Co.* | 123

Jed Rakoff, *23-34 94th St. Grocery v. N.Y. City Bd.* | 123

Patrick Schiltz, *Shiraz Hookah, LLC v. City of Minneapolis* | 124

Patrick Schiltz, *Newton v. Walker* | 125

Not Here, Not Now: Distinguishing | 127

Patricia Wald, *Hubbard v. EPA* | 127

Alex Kozinski, *Mattel v. MCA Records* | 131

Shira Scheindlin, *New York Magazine v. Metropolitan Transit Authority* | 132

Richard Posner, *Indiana Harbor Belt R.R. v. American Cyanamid Co.* | 133

Learned Hand, *Cheney Bros. v. Doris Silk Corp.* | 135

As an Aside: Parentheticals | 136

Michael Ponsor, *Gatti v. Nat'l Union Fire Ins.* | 136

Patricia Wald, *Steffan v. Perry*, dissenting | 137

Shira Scheindlin, *Clark v. Perez* | 137

John Roberts, *Messerschmidt v. Millender* | 138

Michael Kirby, *Green v. The Queen*, dissenting | 139

Diane Wood, *Tarpley v. Allen County, Indiana* | 140

Lead 'Em On: Quoting without Tears | 140

Frank Easterbrook, *In re Sinclair* | 142

Alex Kozinski, *Mattel v. MCA Records* | 143

Michael Kirby, *Green v. The Queen*, dissenting | 144

Beverly McLachlin, *R. v. Keegstra*, dissenting | 144

Antonin Scalia, *Scott v. Harris* | 145

John Paul Stevens, *Scott v. Harris*, dissenting | 146

Troubled Waters: The Footnoters' Dilemma | 147

Antonin Scalia, *Sykes v. United States*, dissenting | 148

Patricia Wald, *Steffan v. Perry*, dissenting | 149

Michael Ponsor, *United States v. Watts* | 150

Patrick Schiltz, *Newton v. Walker* | 151

Ruth Bader Ginsburg, *United States v. Virginia* | 152

Practice Pointers for the Analysis | 153

PART FOUR The Words: Style Must-Haves | 157

Sentence-Level Strategies | 163

A. What a Breeze: Direct, Natural, "Impure" Diction | 163

Elena Kagan, *Arizona Free Enterprise Club v. Bennett*, dissenting | 165

Elena Kagan, *Arizona Free Enterprise Club v. Bennett*, dissenting | 165

Elena Kagan, *Kloeckner v. Solis* | 166

Elena Kagan, *Scialabba v. Cuellar de Osorio* | 166

Lord Denning, *Thornton v. Shoe Lane Parking* | 167

Richard Posner, *United States v. Gutman* | 167

Frank Easterbrook, *In Re Sinclair* | 168

John Roberts, *Rumsfeld v. Forum for Academic & Inst. Rights* | 168

John Roberts, *FCC v. AT&T* | 169

John Roberts, *Rancho Viejo v* Norton, dissenting from a denial of *en banc* rehearing | 170

Benjamin Goldgar, *In Re Brent* | 171

O. Rogeriee Thompson, *United States v. Seng Tan* | 172

B. The Starting Gate: Short Sentence Openers | 174

Edward Carnes, *Hamilton v. Southland Christian School* | 174

Oliver Wendell Holmes Jr., *Abrams v. United States*, dissenting | 174

Beverly McLachlin, *Seaboyer v. H.M. The Queen* | 176

John Roberts, *Already LLC v. Nike, Inc.* | 176

O. Rogeriee Thompson, *United States v. Seng Tan* | 177

Benjamin Goldgar, *In re Earley* | 177

D. P. Marshall, *Little Rock School Dist. v. North Little Rock School Dist.* | 177

Lord Sumption, *Prest v. Petrodel* | 178

Patrick Schiltz, *Newton v. Walker* | 178

Lord Hoffmann, *A(FC) and others (FC) v. Secretary of State for the Home Department*, dissenting | 178

Elena Kagan, *Florida v. Harris* | 179

C. Size Matters: The Pithy Sentence | 179

Frank Easterbrook, *United States v. Dumont* | 181

Edward Carnes, *Southland Christian School v. Hamilton* | 181

Lord Denning, *Thornton v. Shoe Lane Parking* | 182

Lady Hale, *Dunhill v. Burgin* | 182

Lord Sumption, *Prest v. Petrodel* | 183

  D. P. Marshall, *Little Rock School Dist. v. North Little Rock School Dist.* | 183

  Elena Kagan, *Florida v. Harris* | 184

  John Roberts, *Attorney General's Office v. Osborne* | 184

  D. P. Marshall, *Tucker v. Southwestern Energy Co.* | 185

  D. Talk to Me: Variety in Sentence Form | 185

  D.P. Marshall, *Tucker v. Southwestern Energy Co.* | 186

  Lord Hoffmann, *A(FC) and others (FC) v. Secretary of State for the Home Department,* dissenting | 186

  Beverly McLachlin, *Seaboyer v. H.M. The Queen* | 186

  Richard Posner, *Cecaj v. Gonzalez* | 187

  Antonin Scalia, *Scott v. Harris* | 187

  Alex Kozinski, *Mattel v. MCA Records* | 187

  John Roberts, *Attorney General's Office v. Osborne* | 188

  E. Parallel Lives: Parallel Constructions | 188

  Patrick Schiltz, *Newton v. Walker* | 190

  Oliver Wendell Holmes Jr., *Abrams v. United States* | 190

  Lord Hoffmann, *A(FC) and others (FC) v. Secretary of State for the Home Department,* dissenting | 190

  Frank Easterbrook, *In re Sinclair* | 191

  Oliver Wendell Homes Jr., *United States v. Schwimmer* | 191

  Louis Brandeis, *Whitney v. California,* concurring | 192

  Robert Jackson, *Zorach v. Clauson,* dissenting | 192

  Frank Easterbrook, *In re Sinclair* | 193

  Lady Hale, *Dunhill v. Burgin* | 193

  Learned Hand, *NLRB v. Federbush Co.* | 193

  Lord Sumption, *Petroleo Brasileiro S.A. v. E.N.E. Kos 1 Ltd.* | 194

  Benjamin Goldgar, *In re Brent* | 194

  Antonin Scalia, *Scott v. Harris* | 195

  Michael Musmanno, *Schwartz v. Warwick-Phila Corp.* | 196

Word-Level Strategies | 196

  A. Lean and Mean: Words and Phrases to Avoid | 197

    Interlude: 16 Key Edits | 197

      Edward Carnes, *Ash v. Tyson* | 197

Lord Denning, *Cummings v. Granger* | 198

Michael Kirby, *Wurridjal v. Commonwealth of Australia* | 198

Benjamin Goldgar, *In re Earley* | 198

Michael Kirby, *Wurridjal v. Commonwealth of Australia* | 198

Ruth Bader Ginsburg, *Astrue v. Capato* | 199

Frank Easterbrook, *In re Sinclair* | 199

John Roberts, *Snyder v. Phelps* | 199

Patrick Schiltz, *Newton v. Walker* | 200

Benjamin Goldgar, *In re Earley* | 200

Beverly McLachlin, *Seaboyer v. H.M. the Queen* | 200

Lord Hoffmann, *A(FC) and others (FC) v. Secretary of State for the Home Department,* dissenting | 200

Edward Carnes, *Hamilton v. Southland Christian School* | 201

Shira Scheindlin, *New York Magazine v. Metropolitan Transit Authority* | 201

Benjamin Goldgar, *In re Brent* | 201

Lord Denning, *Cummings v. Granger* | 202

Benjamin Goldgar, *In re Brent* | 202

Lord Denning, *Lloyds Bank Ltd. v. Bundy* | 202

Lady Hale, *Dunhill v. Burgin* | 202

B. Zingers: Evocative Verbs | 203

John Roberts, *Attorney General's Office v. Osborne* | 203

Oliver Wendell Holmes Jr., *McFarland v. American Sugar Refining Co.* | 204

Robert Jackson, *Zorach v. Clauson,* dissenting | 204

Lord Denning, *Lazarus Estates Ltd. v. Beasley* | 204

Diane Wood, *JCW Investments, Inc. v. Novelty, Inc.* | 205

Alex Kozinski, *United States v. Alvarez,* concurring | 205

Antonin Scalia, *Scott v. Harris* | 206

John Roberts, *Nike v. Already LLC* | 206

Robert Jackson, *Zorach v. Clauson,* dissenting | 207

John Paul Stevens, *Attorney General's Office v. Osborne,*
dissenting | 207
O. Rogeriee Thompson, *United States v. Seng Tan* | 207
Frank Easterbrook, *In re Sinclair* | 208
John Roberts, *League of United Latin Am. Citizens v. Perry,*
dissenting | 208
Beverly McLachlin, *Seaboyer v. The Queen* | 208
Interlude: 55 Zinger Verbs | 209
C. A Dash of Style: The Dash | 210
John Paul Stevens, *Attorney General's Office v. Osborne,*
dissenting | 210
Patrick Schiltz, *Newton v. Walker* | 210
Frank Easterbrook, *In re Sinclair* | 211
Beverly McLachlin, *Seaboyer v. H.M. The Queen* | 211
Benjamin Goldgar, *In re Earley* | 211
Alex Kozinski, *United States v. Alvarez,* concurring | 212
Antonin Scalia, *Romer v. Evans,* dissenting | 212
Frank Easterbrook, *United States v. Bradley* | 212
Louis Brandeis, *Olmstead v. United States,* dissenting | 212
Lord Denning, *Thornton v. Shoe Lane Parking* | 213
Interlude: the Hyphen | 213
O. Rogeriee Thompson, *United States v. Seng Tan* | 213
Patrick Schiltz, *Newton v. Walker* | 213
Lord Sumption, *Prest v. Petrodel* | 214
D. P. Marshall, *Cunningham v. Loma Systems* | 214
Antonin Scalia, *Scott v. Harris* | 214
Antonin Scalia, *Stenberg v. Carhart,* dissenting | 215
D. Good Bedfellows: The Semicolon | 215
Frank Easterbrook, *FTC v. QT, Inc.* | 215
John Paul Stevens, *Attorney General's Office v. Osborne,*
dissenting | 216
Patrick Schiltz, *Newton v. Walker* | 216
Learned Hand, *Cheney Bros. v. Doris Silk Corp.* | 216
Michael Kirby, *Green v. The Queen,* dissenting | 217

E. Drum Roll: The Colon | 218

 Beverley McLachlin, *Schmeiser v. Monsanto* | 218

 Lord Denning, *Thornton v. Shoe Lane Parking* | 218

 Alex Kozinski, *Mattel v. MCA Records* | 218

 Antonin Scalia, *Romer v. Evans*, dissenting | 219

 Jan Paulsson, *Pantechniki v. Albania* | 219

F. Take Me by the Hand: Seamless Transitions | 219

 Richard Posner, *Cecaj v. Gonzalez* | 221

 Patricia Wald, *Hubbard v. EPA* | 221

 Lady Hale, *Dunhill v. Burgin* | 222

 Patrick Schiltz, *Shiraz Hookah LLC v. City of Minneapolis* | 223

 Benjamin Goldgar, *In re Brent* | 224

 Interlude: 135 Transition Words and Phrases | 225

G. Bridge the Gap: Linked Paragraphs | 228

 Beverly McLachlin, *Seaboyer v. H.M. the Queen* | 228

 John Paul Stevens, *Attorney General's Office v. Osborne*, dissenting | 229

 D. P. Marshall, *Tucker v. Southwestern Energy Co.* | 229

 John Roberts, *Attorney General's Office v. Osborne* | 230

 Benjamin Goldgar, *In re Brent* | 230

 O. Rogeriee Thompson, *United States v. Seng Tan* | 231

 Lord Sumption, *Petroleo Brasileiro S.A. v. E.N.E. Kos 1 Ltd.* | 232

Practice Pointers for Style Must-Haves | 233

 Sentence Strategies | 233

 Word Strategies | 233

PART FIVE *The Words*: "Nice-to-Haves" in Style | 235

It Is What It Is: Metaphors | 237

 Oliver Wendell Holmes Jr., *New York Trust Co. v. Eisner* | 238

 Oliver Wendell Holmes Jr., *Towne v. Eisner* | 238

Oliver Wendell Holmes Jr., *Rock Island A. & L. R. Co.*
v. United States | 238
Oliver Wendell Holmes Jr., *Bain Peanut Co. v. Pinson* | 238
Oliver Wendell Holmes Jr., *United States v. Abrams*,
dissenting | 239
Robert Jackson, *West Virginia State Bd. of Education*
v. Barnette | 239
Louis Brandeis, *New State Ice Co. v Liebmann*,
dissenting | 240
John Roberts, *Virginia Office for Protection & Advocacy*
v. Stewart, dissenting | 240
Antonin Scalia, *Webster v. Reproductive Health Services*,
concurring | 241
Antonin Scalia, *Lee v. Weisman*, dissenting | 241
Learned Hand, *Harrison v. United States* | 242
Learned Hand, *NLRB v. Federbush Co.* | 242
As If: Similes | 243
Richard Posner, *Singletary v. Continental Illinois Nat'l Bank &*
Trust Co. | 243
Robert Jackson, *Edwards v. California* | 243
Robert Jackson, *Korematsu v. United States*,
dissenting | 244
Antonin Scalia, *Lamb's Chapel v. Center Moriches Union Free*
School District, concurring | 244
Brett Kavanaugh, *Belize Social Development Ltd.*
v. Government of Belize, dissenting | 245
Richard Posner, *Mayo v. Lane* | 245
John Roberts, *Brigham City v. Stuart* | 246
That Reminds Me: Examples and Analogies | 247
Oliver Wendell Holmes Jr., *Schenck v. United States* | 247
Frank Easterbrook, *Doe v. Elmbrook School Dist.* | 247
Diane Wood, *JCW Investments, Inc. v. Novelty, Inc.* | 248
Richard Posner, *Cecaj v. Gonzalez* | 248
Alex Kozinski, *Mattel v. MCA Records* | 248

Alex Kozinski, *United States v. Alvarez*, concurring | 249
Frank Easterbrook, *FTC v. QT, Inc.* | 251
Elena Kagan, *Florida v. Jardines*, concurring | 252
Elena Kagan, *Arizona Free Enterprise Club v. Bennett*, dissenting | 253
Elena Kagan, *Arizona Christian School Tuition Org. v. Winn*, dissenting | 254

Treasure Trove: Literary and Cultural References | 255
Diane Wood, *Ritter v. Ross* | 255
Antonin Scalia, *Smith v. United States* | 256
John Roberts, *Already LLC v. Nike* | 256
Oliver Wendell Holmes Jr., *Lochner v. New York*, dissenting | 257
Lord Denning, *The Siskina* | 257
Lord Hoffmann, *A(FC) and others (FC) v. Secretary of State for the Home Department*, dissenting | 258
Antonin Scalia, *Coy v. Iowa* | 258
Ruth Bader Ginsburg, *Shelby County v. Holder*, dissenting | 259
Richard Posner, *Albright v. Oliver* | 260
Frank Easterbrook, *Federal Trade Commission v. QT, Inc.* | 260
Antonin Scalia, *National Endowment for Arts v. Finley*, concurring | 261
Antonin Scalia, *Barnes v. Glen Theatre, Inc.*, concurring | 261
John Roberts, *Already LLC v. Nike* | 262
Elena Kagan, *Scialabba v. Cuellar de Osorio* | 262
John Roberts, *Sprint Comm. Co. L.P. v. APCC Servs. Inc.*, dissenting | 262
John Roberts, *Pennsylvania v. Nathan Dunlap*, dissenting from denial of *certiorari* | 263

That's Classic: Rhetorical Devices | 264
John Roberts, *Shelby County v. Holder* | 264
John Roberts, *Parents Involved in Community Schools v. Seattle* | 265

John Roberts, *Already LLC v. Nike* | 265
Benjamin Cardozo, *People v. Defore* | 265
John Roberts, *Morse v. Frederick* | 266
Robert Jackson, *Brown v. Allen,* concurring | 266
Robert Jackson, *American Communications Associate v. Douds* | 266
Robert Jackson, *Zorach v. Clauson*, dissenting | 266
Benjamin Cardozo, *Berkovitz v. Arbib & Houlberg* | 267
Robert Jackson, *Thomas v. Collins* | 267
Practice Pointers for Style Nice-to-Haves | 268

PART SIX Dissents: The Road Not Traveled | 269

A Sordid Tale: Wrong on the Facts | 272
Robert Jackson, *Chicago v. Terminiello*, dissenting | 273
Richard Posner, *Johnson v. Phelan*, dissenting | 274
Antonin Scalia, *Romer v. Evans*, dissenting | 275
Ruth Bader Ginsburg, *National Federation of Independent Business v. Sebelius*, dissenting | 276
Piercing the Veil: Wrong on the Law | 277
John Paul Stevens, *Citizens United v. Federal Elections Commission*, dissenting | 278
Antonin Scalia, *Morrison v. Olson*, dissenting | 279
Diane Wood, *A Woman's Choice-East Side Women's Clinic v. Newman*, dissenting | 279
Brett Kavanaugh, *In re Sealed Case*, dissenting | 280
Elena Kagan, *Arizona Free Enterprise Club's Freedom Club PAC v. Bennett*, dissenting | 282
Ruth Bader Ginsburg, *Bush v. Gore*, dissenting | 283
John Roberts, *Miller v. Alabama*, dissenting | 284
Robert Jackson, *Korematsu v. United States*, dissenting | 286
John Paul Stevens, *Citizens United v. Federal Election Campaign*, dissenting | 287

Elena Kagan, *Arizona Christian School Tuition Org. v. Winn*, dissenting | 288

Get Real: Wrong on the Policy | 290

  A. Anti-Elitist | 290

    John Stevens, *Citizens United v. Federal Election Commission*, dissenting | 291

    Alex Kozinski, *United States v. Pineda-Moreno*, dissenting from a denial of rehearing | 292

    Robert Jackson, *Terminiello v. City of Chicago*, dissenting | 294

    Oliver Wendell Holmes Jr., *Lochner v. New York*, dissenting | 295

    Antonin Scalia, *Lawrence v. Texas*, dissenting | 297

  B. Anti-Populist | 298

    Lord Hoffmann, *A(FC) and others (FC) v. Secretary of State for the Home Department*, dissenting | 299

    Lord Sumption, *Societe Generale v. Geys*, dissenting | 300

    Michael Kirby, *Wurridjal v. Commonwealth of Australia*, dissenting | 301

    Michael Kirby, *Kartinyeri v. Commonwealth*, dissenting | 302

    Robert Jackson, *Terminiello v. City of Chicago*, dissenting | 303

    John Paul Stevens, *Attorney General's Office v. Osborne*, dissenting | 304

    Ruth Bader Ginsburg, *Shelby County v. Holder*, dissenting | 305

Practice Pointers for Dissents | 305

PART SEVEN Appendices | 309

Biographies | 310

Practice Pointers | 323

NOTES | 331

TABLE OF CASES | 335

INDEX | 341

Introduction

"Who would be so bold as to write on the writing of judgments?" asks Justice Michael Kirby of the High Court of Australia. "As many lawyers as there are, so many opinions and more exist about what makes a good judgment."[1]

Going bold on judicial opinions is the spark behind this book. And I have no qualms about doing so. Although the State stamps its imprimatur on even the most mundane decision, opinion-writing has long been a free-for-all, if not a "Sahara," as Justice Benjamin Cardozo once put it. To help save judges from permanent exile to the desert, this guide will transform the work of some of the world's best judges into a concrete step-by-step method accessible to judges at all levels and across jurisdictions.

In some ways, extracting a strategy for great opinion writing was harder than my earlier work dissecting great written advocacy. In many countries, publicly available decisions are rare. Academics commenting on the bench care far more about jurisprudential theory than jurisprudential craft. And judges almost never get feedback on their writing. For all these reasons, the world's judges face fundamental fuzziness on the end game: For whom is a judgment intended? And whose voice should it adopt?

Judge Learned Hand once mused about these questions in a conversation with his clerk, Archibald Cox, who would become the famed

Watergate prosecutor. "To whom am I responsible?" Hand asked. "No one can fire me. No one can dock my pay. Even those nine bozos in Washington, who sometimes reverse me, can't make me decide as they want. Everyone should be responsible to someone. To whom am I responsible?" Hand paused and then gestured over to a stack of law books. "To those books about us! That's to whom I am responsible!"

And yet how on earth do you address a judicial opinion to "law books"? Even judges need an audience. But which one? Should you address your opinions to the winning party? The losing party? Counsel? An appellate court? As-yet-unnamed judges deciding future disputes? Law students? Academics? The broader bar? The press? The legislature? The general public? Or, as Justice Kirby has put it, the judge's "own conscience"?[2] Do dissents have different audiences? And when it comes to "great opinions," does your intended audience even matter as much as your core writing style, skills, and strategies?

Speaking of style, some commentators have pondered the interplay between an opinion's "voice" and what it projects about the judge's role in the judiciary and the body politic. Dichotomies are all the rage. The great scholar Karl Llewellyn contrasted the *Grand Style* of opinion-writing, which breezes along like an essay, with scant authorities and many nods to pragmatism, with the *Formal Style*, which is wooden and riddled with strings of citations. More recently, Judge Richard Posner, borrowing from Robert Penn Warren's famous formulation about poetry, divided opinion-writing styles into the *Pure* and the *Impure*. Other style splits in the literature include "personal" versus "impersonal," "authoritative" versus "exploratory," and "magisterial" versus "personal."

These distinctions are no mere debaters' points. They strike at the heart of whether a judge should write in a restrained, institutional, authoritative voice that some might call antiseptic and imperious—or in a candid, pensive, expressive voice that some might call maudlin and self-aggrandizing. And that debate itself seeps into political questions about whether judges should be formalists, realists, pragmatists, or all of the above.

And yet as unsettled as these core questions might seem, the bench and bar tend to nominate the same names for the pantheon of great judicial writing. By delving into the work of these famous figures, we can reverse-engineer the best practices. In the modern United Kingdom, for example, Lord Denning is considered peerless. So where did he come down on these debates? As for intended audience, he appears to conjure up an uninitiated but curious reader who is not a party to the case. And as for voice and style, I'll let him speak for himself:

> No matter how sound your reasoning, if it is presented in a dull and turgid setting, your hearers—or your readers—will turn aside. They will not stop to listen. They will flick over the pages. But if it is presented in a lively and attractive setting, they will sit up and take notice. They will listen as if spellbound. They will read you with engrossment.[3]

Reader engrossment and engagement will indeed be our guiding lights in these pages. Our tour will be fueled with example after example. I'll strive to be as granular and realistic as possible, because I've interacted with enough judges and clerks to know how much pressure they feel to churn out the best possible product in a modest amount of time. But for inspirational purposes, I've also included some of the most enduring passages in opinion-writing history, just in case a future Oliver Wendell Holmes happens to be reading my book.

In Part 1, I'll share a four-quadrant system for crafting effective and efficient openings that set the stage for what's to come. We'll discuss the pros and cons of whether you should resolve the legal issues up front and whether you should sacrifice taut syllogistic openings in the name of richness and nuance.

In Part 2, we'll turn to the facts. I will cover strategies for pruning clutter, adding background, emphasizing key points, adopting a narrative voice, and guiding the reader through visual cues.

Part 3 dives into the heart of the legal analysis. Focusing on structure and flow, we'll cover techniques for organizing the discussion at the macro level. Then we'll move on to special considerations for using headings, marshaling authorities, including or avoiding footnotes, and finessing transitions.

Part 4 is about what I call "Must Haves" in style. I'll share a host of edits at the word and sentence level that will add punch and interest, making your prose more vivid, varied, confident, and enjoyable.

Part 5, for the stylistically ambitious, will delve into "Nice to Haves" in style—the sorts of things that turn "great judicial writing" into just "great writing": metaphors, similes, examples, analogies, allusions, and rhetorical figures.

Finally, in Part 6, we will turn to the thorny problem of dissents. I'll cover the best practices for dissents that hinge on facts, dissents that hinge on doctrine, and dissents that hinge on policy.

In the appendix, you'll find a checklist of practice pointers along with biographies of the 34 featured judges.

Now a word about method. In choosing which judges to profile, I cast a wide net, but without any pretense that it's possible to identify "the world's greatest judges" definitively or that great judges are all great writers or vice versa. For practical reasons, I've limited my focus to common-law judges who write opinions in English. I also concede a bias in favor of U.S. judges and particularly U.S. federal judges. One reason such judges dominate the book is that I'm a product of the U.S. legal system myself. But other reasons matter even more. The opinions of U.S. judges, including lower-court judges, are readily available online. U.S. judges play an outsized role in our tripartite government, with their decisions often splashed above the fold on the front page and trumpeted and dissected on cable news. The celebrity-driven legal culture in the United States has many ill effects, but it also spurs the nation's most-ambitious judges to perfect their craft and to develop a powerful voice. Although many American judges are lackluster writers, endless scrutiny also prompts many other judges to embrace the highest possible editing standards. And finally, U.S. judicial culture, for better or for worse, also seeps into much of the rest of the world. In fact, when I read articles and speeches about judicial writing from abroad, the examples and quotations often come from U.S. judges, and when I've taught judges abroad myself, I've encountered a similar fascination.

I also admit a bias in favor of personal writing—or what Judge Posner calls the *Impure* style—because that's what students, lawyers, and the public all appear to prefer. When in my seminars I share excerpts from opinions that are a bit colorful, lawyers often love them, but other judges not always so much. Many of these suspicious judges appear to put opinions into two categories: idiosyncratic and attention-grabbing on the one hand, or clear and straightforward, on the other. But most opinions are neither. Draining an opinion of personality and voice does not necessarily render it easy to follow. That's why I devote so much of this book to organization and analysis.

So who made the final cut? You'll find familiar names like Lord Denning, Holmes, Learned Hand, Posner, and Scalia. But you'll also discover judges who are unknown, even to other judges, but who have exceptional writing skills worthy of your review. Many of these unsung judges are at the trial level. All things equal, I've favored contemporary judges over the inspiring figures of the past, so don't look for Lord Bramwell or Chief Justice Marshall here. I've sought a bit of diversity. And I've also taken pains to present a broad swath of opinions and judgments at many procedural stages and in many practice areas.

That said, I know that some readers might ask "What about so-and-so?" I am the first to agree that I could have easily included scores of additional names, but at a certain point I had to keep the list manageable. Think of those who populate the book as a mere cross-section.

I learned from revising my *Point Made: How to Write Like the Nation's Top Advocates* that some readers crave nitty-gritty stylistic and grammatical analysis, and other readers can't be bothered. So in the name of diplomacy, I've scattered style notes across the bottom of many of these pages. Devour them or ignore them as you wish.

I've also bolded key parts of some of the excerpts for your easy reference. And I've cut most of the citations.

This project was both daunting and exhilarating. I'd especially like to thank my crack Legal Writing Pro team of Daniel Baker, Nichole Best, Sue Hickey, Gale Sterling, and especially Karin Ciano. I'm grateful for the comments of my outside readers: Steve Armstrong, Martha Blue, Ward Farnsworth, Matt Gallaway, Todd Henderson, Joe Kimble, Brian Porto, Wayne Schiess, Mark Tushnet, and Sonja West. Several judge friends offered insights as well. Thanks as always to Heidi and to my children, Sean and Meghan. And I'd also like to thank both the Federal Judicial Center for putting me in front of so many judges and the many other judges around the world I've come to know.

If you have any comments about the book, I'd love to hear from you at Ross@LegalWritingPro.com. Happy reading.

Part 1

Set the Stage

The Opening

Teaser Opener: Succinct and Unresolved 3
    Jed Rakoff, *Garcia v. Bloomberg* 4
    Lady Hale, *Dunhill v. Burgin* 5
    Antonin Scalia, *Smith v. United States* 6
    Michael Ponsor, *Thomas v. Consolidated Rail Corp.* 7
    Roger Traynor, *Drennan v. Star Paving Co.* 8
    Lord Denning, *Cummings v. Granger* 8
    Alex Kozinski, *Flowers v. Carville* 9
    John Roberts, *Blueford v. Arkansas* 9
Teaser Practice Pointers 11
Trailer Opener: Detailed and Unresolved 12
    Richard Posner, *Cecaj v. Gonzalez* 12
    Alex Kozinski, *Mattel v. MCA Records* 15
    Michael Musmanno, *Schwartz v. Warwick-Phila Corp.* 17
    Michael Kirby, *Green v. the Queen*, dissenting 18
    D.P. Marshall, *Little Rock School Dist. v. North Little Rock School Dist.* 19
    Learned Hand, *Cheney Bros. v. Doris Silk Corp.* 20
    Diane Wood, *JCW Investments v. Novelty* 21
Trailer Practice Pointers 23
Sound Bite Opener: Succinct and Resolved 24
    Patricia Wald, *Hubbard v. EPA* 24
    Marsha Berzon, *Reed v. Massanari* 25
    Benjamin Goldgar, *In re Earley* 25
    Elena Kagan, *Florida v. Harris* 26
    Ruth Bader Ginsburg, *United States v. Virginia* 27

Shira Scheindlin, *New York Magazine v. Metropolitan Transit Authority* 28

Sound Bite Practice Pointers 29

Op-Ed Opener: Detailed and Resolved 30

Beverly McLachlin, *Seaboyer v. H.M. the Queen* 30

John Roberts, *Attorney General's Office v. Osborne* 32

Ruth Bader Ginsburg, *Astrue v. Capato* 33

Marsha Berzon, *United States v. Trimble* 34

Benjamin Goldgar, *In Re Brent* 35

Michael Ponsor, *United States v. Watts* 37

Op-Ed Practice Pointers 39

The start of an opinion is your first chance to shine. The best openings soar above the formulaic, granting readers the gift of a self-contained snapshot that's helpful, and even enjoyable. The tone you adopt and the details you stress in your opening lines also say a lot about your approach to the craft of judging.

Although there's no pat formula here, judges with a knack for writing strong openings appear to have thought a lot about three key questions: (1) Should I simply share the issue the court faced, or should I also reveal how the court resolved it up front? (2) How much detail should I provide about the dispute and about the key facts and reasons supporting my decision? (3) How can I engage readers who are not parties to the case?

Unlike the families in *Anna Karenina*, happy introductions are not all happy in the same way. Some could fit on a bumper sticker; others spill onto several pages. Some resolve the issue before the court by the end of the first paragraph; others create an aura of mystery, prompting the reader to peer into the judge's mind before finding out Who Done It on the last page.

All these choices force trade-offs. A short opening has the appeal of a syllogism, but it can oversimplify or even skew the issues in a way that assumes what the opinion seeks to prove. Longer openings offer more context, but they can easily overwhelm the uninitiated.

So too with giving away the ending. Announcing the conclusion up front saves the reader time, but it can also make the analysis sound like an afterthought, or perhaps even preordained. As with catchy but facile newspaper headlines, readers are let off the hook: some will find no need to read on and may be left with only a superficial understanding. And yet as much as the "Leave 'Em Hanging" crowd believes that hiding the ball will inspire readers to stick with the court's step-by-step reasoning, impatient readers will likely skip right to the end anyway.

Of course, you probably already have a position on these issues, and you may even be bound by the practices of your court and your jurisdiction. So let's look at the best practices for each of these four quadrants for openings: (1) *Teaser* Openings: succinct and unresolved, (2) *Trailer* Openings: detailed and unresolved, (3) *Sound Bite* Openings: succinct spoilers, and (4) *Op-Ed* Openings: detailed spoilers.

Teaser Opener: Succinct and Unresolved

The *Teaser* approach—a short, brisk statement of the issue before the court—piques readers' curiosity. It avoids confusion in favor of streamlined prose, but at the risk of oversimplifying the issues and perhaps "stacking the deck" by wording a complex legal problem in a way that makes its resolution seem too pat.

The *Teaser* opening avoids sharing any conclusions up front, a practice promoted by Seventh Circuit Judge Richard Posner. When a decision is announced at the outset, Posner believes, "the impression conveyed is that what follows is simply the rationalization of a result reached on undisclosed grounds."[1] He thus recommends delaying the inevitable until your full analysis has been laid bare.

Let's start with a model *Teaser* opening from a trial court. In the example below, trial judge Jed Rakoff must decide whether to dismiss the civil rights claims of *Occupy Wall Street* protesters arrested for blocking traffic on the Brooklyn Bridge. Here's how he sets the stage:

> **Jed Rakoff, *Garcia v. Bloomberg***
>
> What a huge debt this nation owes to its "troublemakers." From Thomas Paine to Martin Luther King, Jr., they have forced us to focus on problems we would prefer to downplay or ignore. Yet it is often only with hindsight that we can distinguish those troublemakers who brought us to our senses from those who were simply ... troublemakers. Prudence, and respect for the constitutional rights to free speech and free association, therefore dictate that the legal system cut all non-violent protesters a fair amount of slack.
>
> These observations are prompted by the instant lawsuit, in which a putative class of 700 or so "Occupy Wall Street" protesters contend they were unlawfully arrested while crossing the Brooklyn Bridge on October 1, 2011. More narrowly, the pending motion to dismiss raises the issue of whether a reasonable observer would conclude that the police who arrested the protesters had led the protesters to believe that they could lawfully march on the Brooklyn Bridge's vehicular roadway.

Judge Rakoff's terrific opening lines pit the protestors' rights of free speech and assembly against the public's desire for order, not to mention its need to navigate the Big Apple's roadways. By the end of the second paragraph, Rakoff has squeezed the saga into a single-sentence narrative, stated the legal issue clearly, and, through his references to Paine and King and his play on "troublemakers," shown us why the case is about far more than just a blocked bridge. And yet he also leaves us hanging, *Teaser*-style. Although the "fair amount of slack" language suggests that he will find in the protestors' favor, he actually ends up dismissing their claims.*

---

* I appreciate the all-important short, thematic opening line, the crisp "Yet it is often only through" transition, and the smooth "These observations" bridge between the end of the first paragraph and the beginning of the next. But let's

Rakoff provides a great model for a single-issue case. But what if you face several issues? On the other side of the Atlantic, Lady Hale of the U.K. Supreme Court streamlines a complex civil-rights case by conceding that the issues are difficult. She then lists those issues in a clear numbered format. In an opening this taut, something has to give, of course, and so unlike Rakoff she forgoes any semblance of a narrative:

Lady Hale, *Dunhill v. Burgin*

There are two issues in this case, both of them simple to state, but neither of them simple to answer. First, what is the test for deciding whether a person lacks the mental capacity to conduct legal proceedings on her own behalf (in which case the Civil Procedure Rules require that she have a litigation friend to conduct the proceedings for her)? Second, what happens if legal proceedings are settled or compromised without it being recognised that one of the parties lacked that capacity (so that she did not have the benefit of a litigation friend and the settlement was not approved by the court as also required by the [Civil Procedure Rules])? Can matters be re-opened long after the event or does the normal rule of English law apply, which is that a contract made by a person who lacks capacity is valid unless the other party to the contract knew or ought to have known that she lacked that capacity in which case it is voidable (the rule in *Imperial Loan Co Ltd v Stone*)?

Styling the issues as direct questions offers the added psychological benefit of making the court look open-minded and curious.*

---

add a "that" after "contend" for clarity, and let's change the stale "instant lawsuit" language to "this suit."

* "Without it being recognised" is a good example of why the passive voice can confuse: If the proceedings are settled pre-trial, who would be doing the recognizing?

Some *Teaser* openings are even shorter than Rakoff's or Hale's.
U.S. Supreme Court Justice Antonin Scalia is known for his fiery dissents, but below you'll find a surprisingly austere Scalia opener to a
majority opinion. He manages to crystallize the issue without showing his cards:

Antonin Scalia, *Smith v. United States*

Upon joining a criminal conspiracy, a defendant's membership
in the ongoing unlawful scheme continues until he withdraws.
A defendant who withdraws outside the relevant statute-of-
limitations period has a complete defense to prosecution. We
consider whether, when the defendant produces some evidence supporting such a defense, the Government must prove
beyond a reasonable doubt that he did not withdraw outside the
statute-of-limitations period.

In just three sentences, Scalia makes the issue clear: the first sentence
presents the governing principle in its broadest terms, the second
adds a confounding fact, and the third branches into the novel problem before the Court.*

I'm not sure about the last sentence, either. The relationship between the "matters" and the "normal rule" is hazy, plus the "which is that" language toward the
end is a remote relative. Although it's clear enough that the "which" refers to
the "normal rule," the "apply" in between gets in the way. Perhaps we could try
something like "or is the proceeding subject to the normal rule of English law: a
contract. . . ."

* Scalia repeats key words to link his sentences and to improve flow: "withdraws"
in the second sentence harkens back to "withdraws" in the first; "such a defense" in
the third sentence recalls "defense" in the second. Scalia also presents the defendant's burden neutrally, calling it "some evidence" instead of something slanted
like "scant evidence" or "credible evidence." Note the tightness as well: the defendant withdraws "outside," not "outside of," the limitations period. The Court considers "whether," not "whether or not." The Government "must"—not "is obliged

Criminal conspiracies are sexy, as legal issues go, but do the same techniques work for run-of-the-mill facts and issues? Sure they do. In the example below, for instance, trial judge (and former Rhodes Scholar) Michael Ponsor offers another model *Teaser* opening, stripping a dispute to its essence while juxtaposing the two parties' views:

> **Michael Ponsor, *Thomas v. Consolidated Rail Corp.***
>
> Defendant has moved to preclude any expert testimony from three of the plaintiff's potential witnesses, Dr. Susan Upham, Dr. Marc Linson and physical therapist Edward Palmer, on the ground that plaintiff has failed to comply with the disclosure requirements of Fed. R. Civ. P. 26(a)(2). Plaintiff has responded that he is not obligated to make the disclosures demanded by defendant because the three witnesses were "treating physicians."*

Ponsor got his case down to two sentences. Let's up the ante: former California Supreme Court Justice Roger Traynor gets his own opening down to just one.

---

to" or "is required to"—prove its case. And the Government would do so "when," not "where," the defendant produces some evidence supporting that defense. That said, it's the defendant, not the "defendant's membership," who is joining the conspiracy, so to avoid a dangling participle, Scalia should have centered the first sentence on the defendant himself: "Upon joining a criminal conspiracy, a defendant is a member of the ongoing unlawful scheme until he withdraws."

* How about a colon rather than a comma after "witnesses" to clarify that Dr. Upham is witness number one, not witness number four? A serial comma after Dr. Linson would have made the list clearer as well. And on the plus side, "need not" is a great short substitute for "is not obligated to" or "is not required to."

> **Roger Traynor, *Drennan v. Star Paving Co.***
>
> Defendant appeals from a judgment for plaintiff in an action to recover damages caused by defendant's refusal to perform certain paving work according to a bid it submitted to plaintiff.

In just 30 words, Traynor has framed the dispute and the bare bones of the facts: a bid, a construction contract, a refusal to perform. The sentence orients the reader to a more detailed discussion of the facts to follow.

Of course, the ultimate *Teaser* isn't just clear. It's a gripping opening sentence that invites the reader to read on, as the great Lord Denning did here:

> **Lord Denning, *Cummings v. Granger***
>
> This is the case of the barmaid who was badly bitten by a big dog.

Lord Denning is an acknowledged master of this art. Here are a few more of his most memorable opening lines:

- "It happened on April 19, 1964. It was bluebell time in Kent." (*Hinz v Berry*)
- "Old Peter Beswick was a coal merchant in Eccles, Lancashire." (*Beswick v Beswick*)
- "In Bognor Regis there was years ago a rubbish tip." (*Dutton v Bognor Regis UDC*)
- "There is a 'pop' group of four or five musicians called 'Fleetwood Mac'." (*Clifford Davis Management Ltd v WEA Records Ltd*)

As these Lord Denning chestnuts show, you can show some spark and flair even in a relatively pat *Teaser*. Look how much whimsy Ninth Circuit Judge Kozinski squeezes into his opener below in a case involving the Clintons:

Alex Kozinski, *Flowers v. Carville*

Long after the public spotlight has moved on in search of fresh intrigue, the lawyers remain. And so we find ourselves adjudicating a decade-old dispute between Gennifer Flowers and what she affectionately refers to as the "Clinton smear machine": James Carville, George Stephanopoulos and Hillary Clinton. Flowers charges that said machine destroyed her reputation by painting her as a fraud and a liar after she disclosed her affair with Bill Clinton. We decide whether Flowers's claims are timely and, if so, whether they survive a motion to dismiss.

I hope I'm not suggesting that writing a good *Teaser* opening—or any good opening—is easy. It's anything but. Take, for example, these two openings, each from a recent U.S. Supreme Court opinion in a criminal matter:

John Roberts, *Blueford v. Arkansas*

The Double Jeopardy Clause protects against being tried twice for the same offense. The Clause does not, however, bar a second trial if the first ended in a mistrial. Before the jury concluded deliberations in this case, it reported that it was unanimous against guilt on charges of capital murder and first-degree murder, was deadlocked on manslaughter, and had not voted on negligent homicide. The court told the jury to continue to deliberate. The jury did so but still could not

> reach a verdict, and the court declared a mistrial. All agree that the defendant may be retried on charges of manslaughter and negligent homicide. The question is whether he may also be retried on charges of capital and first-degree murder.

Not for nothing is Chief Justice Roberts considered to have been the greatest advocate of his generation: every sentence is clear, not a word is wasted. The prose is crisp and natural.

Now read the example below from Justice Anthony Kennedy's opinion in a case called *Bailey v. United States*. Like Chief Justice Roberts, Justice Kennedy is trying to condense a complicated criminal issue into a brisk *Teaser* opening paragraph:

> The Fourth Amendment guarantees the right to be free from unreasonable searches and seizures. A search may be of a person, a thing, or a place. So too a seizure may be of a person, a thing, or even a place. A search or a seizure may occur singly or in combination, and in differing sequence. In some cases the validity of one determines the validity of the other. The instant case involves the search of a place (an apartment dwelling) and the seizure of a person. But here, though it is acknowledged that the search was lawful, it does not follow that the seizure was lawful as well. The seizure of the person is quite in question. The issue to be resolved is whether the seizure of the person was reasonable when he was stopped and detained at some distance away from the premises to be searched when the only justification for the detention was to ensure the safety and efficacy of the search.

Roberts and Kennedy both start with a threshold statement about the law, but from that point on, they inhabit different writing universes. Kennedy, the key "swing" vote on the current U.S.

Supreme Court, favors a lofty and grandiloquent style. But this particular opening misses the mark. Stream-of-consciousness organization is one problem: six sentences pass before we learn what question the court is asking. The chronology is also fuzzy: Which came first, the search or the seizure? The sentences themselves sound repetitive because they are all of similar length and structure, and some are wordy or heavy, long on such expressions as "the instant case" and "quite in question." There are usage glitches ("So too a seizure may be" should be "So too may a seizure be"). And the same word ("when") is used to mean different things in the same sentence ("[t]he issue . . . is whether the seizure of the person was reasonable *when* he was stopped . . . *when* the only justification for the detention was to ensure the safety and efficacy of the search").

So let's imagine how this opening might read if someone like Chief Justice Roberts had edited it down to a succinct *Teaser*:

> The Fourth Amendment guarantees the right to be free from unreasonable searches and seizures, whether they occur separately or together. In this case, to ensure a safe and effective search of the defendant's apartment, the police seized the defendant after he had left his apartment and driven nearly a mile away. The question is whether that seizure was reasonable.

Can you condense everything down to seven sentences tops? If so, a *Teaser* could be the ideal way to start your next opinion.

Teaser Practice Pointers

- A great *Teaser* opening asks a compelling question and leaves the reader wanting to learn more.
- It works best for disputes that are legal at their core and that hinge on facts that can be easily grasped.

- It pairs well with a simple, natural style, and it demands ruthless editing.
- A great *Teaser* opening begins with a sentence that frames a legal issue or broad general principle.
- Follow that opening sentence with a couple of sentences either juxtaposing the parties' arguments or presenting the specific factual context.
- Conclude with a final sentence stating the question that the court must resolve.

Trailer Opener: Detailed and Unresolved

Small is beautiful, but a longer and richer narrative-like opening offers rewards of its own. By allowing yourself several paragraphs up front, you can include more facts leading up to the dispute and can engage in a true point-counterpoint treatment of the dueling legal arguments. That said, long, unresolved openings are risky. The more facts you include, the likelier you'll confuse or overwhelm readers on the hunt for a discrete legal issue. And the more analysis you include, the harder it is to avoid tipping your hand, and yet making your views known tacitly has all the vices and none of the virtues of spelling out the disposition up front.

Let's dive into an excellent example of a *Trailer* opening, this time from Seventh Circuit Judge Posner in an immigration appeal:

Richard Posner, *Cecaj v. Gonzalez*

Questor Cecaj, who together with his wife is seeking asylum in the United States, was active in the Democratic Party of Albania at a time when the country was ruled by the Socialist Party. Persecution of Democratic Party activists during this period has been found in a number of cases. In 1998, Cecaj—whom the immigration judge found wholly credible—was arrested following a political protest in which he had participated. He was detained for six days and during that period was beaten by masked police with rubber truncheons and also kicked, suffering injuries that required his hospitalization. A few days after his release from the hospital a member of the Socialist Party accosted Cecaj on the street and fired a gun near his head, an act that Cecaj sensibly interpreted as a threat. He fled to Greece but returned in 2000 and resumed his political activity with the New Democratic Party, which is related to the Democratic Party, though the precise relationship is obscure. The following year, after an unsuccessful run for mayor of his hometown, he stood for the Albanian parliament on the New Democratic Party ticket in his hometown, which was dominated by the Socialist Party. Although he was a well-known local figure and candidate for public office, he was arrested during the campaign and beaten by the police, ostensibly for not having identification papers on him. He also received threatening phone calls, which he believed came from the police. The last straw was the kidnapping of his 10-year-old brother by unknown persons who told the child that he was being kidnapped because of Cecaj's political activity and that the child "would end up dead" if Cecaj "didn't do what they say." The child was released unharmed after a few hours but Cecaj received a call in which "they said that [the kidnapping] was the last warning." Cecaj prudently abandoned his candidacy and left Albania with his wife.

The immigration judge ruled that Cecaj's testimony did not establish that he had been persecuted.

In this excerpt you can see why Judge Posner is one of the world's best-known opinion writers—but you can also see why his style sometimes raises eyebrows.

This long opening paragraph is detailed by design, all the better to expose the immigration judge's apparently flawed decision below. By adopting a true narrative style, Posner tells a story that drip-by-drip—first the arrests, then the beatings, kidnapping, and even death threats—makes Cecaj sound like a classic victim of political persecution. Posner also marshals details—from the rubber truncheons to the "kidnapping is the last warning" threat—suggesting that the immigration judge had his head in the sand.

In just a few lines, Posner offers many examples of how skilled writers use the passive voice on purpose. The passive voice improves the flow of the first two sentences: the construction "was ruled by" helps keep "country" closer to Albania, and the "has been found in a number of cases" helps keep "activists" closer to the previous sentence, which is about politics, not case law. In the third sentence, Posner uses the passive voice to help us focus on what matters most: by writing that Cecaj "was arrested," Posner keeps us focused on Cecaj, and not on who arrested him. Again in the fourth sentence, choosing "was detained" and "was beaten" makes sense, because Posner wants to draw attention to Cecaj, and the best way to do that is to keep him as the sentence's subject.

Also notice Posner's strong, vivid verbs: *fled, fired, ruled, accosted, kicked, dominated, stood for, abandoned, left*. He even adds in some fresh, colloquial language to boot: *also*, not *additionally*, and *after*, not *subsequent to*. And finally, for a bit of flair, he uses dashes to slow the reader down: "Cecaj—whom the immigration judge found wholly credible." (I'll discuss many of these tips in more detail in Part 4.)

And yet Posner's fresh, candid, "impure" style is not always to everyone's liking. For one thing, the authorial intrusions might be a bit *too* frank. Do we really need to know that Posner thinks that Cecaj acted "sensibly" and "prudently"? Shouldn't the facts speak for themselves? Posner appears here to contradict the advice that he has offered other judges: "The handful of impure judicial stylists prefer the bolder approach (to critics, brazen) of trying to persuade without using stylistic devices intended to overawe, impress, and intimidate the reader."[2] And on the substance side, the tone here is so cocksure and so one-sided that the immigration judge is made to sound like a fool. Surely there must be some counterargument or bad fact somewhere that supports the immigration judge's denial of asylum?

As I noted above, Posner favors an unresolved opening, as in this example. And although he does not announce his decision, his word choices and writing style telegraph the ultimate outcome.

Judge Kozinski pens a similarly excellent *Trailer* opening in this next example. Note the clever opening line in particular:

Alex Kozinski, *Mattel v. MCA Records*

If this were a sci-fi melodrama, it might be called Speech-Zilla meets Trademark Kong.

Barbie was born in Germany in the 1950s as an adult collector's item. Over the years, Mattel transformed her from a doll that resembled a "German street walker," as she originally appeared, into a glamorous, long-legged blonde. Barbie has been labeled both the ideal American woman and a bimbo. She has survived attacks both psychic (from feminists critical of her fictitious figure) and physical (more than 500 professional makeovers). She remains a symbol of American girlhood, a public figure who graces the aisles of toy stores throughout the country and beyond. With Barbie, Mattel created not just a toy but a cultural icon.

With fame often comes unwanted attention. Aqua is a Danish band that has, as yet, only dreamed of obtaining Barbie-like status. In 1997, Aqua produced the song Barbie Girl on the album *Aquarium*. In the song, one band member impersonates Barbie, singing in a high-pitched, doll-like voice; another band member, calling himself Ken, entices Barbie to "go party." (The lyrics are in the Appendix.) Barbie

Girl singles sold well and, to Mattel's dismay, the song made it onto the Top 40 music charts.

Mattel brought this lawsuit against the music companies who produced, marketed, and sold Barbie Girl .... MCA in turn challenged the district court's jurisdiction under the Lanham Act and its personal jurisdiction over the foreign defendants . . . ; MCA also brought a defamation claim against Mattel for statements Mattel made about MCA while this lawsuit was pending. The district court concluded it had jurisdiction over the foreign defendants and under the Lanham Act, and granted MCA's motion for summary judgment on Mattel's federal and state-law claims for trademark infringement and dilution. The district court also granted Mattel's motion for summary judgment on MCA's defamation claim.

Mattel appeals the district court's ruling that Barbie Girl is a parody of Barbie and a nominative fair use; that MCA's use of the term Barbie is not likely to confuse consumers as to Mattel's affiliation with Barbie Girl or dilute the Barbie mark; and that Mattel cannot assert an unfair competition claim under the Paris Convention for the Protection of Industrial Property. MCA cross-appeals the grant of summary judgment on its defamation claim as well as the court's jurisdictional holdings.

Kozinski grabs the reader's attention with that audacious (some might say flippant) first sentence, and then parades the key facts supporting his opinion that the song in question was protected speech and not trademark infringement: Barbie, as a known cultural icon, can hardly expect to escape cultural comment. And note how Kozinski calls Barbie a "public figure," a nod to the *New York Times v. Sullivan* test that foreshadows (but does not announce) his ultimate conclusion.

A *Trailer* is a cinematic term—and for good reason. Even in a routine case, a skilled, confident judge can spin an engaging tale in just a few lines, making you want to know more. Look how the late Pennsylvania Supreme Court Justice Michael Musmanno opened his majority opinion in a routine slip-and-fall-on-asparagus-during-a-wedding case below. As a reader, you feel like you're spinning on the dance floor yourself:

Michael Musmanno, *Schwartz v. Warwick-Phila Corp.*

It was a wedding banquet and the guests were enjoying themselves in the traditional custom of nuptial celebrations. There was dining and dancing and then dancing and dining. Fork work interspersed with footwork. The banquetters would enjoy a spell of eating and then amble out to the dance floor to dance. When the music suspended, the dancers returned to their tables and became diners again. The mythical playwright who prepares the script for the strange and sometimes quixotic episodes which eventually end up in court, mixed his stage properties and characters in this presentation because he placed in the center of the dance floor a quantity of freshly cooked asparagus and ladled over it a generous quantity of oleaginous asparagus sauce. In this setting it was inevitable that something untoward would happen, and it did.

Musmanno's narrative gifts and playfulness—"Fork work interspersed with footwork" —remind me of Lord Denning here, though Musmanno has a penchant for longer sentences, and it's hard to imagine Lord Denning using a word like "oleaginous"!

A *Trailer* opening can do more than just share the key facts underlying the issue before the court. It can also explain what makes the case important or at least novel. In the example below, an introduction to a dissent, Justice Michael Kirby of the High Court of Australia starts by explaining what's new—and old—in a high-profile case about whether a same-sex sexual advance can support a provocation defense in a murder case. The tone of the dissent's opening lines is calm and measured:

Michael Kirby, *Green v. the Queen*, dissenting

Once again the Court has before it an appeal concerning the law of provocation and its effect on a person tried for, and convicted of, murder.

In this case, there are two variations from the themes considered in earlier cases, some of them quite recent. The first is factual. The facts alleged to constitute the provocation here were of a sexual advance, homosexual in character, which resulted in the infliction of terrible injuries on the victim, leading to his death. Recent writing, both academic and official, suggests, with reference to numerous cases, that provocation is now quite commonly raised in such circumstances, both in Australia and elsewhere.

The second variation is that in this case, unlike some others which have come to this Court, the trial judge left the issue of provocation to the jury. He did so in circumstances in which it is accepted that errors of a technical kind occurred in his rulings and directions. The Court of Criminal Appeal of New South Wales nonetheless applied the proviso. The question thus presented is whether the accused lost a real chance of being acquitted of murder (although found guilty of manslaughter) on the ground of provocation or whether the trial was so irregular that it should be classified as no trial at all. If the trial did sufficiently conform to the law and if no reasonable jury, properly instructed, could have found provocation in the facts adduced, no injustice will have occurred requiring disturbance of the jury's verdict that the accused was guilty of murder.*

Like Justice Kirby in his dissent, but this time in a trial decision, trial judge D.P. Marshall begins his own *Trailer* introduction with a broad thematic statement—but here the dividing line isn't old versus new, but what the case is (and is not) about. In that sense Marshall is turning down the heat, suggesting that when the case is stripped of its political and emotional subtext, it's at bottom just another contract dispute:

D.P. Marshall, *Little Rock School Dist. v. North Little Rock School Dist.*

Reasonable people of good will disagree about the wisdom and efficacy of charter schools. Those issues are not before this Court. The Little Rock School District and the Joshua Intervenors make no facial challenge to the Arkansas Charter Schools Act of 1999, as amended. LRSD and Joshua argue, instead, that the State, acting through the Department of Education, has broken the parties' 1989 Settlement Agreement in applying the Act to open-enrollment charter

---

* Let's revisit the second sentence of the final paragraph: "[The trial judge] did so in circumstances in which it is accepted that errors of a technical kind occurred in his rulings and directions." First a diagnosis: like Lady Hale's "it is recognised" above, the phrase "it is accepted" muddies who did the accepting—and that matters very much here. It's also confusing to repeat the preposition "in" for different purposes ("in circumstances," "in his rulings"). And although "circumstances" apparently refers to the judge's errors, in a criminal case a reader might expect it to refer to the facts. I believe that Justice Kirby meant something like this: "In doing so, the trial judge made some technical errors both in his rulings and in his directions to the jury." Or, if Justice Kirby finds it indelicate to suggest that the trial judge made errors, perhaps "As the parties concede, technical mistakes were made in the trial judge's rulings and directions."

schools in Pulaski County. These new schools, the argument runs, have grown with the State's blessing to the point where they are substantially interfering with desegregation efforts. The parties' Settlement Agreement is a contract, which this Court approved and adopted as part of its consent decrees governing how the State, LSD, PCSSD, and the North Little Rock School Districts would remedy their constitutional violations. Has the State broken the parties' contract in implementing the Charter Schools Act in Pulaski County? And can the Court decide on the record compiled by the parties or does there need to be a trial to resolve genuine issues about important facts? These are the main questions presented.*

You can try to split the baby when you present the two parties' positions, but how about actually making the losing side's position sound strong up front? Judge Learned Hand did just that in a 1930 case about copyrighted silk designs:

Learned Hand, *Cheney Bros. v. Doris Silk Corp.*

The plaintiff, a corporation, is a manufacturer of silks, which puts out each season many new patterns, designed to attract purchasers by their novelty and beauty. Most of these fail in that purpose, so that no much more than a fifth catches the public fancy. Moreover, they have only a short life, for the most part no more than a single season of eight or nine

---

* Watch how Judge Marshall, like Lady Hale in the *Teaser* example above, shapes the opening sentences to build up to a series of questions that the rest of the opinion will seek to answer. Admire his taut language as well: "*about*" (instead of "regarding"), "*broken*" (instead of "breached"), "the argument *runs*," "the State's *blessing*," "*how*" (instead of "the manner in which"), and "*And*" (instead of "Moreover"). Just lose the commas around "instead" in the fourth sentence.

months. It is in practice impossible, and it would be very oner-
ous if it were not, to secure design patents upon all of these;
it would also be impossible to know in advance which would
sell well, and patent only those. Besides, it is probable that
for the most part they have no such originality as would support a design patent. Again, it is impossible to copyright them
under the Copyright Act, or at least so the authorities of the
Copyright Office hold. So it is easy for any one to copy such as
prove successful, and the plaintiff, which is put to much ingenuity and expense in fabricating them, finds itself without
protection of any sort for its pains.

Note how Hand begins his narrative with the party's business
problem, framed in a way that helps him shift to a gap in the law.
Also look how Hand frames these opening facts to favor the plaintiff,
paying tribute to the "novelty and beauty" of its silks and praising its
hard work—"put to much ingenuity and expense"—even though the
plaintiff ultimately loses.

One final option. Although announcing the decision too soon
may make opinions seem self-satisfied, even Judge Posner allows
for a compromise of sorts: "to say at the outset, 'For reasons to be
explained, the judgment of the district court is affirmed [reversed,
etc.].'"[3] That approach resolves the "Who Won?" suspense while
still giving nothing away about the court's reasoning. Consider this
entertaining example from Judge Diane Wood, Posner's colleague on
the Seventh Circuit:

Diane Wood, *JCW Investments v. Novelty*

Meet Pull My Finger® Fred. He is a white, middle-aged, overweight man with black hair and a receding hairline, sitting in
an armchair wearing a white tank top and blue pants. Fred

is a plush doll and when one squeezes Fred's extended finger on his right hand, he farts. He also makes somewhat crude, somewhat funny statements about the bodily noises he emits, such as "Did somebody step on a duck?" or "Silent but deadly." Fartman could be Fred's twin. Fartman, also a plush doll, is a white, middle-aged, overweight man with black hair and a receding hairline, sitting in an armchair wearing a white tank top and blue pants. Fartman (as his name suggests) also farts when one squeezes his extended finger; he too cracks jokes about the bodily function. Two of Fartman's seven jokes are the same as two of the 10 spoken by Fred. Needless to say, Tekky Toys, which manufactures Fred, was not happy when Novelty, Inc., began producing Fartman, nor about Novelty's production of a farting Santa doll sold under the name Pull-My-Finger Santa.

Tekky sued for copyright infringement, trademark infringement, and unfair competition and eventually won on all claims. The district court awarded $116,000 based on lost profits resulting from the copyright infringement, $125,000 in lost profits attributable to trademark infringement, and $50,000 in punitive damages based on state unfair competition law. The district court then awarded Tekky $575,099.82 in attorneys' fees. On appeal, Novelty offers a number of arguments for why it should not be held liable for copyright infringement, argues that Illinois's punitive damages remedy for unfair competition is preempted by federal law, and contends that the attorneys' fees awarded by the district court should have been capped according to Tekky's contingent-fee arrangement with its attorneys. For the reasons set forth below, we affirm.

Wood's crisp, gently imperative opening sentence starts by poking fun at this amusing litigation. Then she segues into some facts showing that the products are similar enough to infringe, all the while giving very little away and encouraging the reader to forge ahead.

Like *Teasers*, *Trailer* openings invite the reader to peer into the court's thinking step by step. But unlike *Teasers*, they risk overwhelming the uninitiated reader for the sake of richer, fuller background.

If *Teasers* are all about the question, *Trailer* openings are all about the backdrop: factual, procedural, jurisprudential, or historical. A *Trailer* opening signals that the case is complex, that the decision is difficult, and that the court takes its job seriously.

A *Trailer* is appropriate when the procedural history is complicated, when application of the law is novel, when a sympathetic party loses, or when the issues are likely to stir strong emotions. An open-ended introduction is a great way to show that things are not as simple as they seem—or sometimes, as in the Marshall example above, that they are simpler.

Trailer Practice Pointers

- If the narrative speaks for itself, jump right into the tale, keeping details to a minimum.
- If some context would help the reader absorb the facts, start the introduction with an opening line that tells what the case is about, or what it's not about.
- Edit for tone. The point of a *Trailer* opening is to convey open-mindedness and receptivity to all sides' arguments, so resist the temptation to slant the presentation. Strip the introduction of authorial intrusions, especially adverbs, and consider framing the facts in the losing party's favor.
- And finally, edit for style. Replace long words with short ones, and vary sentence length to keep the narrative flowing.

Sound Bite Opener: Succinct and Resolved

The third type of opening compresses the issue and its resolution into a single paragraph. When time is short, when issues are clear, or when readers likely long for a portable holding, defusing the dramatic tension up front allows the reader to explore the court's reasoning in depth. The risk is that sound bite-hungry readers will skip the rest of the opinion altogether, so judges who pen these self-contained openings have tacitly conceded that in the court of public opinion, the beginning of the opinion is often the end as well. (It's no surprise that *Sound Bite* openings are particularly popular in the United States, a nation not known for patience.)

If you'd like a model *Sound Bite* opening, I propose the following four-sentence introduction from former D.C. Circuit Chief Judge Wald:

Patricia Wald, *Hubbard v. EPA*

This case presents a straightforward, but nonetheless hard, question of law: Has the United States waived sovereign immunity for a back pay award to an individual denied federal employment in violation of his constitutional rights? A panel of this court answered "yes" to that question, finding that 5 U.S.C. § 702's waiver of sovereign immunity for "relief other than money damages" encompasses back pay. On revisiting this issue en banc, we find no clear evidence from the language of the statute, its legislative history, or the case law that § 702 waives sovereign immunity for back pay. We thus affirm the district court's decision that Michael Hubbard may not receive back pay as part of a remedy for the Environmental Protection Agency's ("EPA") refusal to hire him in violation of his First Amendment rights.

Wald's opening incorporates three effective *Sound Bite* elements: (1) a sentence that frames the issue and puts it in context, (2) a pair of sentences juxtaposing both sides' arguments, and (3) a final sentence summing up the court's disposition.

Here's another great *Sound Bite* example from Ninth Circuit Judge Marsha Berzon, this time in a reversal:

Marsha Berzon, *Reed v. Massanari*

The Commissioner of Social Security determined that Nadine Reed is not entitled to disability benefits or supplemental security income. The district court granted summary judgment in favor of the Commissioner on Reed's challenge to that decision, and Reed appeals. We find that the Administrative Law Judge rejected for an improper reason Reed's request for a consultative examination. We therefore reverse and remand for further proceedings.

This example, like Judge Wald's, frames the issue that forms the basis for reversal; it focuses not on the parties' contentions but on the case's procedural history.

The *Sound Bite* technique might appear to work best for appellate opinions, because advocates are usually asked to frame the issues on appeal. But it works just as well for trial court decisions. Below, for example, I share a top-notch example from the bankruptcy courts with a slight twist on the *Sound Bite* ingredients, substituting for the parties' arguments a short discussion of the facts:

Benjamin Goldgar, *In re Earley*

This matter presents a question that seems to be arising with increasing frequency. Triad Financial Corporation holds a judgment against debtor Robert Earley and has a lien on his

> wages under the Illinois Wage Deduction Act (the "IWDA"). In his chapter 13 plan, however, Earley proposes to treat Triad's claim as unsecured. The question: must a debtor's chapter 13 plan treat as secured the claim of a judgment creditor holding a garnishment lien on the debtor's wages under the IWDA? The answer: no.

Note that both the Wald and the Goldgar examples adopt a neutral tone and focus entirely on the legal issues—and that's by design. The *Sound Bite* opening is geared toward the parties, legal scholars, and future courts, all of whom prize clear issues and even clearer resolutions.

Sometimes, however, although a *Sound Bite* opening seems fair and balanced, upon closer inspection, wording choices have stacked the deck. Take this bite-sized opening from U.S. Supreme Court Justice Elena Kagan in a criminal-procedure matter:

> **Elena Kagan, *Florida v. Harris***
>
> In this case, we consider how a court should determine if the "alert" of a drug-detection dog during a traffic stop provides probable cause to search a vehicle. The Florida Supreme Court held that the State must **in every case** present an **exhaustive** set of records, including a log of the dog's performance in the field, to establish the dog's reliability. We think that demand inconsistent with the "flexible, common-sense standard" of probable cause.

Kagan's opening here is clear, powerful, and convincing. As with all of her writing, not a word is wasted, and you won't find even a whiff of pretension. And yet some might say that the opening isn't quite fair. We can see in this opening, in fact, all the risks of the *Sound Bite*. As soon as Kagan refers to the "exhaustive" documentation required "in every case," she has already doomed the state court's ruling. It's almost as if the legal issue were "Does an inflexible and impractical requirement meet a 'flexible, common-sense standard?'" Well when you put it that way. . . .

To give the lower courts a better sense of where to draw the line, Kagan could have drafted a *Sound Bite* opening that's a bit more even-handed:

> In this case, we consider whether a drug-detection dog's "alert" during a traffic stop provides probable cause to search a vehicle. The Florida Supreme Court held that to establish the alert's reliability, the State must produce a specific set of comprehensive records, including a log of the dog's performance in the field. The performance-log requirement would apply even if the State could produce other abundant evidence of the alert's reliability. We think that demand inconsistent with the "flexible, common-sense standard" of probable cause.

Adding a sentence about the apparent flaw in the Florida Supreme Court's rule helps the reader understand why such rules don't pass muster under the Fourth Amendment. Otherwise, it sounds like the holding is simply "Don't require dog-performance logs."

Here's another some-would-say-slightly-slanted *Sound Bite*, this time from Kagan's colleague Justice Ruth Bader Ginsburg in a case about whether a state could finance a single-sex military college:

> **Ruth Bader Ginsburg, *United States v. Virginia***
>
> Virginia's public institutions of higher learning include an **incomparable** military college, Virginia Military Institute (VMI). The United States maintains that the Constitution's equal protection guarantee precludes Virginia from reserving

> **exclusively** to men the **unique** educational opportunities VMI affords. We agree.

Like Kagan's, Ginsburg's three-sentence *Sound Bite* opening chooses words—"incomparable," "exclusively," "unique"—that make the outcome seem preordained. Although Ginsburg doesn't lead with a "this case is about" sentence, she pivots from introducing VMI to explaining why it stands before the Court. Ginsburg invokes the winner's position, and then endorses it. The Commonwealth of Virginia might object that it did, after all, provide an alternative for women that Ginsburg never mentions here, but not even the very-much-dissenting Justice Scalia claims that the alternative program was as good as VMI's. Balance struck.

Let me end with a slightly fiery example, this time from the brash world of the New York trial courts. Below, Judge Shira Scheindlin had to decide whether then-New York City Mayor Rudy Giuliani has a right to control the use of his name. Her *Sound Bite* opener front-loads the facts:

> **Shira Scheindlin, *New York Magazine v. Metropolitan Transit Authority***
>
> Who would have dreamed that the Mayor would object to more publicity? But that is what this case is all about. Our twice-elected Mayor, whose name is in every local newspaper on a daily basis, who is featured regularly on the cover of weekly magazines, who chooses to appear in drag on a well-known national TV show, and who many believe is considering a run for higher office, objects to his name appearing on the side of city buses. He staunchly asserts, through his designated officials, that he has a "right to publicity," namely the right to *control* the use of his name when it is used for

> advertising or trade purposes. However, one who has chosen to be Mayor, and therefore to be the subject of daily commentary and controversy, cannot avoid the limelight of publicity—good and bad. Because of the "incidental use" and "public importance" limitations on the right to publicity, the Mayor's assertion of his right must yield to the Plaintiff's assertion of its First Amendment right.

I like Scheindlin's candid style, her effective use of an opening question, her inclusion of enough facts in the series of "who" phrases to give the issue some teeth, and her clean and confident concluding line. That said, the tone might strike some as a bit brusque (the italicizing of "control" doesn't help in this regard, nor does the insertion of "staunchly").

In the end, then, the virtues of *Sound Bite*—its speed and portability—are also its potential vices. I can neither recommend nor condemn the strong stacking-the-deck "To the victors go the spoils" approach that many judges favor. Whether it's appropriate depends on how you see the role of the judge. Should a judge aim for a sterile, even bland, tone that bends over backward to respect the losing side? Or, on the other hand, should a judge inspire and instill confidence through slightly slanted but compelling prose? Either way, a well-crafted *Sound Bite* can win you some very grateful readers.

Sound Bite Practice Pointers

- Start with a sentence that frames the legal issue ("This case is about"). For more color, consider styling the opening sentence as a question.
- Add a pair of sentences that either juxtapose both sides' arguments or provide necessary factual and legal context to explain the court's decision.

- Conclude with a final sentence announcing your decision.
- Edit for tone, seeking a balanced presentation of the facts. Does the losing party get a fair shake?
- Edit for style, cutting unnecessary qualifiers and heavy connecting words that will slow the reader down.

Op-Ed Opener: Detailed and Resolved

As one commentator has noted, "[t]he more impressive and useful introductions are thoughtful essays in which the judges identify the issue to be resolved in broader historical and philosophical legal contexts."[4] "Essay" might be a little ambitious for many opinions, and not every lawsuit has a "historical and philosophical context," but crafting an opening with the self-contained feel of a short essay is a laudable goal all the same. I call an essay-like opening an *Op-Ed*, because it's a somewhat free-form thought piece on the legal issues raised and their proper resolution.

Let's start with this great example from Chief Justice Beverly McLachlin of the Supreme Court of Canada. Her *Op-Ed* opening is for a case about the constitutionality of Canada's rape-shield statutes. McLachlin winds up striking down one of those statutes because it goes too far in limiting the defendant's right to present evidence. By endorsing a "middle way," she suggests that the court is seeking a reasonable, practical solution that will balance competing interests, though her conclusion will prove to be more controversial than meets the eye:

Beverly McLachlin, *Seaboyer v. H.M. the Queen*

These cases raise the issue of the constitutionality of ss. 276 and 277 of the Criminal Code, commonly known as the "rape-shield" provisions. The provisions restrict the right of the defence on a trial for a sexual offence to cross-examine and lead evidence of a complainant's sexual conduct on other occasions. The question is whether these restrictions offend the guarantees accorded to an accused person by the Canadian Charter of Rights and Freedoms.

My conclusion is that one of the sections in issue, s. 276, offends the Charter. While its purpose—the abolition of outmoded, sexist-based use of sexual conduct evidence—is laudable, its effect goes beyond what is required or justified by that purpose. At the same time, striking down s. 276 does not imply reversion to the old common-law rules, which permitted evidence of the complainant's sexual conduct even though it might have no probative value to the issues on the case and, on the contrary, might mislead the jury. Instead, relying on the basic principles that actuate our law of evidence, the courts must seek a middle way that offers the maximum protection to the complainant compatible with the maintenance of the accused's fundamental right to a fair trial.

Although McLachlin's opening is short and easily digestible, the *Op-Ed* format allows her to preempt a likely criticism: that the judgment heralds a return to the biases of the past. The use of "I" and "my," a practice that U.S. judges use mainly in dissents, also makes McLachlin's conclusions sound immediate and personal. (In the early years of the United States, Chief Justice John Marshall did away with the English practice of separate opinions for the majority, but the tradition remains across the Commonwealth.)

Speaking of chief justices, McLachlin's U.S. counterpart, Chief Justice John Roberts, is another master of the *Op-Ed* opening. Below, in a case about the extent to which convicted criminal defendants have a right to DNA testing, he appears to endorse such testing in theory—and in purposely vague terms—but then rejects the notion that DNA testing is a "freestanding and far-reaching" constitutional right:

John Roberts, *Attorney General's Office v. Osborne*

DNA testing has an unparalleled ability both to exonerate the wrongly convicted and to identify the guilty. It has the potential to significantly improve both the criminal justice system and police investigative practices. The Federal Government and the States have recognized this, and have developed special approaches to ensure that this evidentiary tool can be effectively incorporated into established criminal procedure—usually but not always through legislation.

Against this prompt and considered response, the respondent, William Osborne, proposes a different approach: the recognition of a freestanding and far-reaching constitutional right of access to this new type of evidence. The nature of what he seeks is confirmed by his decision to file this lawsuit in federal court under [Section 1983], not within the state criminal justice system. This approach would take the development of rules and procedures in this area out of the hands of legislatures and state courts shaping policy in a focused manner and turn it over to federal courts applying the broad parameters of the Due Process Clause. There is no reason to constitutionalize the issue in this way. Because the decision below would do just that, we reverse.

The magic of Roberts's writing is that he always manages to sound reasonable—even when, as here, he is denying a prisoner access to vital DNA evidence that the prisoner is willing to pay for himself. In his trademark spare style (although Roberts follows an *Op-Ed* pattern, his opening is closer to the length of the typical *Trailer*), Roberts at once concedes DNA's "unparalleled ability" to free the innocent and denies access to that testing for a defendant who claims innocence.*

Justice Ruth Bader Ginsburg offers a slightly different (and longer) model for an *Op-Ed* opening, one that weaves together four threads: (1) a pure and accessible narrative, (2) helpful context, (3) the parties' main arguments, and (4) a succinct conclusion:

Ruth Bader Ginsburg, *Astrue v. Capato*

Karen and Robert Capato married in 1999. Robert died of cancer less than three years later. With the help of in vitro fertilization, Karen gave birth to twins 18 months after her husband's death. Karen's application for Social Security survivors benefits for the twins, which the Social Security Administration (SSA) denied, prompted this litigation. The technology that made the twins' conception and birth possible, it is safe to say, was not contemplated by Congress when the relevant provisions of the Social Security Act (Act) originated (1939) or were amended to read as they now do (1965).

Karen Capato, respondent here, relies on the Act's initial definition of "child" in 42 U.S.C. § 416(e): "'[C]hild' means . . . the child or legally adopted child of an [insured] individual."

---

* Roberts properly splits an infinitive here, writing that DNA testing "has the potential to significantly improve" justice and policing. Had he written "DNA testing has the potential significantly to improve" instead, he would confuse the reader: Is the potential significant? And there are three other Roberts hallmarks here: First, inserting a bridge transition to open the second paragraph: "Against this prompt and considered response." Second, deftly using a dash to emphasize that most states adopt DNA testing by statute. And third, preferring a participle over a "that" or "which" phrase: "courts applying constitutional principles," and not "courts that apply constitutional principles." But I'm not sold on the ambiguous use of "this" after "recognized," all the more because he uses "this" again later in the same sentence: "The Federal Government and the States have recognized **this**, and have developed special approaches to ensure that **this** evidentiary tool. . . . " It would have been better to replace "recognized this" with "recognized these advantages" or whatever else he meant.

Robert was an insured individual, and the twins, it is uncontested, are the biological children of Karen and Robert. That satisfies the Act's terms, and no further inquiry is in order, Karen maintains. The SSA, however, identifies subsequent provisions, § 416(h)(2) and (h)(3)(C), as critical, and reads them to entitle biological children to benefits only if they qualify for inheritance from the decedent under state intestacy law, or satisfy one of the statutory alternatives to that requirement.

We conclude that the SSA's reading is better attuned to the statute's text and its design to benefit primarily those supported by the deceased wage earner in his or her lifetime. And even if the SSA's longstanding interpretation is not the only reasonable one, it is at least a permissible construction that garners the Court's respect under [*Chevron*].

Like a *Trailer*, an *Op-Ed* aims to be patient, balanced, and neutral—communicating to the reader through its length and tone that the court is immersed in the details. Ginsburg's conclusion here does not just declare that the government's interpretation of the statute carries the day. She also explains *why*.

What works for the law also works for the facts. When an outcome turns on an unexpected event or unusual set of facts, an *Op-Ed* opening can allow a skilled judicial writer to play essayist, as Ninth Circuit Judge Berzon does below:

Marsha Berzon, *United States v. Trimble*

The Bill of Rights was ratified in 1791. The United States produced its first automobile in 1877, and the first traffic ticket issued in 1904.

Fast forward to 2005: Sahneewa Trimble was issued several traffic tickets, fairly serious ones, on a military base. She believed that she was charged too much—more than other drivers who did the same thing on federal property on the same day. When Trimble appeared in court to plead guilty to the violations, the magistrate judge dismissed two of the six original citations but imposed a twenty-five dollar processing fee for three of the remaining ones. Standard stuff, except that some individuals, like Trimble, were charged the fee while the others were not. Why? Because Trimble received a new version of the citation notice and the fortunate others received an older version. So what follows is a tale of two forms, old and new. We reverse—demonstrating, again, that our Constitutional principles protect against monetary injuries large and small.

In a fact-heavy trial opinion, a detailed *Op-Ed* opening can be particularly helpful—especially if you have an eye toward appellate review. In just two short paragraphs below, for example, Bankruptcy Judge Goldgar distills the factual background, the procedural history, and the outcome.

Benjamin Goldgar, *In Re Brent*

Timothy K. Liou is one of the most active consumer bankruptcy attorneys in this district, filing nearly 8,000 cases from mid–1996 to the present. More than once, though, Liou's efforts to get paid have drawn the court's attention and resulted in sanctions. Now he faces sanctions again. Earlier this year, seven bankruptcy judges issued orders asserting that Liou had filed false applications for compensation as counsel for the debtors in 317 pending chapter 13 cases.

The applications were false, the orders said, because in them Liou represented that he had entered into the court's form retention agreement with the debtor, entitling him to receive a fixed fee of $3,500 (a "flat" or "no look" fee), when in fact he had modified the agreement to charge additional fees. The orders required him to show cause why he should not be sanctioned for violating Bankruptcy Rule 9011(b).

The Rule 9011 proceedings were consolidated for hearing before the undersigned judge. Based on the evidence adduced at the hearing and on the court's own records in the 317 Chapter 13 cases, the court makes the following findings of fact and conclusions of law pursuant to Bankruptcy Rules 7052 and 9014(c). For the reasons discussed below, Liou will be sanctioned for his multiple misrepresentations to the court in violation of Rule 9011(b).

This accessible *Op-Ed* opening features both the substance and the style of a true narrative.

First, the substance: the paragraph is built through a *who-what-when-why-how* exposition that draws the reader in by introducing the dispute and answering core questions.

And second, the style: Goldgar's fresh, confident language is easy on the eye and ear. Not "on more than one occasion," but "*more than once.*" Not "obtain payment," but "*get paid.*" Not "however," but "*though.*" Not "at present," but "*now.*" He also sprinkles in some strong, active verbs: "*drawn*" and "*faces*" as well as "*filing*" and "*entitling.*" And yet his style also stands out for what is missing: no dates, no citations, no defined terms, no "regarding" or "concerning," and, thank goodness, no "the instant dispute."

In other words, we have the makings of a real story here—perhaps even one that you'd like to read more about.

Sticking with trial judges, let's look at ways to exploit an *Op-Ed* opening for decisions that will be more newsworthy or controversial that Goldgar's. Here's a great example in a routine case that nevertheless carries broader implications about sentencing:

Michael Ponsor, *United States v. Watts*

The narrow question raised by this pretrial motion is whether, if Antoine Watts is convicted of possessing with intent to distribute five grams or more of crack cocaine, the court will be compelled to impose a minimum mandatory sentence of at least five years on him, or will have the discretion to impose a lower sentence as permitted by the recently enacted Fair Sentencing Act of 2010 ("FSA").

The broader question is whether federal trial courts will be required, for roughly the next five years, to perpetuate a congressionally recognized injustice. It is disturbing enough when courts, whose primary task is to do justice, become themselves the instruments of injustice, as in the history of our nation it must be acknowledged they sometimes have. But this discomfort reaches its zenith when the injustice has been identified and formally remedied by Congress itself. For a trial judge, the distastefulness of being forced to continue imposing a rejected penalty becomes unendurable in light of the fact that Congress acted partly because the injustice is racially skewed and, as everyone now agrees, will fall disproportionately upon Black defendants such as Mr. Watts.

The government's position here is that this court, and all federal trial courts in this country, must robotically continue to impose penalties that all three branches of government—executive, legislative, and judicial—and all elements of our political system—Republicans and Democrats from the most conservative to the most liberal—have now formally condemned as racially tainted and have explicitly rejected as not only unjust but mistaken from the outset. For the reasons set forth below, the affront to manifest and undisputed congressional intent advocated by the government here is not required by law.

A few more introductory words. The government's contention that the General Saving Statute ("Saving Statute"), 1 U.S.C. § 109, demands this result—that is, that the Saving Statute makes perpetuation of obvious injustice a regrettable but necessary expression of respect for the law, however harsh its consequences—cannot survive a close examination of the Saving Statute itself or its legal context. The Saving Statute is simply not the straitjacket the government has tried to tailor.

As will be seen, the case most heavily relied upon by the government for its crabbed interpretation of the Saving Statute, *Warden, Lewisburg Penitentiary v. Marrero*, states that when a statute such as the FSA contains a "specific directive" that can be said "*by fair implication* or expressly to conflict with § 109" a court is empowered to hold that the new statute supersedes the Saving Statute. Thirty years after *Marrero*, Justice Scalia, in discussing whether a new statute superseded a prior one, pungently noted that "[w]hen the plain import of a later statute directly conflicts with an earlier statute, the later enactment governs, *regardless* of its compliance with any earlier-enacted requirement of an express reference or other 'magical password.'"

It cannot be disputed that the situation before the court now is precisely what Justice Scalia described. When the intent of Congress and the interests of justice coincide as exactly as they do with regard to the question of the application of the FSA here, it ill behooves a court (or a prosecutor) to engage in contortions to thwart both. For this reason, elaborated below, the court has allowed Defendant's motion and will consider his sentence in light of the applicable statutes as amended by the FSA.*

---

* Ponsor bridges his first and second paragraphs beautifully, tying the "narrow question raised" by the motion at hand to the "broader question" of the impact of the Fair Sentencing Act. Note, too, his strong, vibrant verbs: *"compelled"*

Federal trial judges across the United States had confronted this very issue in the wake of the Fair Sentencing Act. Ponsor's *Op-Ed* opening previews the parties' arguments and the court's options, in language that's both heartfelt and accessible. Because the result is controversial, and because the context is essential to understanding the result, his thoughtful and extended treatment prepares the reader (and, presumably, the appellate court) for the discussion to follow.

Unlike the *Trailer* openings discussed above, *Op-Ed* openings show you your destination before the journey begins.

Op-Ed Practice Pointers

- Lead off with a short and memorable opening line.
- Narrate the factual and procedural context.
- Introduce the parties and juxtapose their competing legal positions.
- Conclude with a sentence or paragraph summarizing the result and offering at least one reason in support.

Introductions to judicial opinions are prime real estate. They set the stage for what's to come and telegraph your approach to both writing and the law. When the issues are short, simple, and of interest mainly to the parties, a *Sound Bite* opening may serve. When the decision is fact-dependent or appeals to a broader readership, a *Teaser* or *Trailer* opening may be the ticket. But when the decision is complicated or controversial, a longer essay-like *Op-Ed* opening may strike the best balance between portability and self-containment.

(instead of "required"), *"perpetuate"* (instead of "continue"), *"condemned"* (instead of repeating "rejected"), *"ill behooves"* (instead of "should not"), *"thwart"* (instead of "avoid"). He also spices up his punctuation, using em dashes to emphasize the universal denunciation of the mandatory sentencing regime that the Government advocates. (He wisely buttresses his argument with some choice quotes from the conservative Justice Scalia.) Finally, he adds some colorful imagery and alliteration in his "The Savings Statute is simply not the straitjacket the government has tried to tailor."

Part 2

The Tale

The Facts

Robert Megarry, *In re Vandervell's Trusts (No 2)* 42

Lord Denning, *In re Vandervell's Trusts (No 2)* 43

The Signal and the Noise: Cut Clutter 44

Benjamin Cardozo, *Palsgraf v. Long Island Rail Road* 44

Patricia Wald, *United States v. Morris* 45

Benjamin Goldgar, *In re Brent* 48

Jan Paulsson, *Pantechniki S.A. Contractors & Engineers (Greece) v. Republic of Albania* 48

Richard Posner, *University of Notre Dame v. Sebelius* 49

Roger Traynor, *Drennan v. Star Paving Co.* 50

Oliver Wendell Holmes Jr., *Baltimore & Ohio R.R. v. Goodman* 51

Patricia Wald, *Hubbard v. EPA* 52

Michael Ponsor, *United States v. Binette* 52

Brett Kavanaugh, *Belize Social Development Ltd. v. Government of Belize*, dissenting 54

Edward Carnes, *Ash v. Tyson* 54

Alex Kozinski, *Mattel, Inc. v. MCA Records, Inc.* 55

D.P. Marshall, Jr., *Little Rock School Dist. v. North Little Rock School Dist.* 56

Big Picture: Add Background 57

Shine a Light: Emphasize Key Facts 59

Michael McHugh, *Green v. The Queen* 61

Michael Kirby, *Green v. The Queen*, dissenting 62

Do You See What I See: Adopt a Narrative Voice 67

Diane Wood, *JCW Investments v. Novelty, Inc.* 67

Richard Posner (sitting by designation), *Apple v. Motorola* 68

Lord Denning, *Cummings v. Granger* 69
Clean-Up: Enhance Visual Appeal 73
Frank Easterbrook, *FTC v. QT, Inc.* 73
Benjamin Goldgar, *In Re Brent* 74
Michael Ponsor, *Angiodynamics, Inc. v. Biolitec, Inc.* 76
Michael Kirby, *Green v. The Queen* 76
Practice Pointers for Fact Statements 77

As I pointed out in Part 1, when judges write the opening paragraphs of their opinions, they face three decisions: how much detail they want to provide, how much of their ultimate conclusion they want to reveal, and how much effort they want to devote to engaging readers from the outset.

Similar choices infuse statements of facts and background sections. Buckling under time pressure, however, judges often take the path of least resistance, essentially regurgitating the facts and record citations in the parties' filings. There's nothing wrong with that, especially when time is short or when a fact section needs to be numbered "findings of fact." But in many cases, a shorter and more focused background section will yield a more persuasive and enduring decision.

To give you an idea of how different judges treat the same facts very differently, I want to share a pair of contrasting facts from two prominent English jurists.[1]

Version One is from Sir Robert Megarry, then Justice Megarry, writing a judgment in an important English trusts case called *In re Vandervell's Trusts*:

Robert Megarry, *In re Vandervell's Trusts (No 2)*

An important consideration was that under the articles the VP Company could distribute its profits as dividends among the ordinary shares, the 'A' shares or the 'B' shares, or to any one or two of these classes to the exclusion of the others or other, as the Company determined in general meetings; and in practice this meant that Mr Vandervell had complete control over whether or not any dividends were paid on any of these shares.

Version Two is by Lord Denning:

Lord Denning, *In re Vandervell's Trusts (No 2)*

In 1949 he set up a trust for his children. He did it by forming Vandervell Trustees Ltd.—the trustee company, as I will call it. He put three of his friends and advisers in control of it. They were the sole shareholders and directors of the trustee company. Two were chartered accountants. The other was his solicitor. He transferred money and shares to the trustee company to be held in trust for the children. Such was the position at the opening of the first period.

Both passages are about the same length, but while Lord Denning includes eight sentences, Justice Megarry writes just a single sentence that runs 76 words. Justice Megarry also centers his facts on an abstraction—"an important consideration"—while Lord Denning tells a story, front-loading his sentences with people, not concepts. For some readers, Lord Denning's breezy approach might be too much of a good thing, but the stark contrasts here show how much liberty judges enjoy when they relay facts.

In that spirit, let's explore five ways to craft a top-notch background section: (1) cut clutter, (2) add background, (3) emphasize key points, (4) adopt a narrative voice, and (5) enhance visual appeal.

The Signal and the Noise: Cut Clutter

The easiest way to improve a fact or background statement is to prune it. Consider this classic passage by then-Judge Cardozo:

> ### Benjamin Cardozo, *Palsgraf v. Long Island Rail Road*
>
> Plaintiff was standing on a platform of defendant's railroad after buying a ticket to go to Rockaway Beach. A train stopped at the station, bound for another place. Two men ran forward to catch it. One of the men reached the platform of the car without mishap, though the train was already moving. The other man, carrying a package, jumped aboard the car, but seemed unsteady as if about to fall. A guard on the car, who had held the door open, reached forward to help him in, and another guard on the platform pushed him from behind. In this act, the package was dislodged, and fell upon the rails. It was a package of small size, about fifteen inches long, and was covered by a newspaper. In fact it contained fireworks, but there was nothing in its appearance to give notice of its contents. The fireworks when they fell exploded. The shock of the explosion threw down some scales at the other end of the platform many feet away. The scales struck the plaintiff, causing injuries for which she sues.

Cardozo gives us a play-by-play account of the accident in eleven short sentences. Only the first and last even mention the plaintiff.

The prose is clear, vivid, and engaging. Although we see precisely what happened, Cardozo spares us the details of the two running men, the guard, and even the plaintiff's injuries.

But how can you distill a stack of filings into something this taut? By cutting with abandon. Parties flood the court with excess details, so to avoid drowning, you should allow only some facts to rise to the surface.

"At once too many and too few," says Judge Posner of the facts presented in most judicial opinions.[2] Posner chides judges who include details that are "irrelevant as well as uninteresting," such as gratuitous names and dates, and who yet say nothing about "obscure business practices, arcane foreign customs, rare medical mishaps, and other esoterica" that are "interesting and important" and that are also readily available online—more about that later.[3]

Posner puts his point to the test by "rewriting" a section of a 3,237-word opinion penned by former D.C. Circuit Chief Judge Wald, whom I feature in this book (and who Posner concedes is a great judge). His rewrite comes in at a spare 602 words.[4] Compare the first paragraphs:

Patricia Wald, *United States v. Morris*

Appellant Robert Morris was convicted of possession of cocaine with intent to sell, in violation of 21 U.S.C. § 841(a)(1) and § 841(b)(1)(B)(iii), and for using or carrying a firearm during and in relation to a drug trafficking offense, in violation of 18 U.S.C. § 924(c)(1). He appeals both convictions on the ground that the evidence was insufficient to support either charge. We reject both challenges and affirm the judgment below.

This is all standard fact-writing fare, but for Posner it is still "over-particularized." Here's his 38-word edit:

> A jury convicted the defendant of possession of cocaine with intent to sell it, and of using or carrying a firearm during and in relation to a drug offense. The judge sentenced him to 130 months in prison.

What's missing? Posner has axed all proper nouns, statutory cites, and even the "official" names of the crimes. (He has also avoided the passive voice, added information about sentencing, and decided not to announce the result for reasons I discussed in Part 1.)

What are some other candidates for the chopping block? Let's look at another before-and-after contrast for more ideas. First the original:

> **Patricia Wald, *United States v. Morris***
>
> On December 11, 1990, officers of the Metropolitan Police Department executed a search warrant on a one-bedroom apartment at 2525 14th Street, N.E., in the District of Columbia. Upon entering the apartment, the officers found appellant seated on a small couch in the living room; they detained him while they searched the apartment. The search produced two ziplock bags containing a total of 15.7 grams of crack cocaine divided among one hundred smaller ziplock bags, $500 in cash, empty ziplock bags, razor blades, and three loaded and operable pistols. Two of the guns were under the cushions of the couch on which appellant sat; the third was in a nightstand in the bedroom.

Again, Wald's facts are just fine. The details of the search are vivid, and we assume that they serve a purpose. In the end, though, few of these details have anything to do with the questions before the court: whether the defendant was living at the apartment, and whether he used guns during the crime. As Chekhov famously put it, "If you say in the first chapter that there is a revolver on the mantel, it absolutely must go off by the second or third chapter." Posner's rewrite thus knocks any needless details off the mantel, so to speak:

> Police had a warrant to search a one-bedroom apartment. Upon entering they found the defendant sitting on a small couch in the living room. The search revealed drugs, cash, and drug paraphernalia, and also three pistols—two under the cushions of the couch and the third in a nightstand in the bedroom.

What's cut this time around? The date of the search, the proper name of the police department, the address where the warrant was executed, and the full inventory. And what was spared? Only those details that will matter to the court's analysis: the one-bedroom apartment, and defendant's location in relation to the contraband.

The first thing to consider cutting: dates. When I ask judges what they hate about briefs, the cry of "too many dates" often tops the list. Certainly some dates are necessary, but most are not, I'm told. After all, bemoan these judges, it's painful to read sentence after sentence that starts with "On October 21, 2013," "On October 23, 2013," and "On October 29, 2013." But guess what, judges—the same is true of your opinions! Even when the time sequence matters, one solution is to replace exact dates with words and phrases that explain what happened, in what order, and for how long. Bankruptcy Judge Goldgar gets it:

> **Benjamin Goldgar, *In re Brent***
>
> **In May 2010**, [the] attorney filed a chapter 13 bankruptcy case .... **Shortly after filing the case**, [he] filed a form fee application ....
>
> **Some months later**, [the] chapter 13 trustee objected to his application ....

For most events, the month and year will orient the reader; an exact date is too fussy. Phrases like "shortly after" and "some months before" allow us to follow the story without making us wonder whether a particular date is significant. Remember Chekhov's revolver on the mantel.

When events span years, you might need to give more than one point of orientation. In that case, following a strict chronology is ill advised if doing so would highlight facts that don't matter. Here's Jan Paulsson, an arbitrator at the International Centre for Settlement of Investment Disputes, describing a years-long sequence of events:

> **Jan Paulsson, *Pantechniki S.A. Contractors & Engineers (Greece) v. Republic of Albania***
>
> In the **summer of 1994** the Claimant was selected **after** an international tender for works on bridges and roads in Albania. Two contracts were concluded by the General Road Directorate and the Claimant:
>
> - Contract No. 4 ... dated **18 August 1994** ...
> - Contract No. 6 ... dated **14 October 1994** ...
>
> The Claimant commenced work **promptly after signature** of the Contracts. The works were interrupted by **several days of riots in March 1997**. Violent incidents led the Claimant

to abandon its work site and to repatriate its personnel. Armed bands stole everything that could be carried away and destroyed almost everything they left behind.

Here, full calendar dates aren't needed to convey a sense of time; they're used only to identify particular contracts. And when all that matters is the sequence—"after an international tender"—no dates are needed at all.

For events that are recent or close together, the focus should zoom in from years to days, as in this example from Judge Posner:

Richard Posner, *University of Notre Dame v. Sebelius*

When the new regulations [about covering birth control] were promulgated in **July of last year**, Notre Dame did not at first bring a new suit .... **Months passed. Not until December** did the university file the present suit. The delay in suing was awkward, since the regulations were to take effect with respect to the employee health plan—and did take effect—on **January 1 of this year**.

With the January deadline for compliance with the regulations applicable to the employee plan **looming**, the university, **less than a week after filing its second suit on December 3**, moved for the entry of a preliminary injunction. The district court **denied the motion on December 20**, and Notre Dame filed its appeal from that denial **the same day**.

What matters here is sequence and timing—after months of delay, a party sues, moves for a preliminary injunction, and then appeals. The year doesn't matter, and it's obvious anyway, so Posner waves it goodbye.

Of course, sometimes you do need a full date. In the example below by California Supreme Court Justice Traynor, there's one key date (and even time) that provides needed context and that anchors the other events in question:

Roger Traynor, *Drennan v. Star Paving Co.*

On **July 28, 1955**, plaintiff, a licensed general contractor, was preparing a bid on the "Monte Vista School Job" in the Lancaster school district. Bids had to be submitted **before 8:00 p.m.** Plaintiff testified that it was customary in that area for general contractors to receive the bids of subcontractors by telephone on the day set for bidding and to rely on them in computing their own bids. Thus **on that day** plaintiff's secretary, Mrs. Johnson, received by telephone between fifty and seventy-five subcontractors' bids for various parts of the school job....

Late in the afternoon, Mrs. Johnson had a telephone conversation with Kenneth R. Hoon, an estimator for defendant. He gave his name and telephone number and stated that he was bidding for defendant for the paving work at the Monte Vista School according to plans and specifications and that his bid was $7,131.60. At Mrs. Johnson's request he repeated his bid. Plaintiff listened to the bid over an extension telephone in his office and posted it on the master sheet after receiving the bid form from Mrs. Johnson. Defendant's was the lowest bid for the paving. Plaintiff computed his own bid accordingly and submitted it with the name of defendant as the subcontractor for the paving. When the bids were opened on **July 28th**, plaintiff's proved to be the lowest, and he was awarded the contract.

On his way to Los Angeles **the next morning** plaintiff stopped at defendant's office....

Cutting clutter isn't just about saving words. It's also about turning down the noise so the signal shines through. As the examples above show, what's signal in one opinion may be noise in another, depending on the issue before the court. In the example below, when the issue was negligence, Justice Holmes focuses on only the details that matter:

> **Oliver Wendell Holmes Jr., *Baltimore & Ohio R.R. v. Goodman***
>
> **Goodman was driving an automobile truck in an easterly direction and was killed by a train running southwesterly across the road at a rate of not less than 60 miles an hour.** The line was straight but it is said by the respondent that Goodman **"had no practical view"** beyond a section house 243 feet north of the crossing **until he was about 20 feet from the first rail**, or, as the respondent argues, 12 feet from danger, and that then the engine was still obscured by the section house. He had been driving at the rate of 10 or 12 miles an hour but had cut down his rate to 5 or 6 miles at about 40 feet from the crossing. It is thought that **there was an emergency** in which, so far as appears, Goodman did all that he could. **We do not go into further details as to Goodman's precise situation**, beyond mentioning that **it was daylight and that he was familiar with the crossing**, for it appears to us plain that nothing is suggested by the evidence to relieve Goodman from responsibility for his own death.

The opinion mentions only what's relevant to determining fault for the fatal collision: train speed, truck speed, visibility at the crossing, and the emergency that might have prompted the deceased to risk crossing ahead of an oncoming train. What noise do we not hear? Full proper names, calendar dates, the nature of the emergency, the precise location of the collision, and the details of the investigation.

(If anything, Holmes might have given more detail on speeds, directions, and distances than he needed to.)

Incidentally, take a cue from Holmes's "We do not go into further details." It's appropriate, and even desirable, to let the reader know that you're screening out noise to highlight signal, as Judge Wald does below.

Patricia Wald, *Hubbard v. EPA*

Michael Hubbard's dispute with the EPA has dragged on for more than a decade. A "frequent flyer" with this court, the facts of Hubbard's conflict with the EPA are chronicled in several prior opinions.* **We highlight only the most salient details here.**

Cutting clutter should be a goal for trial courts as well—and no, the possibility of appellate review does not mean that you should regurgitate the entire record wholesale. Here's an example from a case in which a defendant had moved to dismiss an obstruction-of-justice charge. The trial court's mission? To decide whether the conduct fits the charge. Judge Ponsor streamlines the allegedly illegal conduct, and then describes what happened next:

Michael Ponsor, *United States v. Binette*

Meanwhile, **the Securities and Exchange Commission ("SEC") began an investigation** into suspicious trading activity surrounding Safeco equities in the days before Liberty Mutual's acquisition was announced. As part of

---

* "A "'frequent flyer' with this court" is a dangling modifier. This opening phrase modifies Hubbard, not "the facts of Hubbard's conflict." Nor do you need to put quotation marks around idiomatic phrases like "frequent flyer."

that investigation, **the SEC contacted Defendant and asked to speak with him** about his purchases of Safeco options. According to the record, a group of SEC attorneys and investigators made a conference call to Defendant at the car dealership where he worked as a salesman. It is unclear whether Defendant was ever given *Miranda* warnings or even told that a failure to tell the truth could lead to criminal charges.

What happened next is undisputed. **Defendant decided to take the SEC's call and answer questions.** He told the SEC attorneys that he had not spoken to anyone else about his investment in Safeco. Instead, **he claimed he had read about Safeco in internet chatrooms and had a dream that the company would be acquired.** In a subsequent proffer session with the agency, according to the government, he later admitted that **none of these statements were true.**

What's gone? Dates, times, quotations (we don't know the exact words that defendant said to the SEC), the name and address of the car dealership where the defendant made the statements, and the proper names of the SEC attorneys and investigators who heard them. This pruning allows the reader to focus on what's going to be important: is this kind of statement, on this type of conference call, tantamount to obstruction of justice?

What works for background facts also works for procedural history. Heavy-handed citations to "Plaintiff's Memorandum In Support Of Its Motion In Limine To Exclude Irrelevant, Prejudicial Documents" are, as Judge Posner would say, over-particularized, not to mention just plain annoying (I say the same to brief-writers, by the way). So use shorthand for filings, too. Consider the following example by D.C. Circuit Judge Kavanaugh, who distills proceedings in three countries into five simple sentences.

> **Brett Kavanaugh,** *Belize Social Development Ltd. v.*
> *Government of Belize,* **dissenting**
>
> This case arises out of a messy commercial dispute between a Belize company and the Government of Belize. A London arbitration panel **ruled** in favor of the Belize company. The company then **sued** in U.S. District Court to enforce the arbitration award. Because of ongoing judicial proceedings in Belize related to this matter, the Government of Belize **asked** for a temporary stay, which was uncontested by the company. The District Court then **entered** a temporary stay—understandably, since the stay is only temporary and the company did not oppose it.

Or consider how much procedural mumbo-jumbo Eleventh Circuit Judge Carnes had to purge to end up with this summary:

> **Edward Carnes,** *Ash v. Tyson*
>
> **This case at one time involved multiple plaintiffs and multiple claims. It is now down to one plaintiff and one claim.** This appeal involves that one remaining plaintiff, John Hithon, who is African-American, and his one remaining claim, which is a 42 U.S.C. § 1981 racial discrimination claim based on Tyson Foods' failure to promote him to shift manager at its Gadsden, Alabama chicken processing plant.
>
> . . .
>
> In December of 1996, **this lawsuit was filed.** In it Hithon claimed that Tyson discriminated against him based on his race by promoting King and Dade to the two shift manager positions.

> *Ash I* involved Hithon and five other plaintiffs who brought, among other claims, race and sex discrimination and retaliation claims against Tyson. In an 89-page opinion, the district court denied Tyson's motion for summary judgment on: Hithon and Anthony Ash's promotion discrimination claims, two other plaintiffs' retaliation claims, and one other plaintiff's fraudulent inducement of employment claim. The court granted Tyson's motion for summary judgment as to all of the other claims.

Carnes excises every procedural detail but the one the reader needs to know: which plaintiffs' claims survived summary judgment, and which did not. Needless to say, he does not identify a single pleading by name.* And nor does Ninth Circuit Judge Kozinski below:

> **Alex Kozinski, *Mattel, Inc. v. MCA Records, Inc.***
>
> **Mattel brought this lawsuit** against the music companies [*not* "Mattel filed its Complaint"] . . .
>
> **MCA in turn challenged the district court's jurisdiction** [*not* "MCA filed a Motion to Dismiss for Lack of Jurisdiction"] . . .
>
> **MCA also brought a defamation claim against Mattel** [*not* "MCA filed its Answer and Counterclaim"] . . .

---

* The passive construction "this lawsuit was filed" helps Judge Carnes avoid having to name all the plaintiffs. "Among other claims" is so much better than "*inter alia*." And two punctuation points: First, you should generally include a comma after introductory phrases of two or more words. So "In it, Hithon denied," not "In it Hithon denied." And second, no colon after a lead-in to a list that's just a phrase, not a clause. So no colon after "on" and before "Hithon."

Or trial judge D.P. Marshall here:

> **D.P. Marshall, Jr.,** *Little Rock School Dist. v. North Little Rock School Dist.*
>
> In 2010, the Little Rock School District, joined eventually by the Joshua Intervenors, **moved to enforce** the parties' 1989 Settlement Agreement.
>
> . . .
>
> A group of open-enrollment charter schools **moved to intervene** [*not* "filed their Motion to Intervene"]. The Court agreed, and granted permissive intervention. The Court rejected the charter schools' **request to reorient** the case immediately toward what may be called the *Parents Involved* issues . . . .

Remember that judges can call a motion as they see it, the filings' official names be damned. Note, for example, how Judge Marshall calls the charter schools' motion to intervene a "request to reorient" the litigation, which is almost certainly not the title splashed across the caption. As the judge, you know more about what's happening in the litigation than the reader does, so you can help by describing pleadings and arguments based on what they seek, rather than on what they're titled.

To sum up, if your legal analysis does not turn on one of these details, consider purging them from your fact or background statement:

- Dates and times
- Street addresses
- Dollar amounts and other currencies
- Weights, quantities, and other measures

- Quotations from the record
- Proper names (of people, places, entities, and pleadings)
- Record cites (unless making appealable findings of fact)

Judges of the world, declutter!

Big Picture: Add Background

Pruning surplus facts is a blessing to all readers, and most judges who fail to trim do so for lack of time, not lack of will. Adding background, by contrast, is more controversial—especially when "background" includes facts not in the record.

The world does not, of course, expect judges to live in a bubble. Even at trial, a court may take judicial notice of facts "generally known" within its jurisdiction, or facts that "can be accurately and readily determined from sources whose accuracy cannot reasonably be questioned."[5] So certain contextual details–that October 23 fell on a Thursday, that Tallinn is the capital of Estonia, that an inch of rain fell at a particular location on a particular date—may be cited with no worries.

But the more elaborate the research, the more eyebrows will raise. Sure, it's not unheard of for courts to review news articles, or the parties' websites, or Wikipedia entries to establish background facts or to get a sense of who the parties are and what they do when they're not litigating. But doing so risks bringing in facts that the parties have not had a chance to consider or to cross-examine.

Judges who dip their toes even further sometimes even research issues that the parties never raised but should have—or that they simply failed to address adequately. Now the judge is lurking well beyond the realm of Wikipedia, poring over law-review articles, scientific studies, economic analyses, or other background material. One famous example involved U.S. Supreme Court Justice Harry

Blackmun's trip to the Mayo Clinic library while he was pondering the abortion-rights case *Roe v. Wade*. By donning a medical-researcher hat, Blackmun might have penned a decision that was both broader than need be and anchored on grounds not raised by the parties. In a 2013 speech at the University of Chicago Law School, in fact, Justice Ruth Bader Ginsburg critiqued Blackmun's *Roe* opinion for focusing on medical data and privacy interests rather than on women's rights.

Closer to our time, Judge Posner has also embraced extrinsic research. In a 2014 oral argument in a controversial case about whether the University of Notre Dame must provide contraception coverage to its employees, he asked the university's lawyer whether contraception was a mortal sin or a venial one in Catholic theology (the lawyer didn't know, and Posner countered that he should). In his subsequent opinion for the court, Posner cited a broad swath of secondary authorities about contraception, many of which he found on the Web. These sources, few of which were in the record, ranged from medical journals to the Mayo Clinic's guide to selecting a birth-control pill. In another 2014 opinion affirming lower courts' decisions striking down same-sex-marriage bans in Indiana and Wisconsin, Posner asserted that "there [was] little doubt" that sexual orientation was an immutable characteristic, citing a study published in the journal *Sexuality Research and Social Policy*, as well as information found on the website of the American Psychological Association—even though neither state argued the point.[6]

Critics argue that information outside the record is untested by the adversarial process and is thus more likely to be inaccurate. Even the facts presented in an amicus brief might "not pass muster in a high school research paper," as *New York Times* Supreme Court reporter Adam Liptak recently observed, noting that some of the "facts" that the U.S. Supreme Court had learned of in friend-of-the-court filings had a shaky empirical foundation at best.[7]

At the outer reaches, a judge may decide to test the parties' assertions personally. Judge Posner, for his part, ruffled feathers when he discussed in an appellate opinion videotaped experiments in his chambers that involved having court staff don and doff work clothes at issue in a case about how long it took workers to change into them[8]—and when he included in another opinion a photograph not in the record of an ostrich with its head in the sand.[9]

In Posner's view, such facts add a pragmatic, down-to-earth dimension that he suggests is conspicuously absent from most advocates' (and judges') work. In essence, Posner is inviting the fact-statement writer to be more of a storyteller, adding perspective or context that makes the tale come alive. He has also argued that judges consider extrinsic knowledge anyway, so he is simply being candid in his opinions about what other judges suppress.

So who's right? For most opinions, I'm inclined to think the truth lies in the middle: it can help to add tested facts to establish context, but it's risky to rely on research that may prove to be unsupported (or disputed). Consider how you would react at trial if you learned that jurors spent their evenings on the Web researching articles and studies about, say, the sort of DNA testing that an expert had discussed that morning. Yet Posner also makes points that can't be easily dismissed: that the parties often neglect to include enough context to make their dispute understandable, that he's only doing what the lawyers failed to do, and that if judges do their own research whether they admit it or not, they owe it to the parties to reveal exactly what they considered when making their decisions.

Shine a Light: Emphasize Key Facts

Now you've purged "over-particularized" facts that are irrelevant to the analysis, and perhaps you've also sprinkled in some extrinsic background for good measure. So much for what facts to include in the first place. But what about which of those facts to emphasize? Which should be surveyed from the clouds, and which should be placed under a microscope?

In a few high-profile cases, choices about which facts to stress can even help shape the course of the law. In his excellent book *Opinion Writing*, Judge Ruggero Aldisert offers the example of *Rylands v. Fletcher*, the famous 1868 torts judgment from the House of Lords. By stressing that the defendant had built a reservoir on his land that allowed water to escape, and by declining to discuss any negligence on the defendant's part, the House of Lords essentially established the doctrine of strict liability. Judge Aldisert quotes Jerome Frank on this point: "[The judge] unconsciously selects those facts which, in combination of the rules of law which he considers to be pertinent, will make 'logical' his decision."[10]

And yet I'm not sure that the selection of facts is—or should be—truly unconscious. I doubt it's a coincidence, for example, that in the U.S. Supreme Court's landmark death-penalty cases in the 1970s and '80s, the justices who voted against death sentences said nary a word about the underlying crimes, while those who upheld death sentences sometimes sounded like they were writing smut fiction. Neither side did anything misleading, let alone unethical; each simply shone a light on the parts of the record that supported its conclusions.

"[O]ne cannot simply reprint the record of the trial below, and the task of interpreting and condensing the record requires that the judge frequently dip his pen into the well of rhetoric," says former D.C. Circuit Chief Judge Wald. "This is not," she adds, "just a matter of being selective about which facts to emphasize (or even to mention), but also a matter of characterization; the facts can—and indeed must—be retold to cast the party as an innocent victim or an undeserving malefactor, to tow the storyline into the safe harbor of whatever principles of law the author thinks should control the case."[11]

As an example of how to "tow the storyline into the safe harbor," let's take a close look at dueling facts in an Australian case. A man killed a male friend who he claimed had made a sexual advance toward him. At trial, the defendant sought to present evidence that his father had sexually abused his sisters in the past, evidence that might support a homosexual-provocation defense that the victim's sexual advance had provoked him to lose self-control and to commit the crime. The Australian High Court issued several opinions concluding that the defendant should have been allowed to assert this defense, along with two dissents to the contrary. Justice Michael McHugh wrote a majority opinion, and Justice Kirby wrote a dissent.

Here's how the two judges described the interactions between defendant and victim the evening of the killing. From 30,000 feet (or should I say 10,000 meters?), we have McHugh's account:

Michael McHugh, *Green v. The Queen*

On the night of the killing, the deceased had invited the accused to dinner. They dined and watched a number of television programmes. According to the accused, each of them consumed a significant amount of alcohol during the evening. The deceased asked the accused if he would like to stay overnight. After initially refusing the offer, the accused decided to stay. The deceased said that he would sleep in his mother's bedroom and that the accused could sleep in the deceased's bedroom.

And now contrast that somewhat antiseptic presentation with Justice Kirby's dissent. Kirby shares much more detail about the defendant's preexisting problems, his long-standing relationship with the victim, and the context of the overnight visit. It's no surprise, given these points of emphasis, that Kirby goes on to conclude that the homosexual-provocation defense should have never been allowed:

Michael Kirby, *Green v. The Queen*, dissenting

The appellant had no steady job. For a time, he had a de facto relationship with a girlfriend. But she left him about a week before the events giving rise to the charge. The day before those events, the appellant went to the home of Mr. and Mrs. Sirola. There was a dispute as to exactly what was said during this visit. But both Mr. and Mrs. Sirola recalled that the appellant said something to the effect that he intended to "knock somebody off" or "put someone down". The Sirolas were reminded of these statements some time later when watching a television programme.

They tried to make sense of their recollections. They reported them to the police. They gave evidence about them at the trial.

Early in the morning of 20 May 1993 the appellant killed Mr Don Gillies ("the deceased") at the latter's home in Mudgee, New South Wales. The deceased had been a friend of the appellant for between 5 and 6 years. He was described by one of the appellant's sisters as someone who was "always there" to help the appellant. No reason was established by the evidence, or suggested by the appellant, for any dislike on his part towards the deceased. On the contrary, they went swimming, diving, drinking and jogging together. They worked together at a local church where the deceased played the organ. On a number of occasions, the deceased had organised work for the appellant. The appellant did not allege that, prior to the killing, the deceased had demonstrated any sexual interest in him.

The appellant had never previously stayed overnight at the deceased's premises. However, on the evening of 19 May 1993, at the invitation of the deceased, the appellant went to the latter's home. They shared a meal, drank wine and later whisky together whilst watching television. According to the appellant, later in the evening, when both of them were much affected by the alcohol they had consumed, the deceased invited him to sleep there overnight. This would save the appellant walking to his sister's home where he was then residing. It was proposed that the appellant should sleep in the deceased's bed. The deceased would sleep in another bedroom, sometimes occupied by his mother, but unoccupied on that evening.

That's all for the backstory. But when the two justices shift their gaze to the moments just before the killing, they exchange roles: McHugh zooms in, while Kirby zooms out. McHugh appears to adopt the defendant's perspective and state of mind:

Michael McHugh, *Green v. The Queen*

In a record of interview made a few hours after the killing, the accused said: "and he showed me to the bed I was sleeping in. After a while when I was fully unclothed Don entered the room I was in, slid in beside me in the bed and started talking to me how a great person I was. Then he started touching me. I pushed him away. He asked what was wrong. I said, 'What do you think is wrong? I'm not like this.' He started grabbing me with both hands around my lower back. I pushed him away. He started grabbing me harder. I tried and forced him to the lower side of me. He still tried to grab me. I hit him again and again on top of the bed until he didn't look like Don to me. He still tried to grope and talk to me that's when I hit him again and saw the scissors on the floor on the right hand side of the bed. When I saw the scissors he touched me around the waist shoulders area and said, 'Why'? I said to him, 'Why, I didn't ask for this.'"

Kirby, by contrast, avoids the defendant's point of view almost entirely, choosing instead to summarize and paraphrase like a distant observer. He includes almost no quotes from the defendant at all, other than a quote suggesting that the victim was "trying to soothe" him:

Michael Kirby, *Green v. The Queen*, dissenting

The appellant lay on the deceased's bed. He removed his upper garment but left his underpants and tracksuit pants on. The appellant alleges that, before he had fallen asleep, the deceased entered the bedroom, apparently naked. He lay beside the appellant and started grabbing with both hands towards the appellant's backside and penis. As described in the evidence, the deceased initially did so gently and not aggressively or brutally. The appellant verbally protested to the deceased against these advances. Then, as the deceased started grabbing the appellant more insistently, the latter began hitting the deceased. He hit him repeatedly. The deceased tried to hold the appellant, as the latter interpreted it, "trying to soothe" him. The appellant saw and grabbed a pair of scissors on the floor on the right side of the bed. He stabbed the deceased repeatedly with the scissors. The deceased rolled off the bed. He was left on the floor, face-downward, in a pool of his own blood.

These competing treatments of facts are a harbinger of the competing legal analyses to come: McHugh, who appears to put himself in the shoes of the defendant, prefers a subjective approach, while Kirby steers clear of the defendant's testimony, focusing instead on the objective standard of whether the earlier acts would have provoked an "ordinary man."

Finally, when it comes time to relay the killing itself, the two justices revert to their original roles, with McHugh zooming out at cruising altitude and Kirby zooming in like a character on *CSI: Sydney*. McHugh glosses over the brutality of the killing, occupying himself instead with the defendant's regrets immediately thereafter:

Michael McHugh, *Green v. The Queen*

"I grabbed the scissors and hit him again. He rolled off the bed as I struck him with the scissors. By the time I stopped I realised what had happened. I just stood at the foot of the bed with Don on the floor laying face down in blood. I thought to myself how other people can do something like this and enjoy what they do. I didn't get off on this and like it not just because he was someone I knew even though he resembled someone I knew. I didn't know what to do, didn't know where to go."

But Kirby, for his part, cloaks himself in the perspective of a medical examiner confronted with the deceased's wounded and bloody corpse:

Michael Kirby, *Green v. The Queen*, dissenting

According to the appellant's evidence, he punched the deceased about 35 times and then stabbed him as he rolled off the bed. He admitted to stabbing the deceased up to half a dozen times. However, the post mortem examination showed the ferocity and brutality of the appellant's attack upon the deceased. . . . Ten stab wounds were found. They were described as being in the shape of a butterfly. After describing them, the examiner (Dr. Du Flou) went on:

"Broadly speaking there were three large grazes on the left side of the head in the area of the temple which appeared to be 12 mms apart. In addition there was an area of grazing and bruising over the left temple and an area of grazing immediately behind the left ear. . . ."

[After additional presentation of Dr. Du Flou's testimony, Kirby concludes:]

These findings led Dr. Du Flou, to conclude, when taken with evidence of blood spray patterns and other physical indications at the scene of the crime:

"[W]hat I believe is that the head was brought into contact forcibly with that part of the wall and that the head which at that stage had blood on it on coming into contact with the wall caused blood to spray outwards ... I would strongly favour that in fact the face was brought into contact with the wall."*

Not that there's nothing untoward here. Whether any account can be truly "objective" is an open question. After all, even seemingly antiseptic online or print accounts of events are often accused of bias and hidden agendas these days. Indeed, both McHugh and Kirby will have fans and foes here. Critics will accuse McHugh of glossing over the parties' relationship and the killing itself, but his admirers will insist that he is properly focusing on the core legal issue of the defendant's right to present his best defense. And while Kirby's foes will accuse him of trying to exploit graphic testimony to arouse the reader's sympathies, his fans will praise him for being candid about

---

* The sentence introducing Dr. Du Flou's conclusion is a good example of why it's best to keep like parts of the sentence together. Rather than "These findings led Dr. Du Flou, to conclude, when taken with evidence of blood spray patterns. . .," which is both confusing and syntactically unsound, Justice Kirby could have written "These findings, when taken with evidence of blood spray patterns and other physical indications at the scene of the crime, led Dr. Du Flou to conclude the following."

important facts in the record that cast doubt on the defendant's theory of the case.

Speaking of candor, judges should probably concede that there's no such thing as a "Just the Facts, Ma'am" approach. No matter what you do, and no matter how hard you strive to be "fair," someone can justifiably criticize you for what you include and what you omit, and for what you relay in glorious detail and what you gloss over as fast as you can. It's essential to be fair to the losing side when you present facts. But you shouldn't be afraid to slow down and enjoy the record as you highlight key facts that make your legal conclusions all the more compelling.

Do You See What I See: Adopt a Narrative Voice

All factual accounts have a voice. On one extreme you have *The Economist*, where you won't even find the author's byline—and yet the style is distinctive. On the other extreme you have narrative and literary nonfiction, genres that demand strong authorial identities and intrusions.

Judicial fact statements span the gamut as well. If you agree with Judge Posner's edict that judges should be candid about what they considered and rejected, you'll probably need to include at least the occasional "author's note." In the example below, for instance, Posner's Seventh Circuit colleague Judge Diane Wood engages with the reader directly when she says that "Somewhat to our surprise, it turns out that there is a niche market for farting dolls":

Diane Wood, *JCW Investments v. Novelty, Inc.*

Somewhat to our surprise, it turns out that there is a niche market for farting dolls, and it is quite lucrative. Tekky Toys, an Illinois corporation, designs and sells a whole line of them. Fred was just the beginning. Fred's creators, Jamie Wirt and Geoff Bevington, began working on Fred in 1997, and had a finished doll in 1999. They applied for a copyright registration on Fred as a "plush toy with sound," and received a certificate of copyright on February 5, 2001; later, they assigned the certificate to Tekky.

Rather than simply recite a chronology of events, Judge Wood shares with the reader an honest wonder at Tekky Toys's improbable rise to stardom. And by not taking itself too seriously, the opinion lets the reader chuckle over the subject matter and focus on the law instead.

When the court becomes an active narrator in this way, the reader can appreciate the facts through the court's eyes. Such a perspective is especially helpful when the facts are complex or technical. As a sympathetic narrator, the judge can explain, analogize, simplify, and reassure, as Judge Posner does in a trial opinion in an intellectual-property case below:

Richard Posner (sitting by designation), *Apple v. Motorola*

Apple '002 is the patent feature on the toolbar notification window that gives the user basic information about the state of his device, such as battery strength; it's analogous to an automobile's dashboard. Apple contends that Motorola infringes the patent by including on its cell phones (and other handheld devices, such as tablets—but for simplicity I'll pretend in this opinion that the case involves just cell phones) Apple's patented invention of a software program that prevents the notification window from being partially obstructed by an application program selected by the user. Total, as opposed to partial, obstruction occurs when, for example, the user selects the camera program on the iPhone, which fills the entire screen; the patented invention does not prevent total obstruction.

Notice that even in this high-tech case, Judge Posner tells a story about people. He describes the technology first from the user's perspective, then from the inventor's, and finally from the court's perspective as the entity overseeing the patent dispute. By creating a role for himself in the story as a user and explainer of technology, Judge Posner encourages the reader to trust his presentation of complex facts.

Lord Denning was an acknowledged master of this technique (Posner, in fact, might be Lord Denning's modern American incarnation). It's worth sharing some longish excerpts from Lord Denning's conversational factual account in the famous dog-bite judgment. After the opening sentence we discussed in Part 1, Denning segues into a dinner-party-like recounting of the facts:

Lord Denning, *Cummings v. Granger*

This is the case of the barmaid who was badly bitten by a big dog. It was a guard dog, an Alsatian [German Shepherd] about two years old. It kept guard over a yard next to the Maypole public house in East London. The yard was used for storing and selling scrap motor cars and scrap metal, and so forth. It was enclosed by high walls and a high wire fence. During the day-time customers came to the yard. To protect them, the owner, the defendant, kept the dog secure in an old van from which it could not escape. During the night-time, and also during weekends, there were no customers coming to the yard. The big gates were shut. At those times, to scare intruders, the defendant let the dog run loose about the yard; but it could not get out. The walls and fences were too high.

The big gates had a warning on them in huge letters "Beware of the Dog." Alongside the big gates there was a small wicket gate. It was padlocked at night, but the defendant put the key in a secret place near the gate so that he (or anyone whom he authorised) could get in. The defendant said that the dog took particular objection to coloured people. If people came round near to his cage in the day-time, the dog would bark and run round in circles. At night if the gate was rattled the dog would come to the gate and bark.

Coming now to the particular night, it was November 4, 1971. Closing time in the public house was at half past 11. The customers were leaving. The barmaid, the plaintiff, and her friend Mr. Hobson had just left too. They were going to her car. It was parked in the street outside the scrap-yard. Her friend Mr. Hobson had his car in the scrap-yard. He wanted to get some tools out of it. He knew where to find the key of the yard. He got the key. He unlocked the padlock and went in by the wicket gate. The plaintiff says that she stayed outside on the pavement, but the judge did not believe her. The judge found that she followed her companion in. She got nearly to the middle of the yard when the dog attacked her.

A neighbour in the house opposite saw what was happening. He had just got into bed when he heard the dog barking. He jumped out of bed and looked. He saw the dog in the yard attacking the plaintiff. She was in the middle of the yard. Her man friend was trying to get the dog away by beating it with a piece of wood or iron. He saw him helping the plaintiff to the car to drive her to hospital.

Her cheek was torn open and she was badly injured. She has had plastic surgery, but she has a very severe scar still remaining on her cheek. She now claims damages against the owner of the dog.

. . .

After the accident the plaintiff's handbag and shoe were found in the middle of the yard. She had to explain how this came to be. She did it this way. She said she was standing outside on the pavement waiting for her friend to come out. Then she heard a noise. She turned round and there was the dog. She was terrified of it, but she says that she tried to make friends with it. She patted it on the head. This seemed to infuriate the dog. It went at her and dragged her from the pavement through the gate and then back into the yard. That is why she was seen to be in the yard and that is why her handbag and shoe were there in the middle of the yard. The judge did not believe that the plaintiff stayed outside. He found that she had gone inside. She had followed her companion without any authority at all. She was a trespasser in the yard. That must be accepted. Mr. Irvine took us through the evidence. He asked us to find that the plaintiff's story was correct, but I am quite clear that we cannot interfere with the judge's finding. She was a trespasser.

As with his "rewrite" of Justice Megarry's facts above, Lord Denning uses short and conversational narrative sentences. He identifies no party by name. He depicts the scrap yard, the gates, the warning signs, and the padlock, with each sentence building on a fact introduced in the sentence before. (Although I've cut the citations from nearly all the excerpts in this book, in Lord Denning's judgment there were no citations in the first place.) He presents the facts almost as a beat reporter would, guiding the reader through closing time, the dog's bite, the victim's insistence that she did not go into the yard, and the trial judge's finding that she did. Like Judge Wood, Lord Denning also gives the court a cameo appearance in the narrative (plaintiff's counsel "asked us to find" in her favor, but "I am quite clear that we cannot interfere" with the lower court's ruling).

Even when Lord Denning turns to expert testimony, he preserves his natural narrative voice:

> A veterinary surgeon gave evidence as to the behaviour of this Alsatian. Was it exceptionally ferocious? He answered: "No, I think this is perfectly normal behaviour for a good number of Alsatians or, indeed, many other breeds of dogs." The judge asked: "What—to leap up and seize somebody by the face?"
>
> [*After presenting more of the expert's testimony, Lord Denning continues:*]
>
> A little later he was asked whether it was not unusual for an ordinary house Alsatian to seize somebody's face because she bends down to pat it. The veterinary surgeon answered:
>
> No, many house dogs will not accept strangers, and this sort of behaviour where you bend down straight out of the blue, you are likely to get attacked by many dogs—Alsatians and many other sorts of dogs.
>
> So this Alsatian was just a typical guard dog.

"So this Alsatian was just a typical guard dog." That's not a conclusion you'd see in most opinions. Much more likely, you'd read something like this: "Dr. Smith testified this was customary behavior with regard to guard dogs."

The barmaid's case is justly famous as an example of superb legal analysis, precisely because Denning adopts and maintains an authentic voice, becoming the story's narrator instead of merely parroting back the facts in the record. Don't be afraid to play storyteller.

Clean-Up: Enhance Visual Appeal

Some judges are so adept at narrating facts that they need no structural subparts or other visual cues. But many fact statements could use some thoughtful formatting. Numbered lists and bullet points can make particular "chunks" of facts visible and memorable, and longer sections can benefit from headings as well.

Numbered lists can be an effective way to organize a fact section and to prove that the court has done its homework. In the following example, Seventh Circuit Judge Easterbrook uses bullet points to contrast the defendants' representations with the truth:

Frank Easterbrook, *FTC v. QT, Inc.*

According to the district court's findings, almost everything that defendants have said about the bracelet is false. Here are some highlights:

- Defendants promoted the bracelet as a miraculous cure for chronic pain, but it has no therapeutic effects.
- Defendants told consumers that claims of "immediate, significant, or complete pain relief" had been "test proven"; they hadn't.
- The bracelet does not emit "Q-Rays" (there are no such things) and is not ionized (the bracelet is an electric conductor, and any net charge dissipates swiftly). The bracelet's chief promoter chose these labels because they are simple and easily remembered—and because Polaroid Corp. blocked him from calling the bangle "polarized".
- The bracelet is touted as "enhancing the flow of bio-energy" or "balancing the flow of positive and negative energies";

> these empty phrases have no connection to any medi-
> cal or scientific effect. Every other claim made about the
> mechanism of the bracelet's therapeutic effect likewise is
> techno-babble. . . .

(For those of you who are so inclined, Q-Ray bracelets are still sold online at www.qray.com in "gold" and "silver" varieties ranging from $50 to $250 per bracelet.)

Bankruptcy Judge Goldgar similarly condenses dense facts into a reader-friendly bulleted-pointed list:

Benjamin Goldgar, *In Re Brent*

The addendum went on to describe six charges for which the debtor would be liable:

- "[L]ate fees of 18% per annum from the date below plus reasonable Attorney's fees and court costs" for "any balance due Attorney which is overdue 30 days or more . . . ."
- A fee of "$65.00 for processing each NSF check" presented for the payment of attorney's fees.
- Attorney's fees at Liou's standard hourly rate "for prospective work to cover necessary post-termination work such as drafting itemizations of work performed, collection/skip-tracing, etc.," along with "all costs Attorney incurs on behalf of Client . . . ."
- Attorney's fees at "the hourly rate of $295.00 for services not specified in the Model Retention Agreement . . . ."
- A "'convenience fee' of 5%" if the debtor elected to pay a portion of the attorney's fees and costs "by debit card from a checking account or by someone else's credit card . . . ."

- The filing fee and attorney's fees for "two hours of Attorney time . . . to draft a motion to reopen the bankruptcy case" if the court closed the case without discharge because the debtor had not filed either the credit counseling certificate required under section 109(h) of the Code or the personal financial management certificate required under sections 111 and 1328(g)(1).

In everyday writing, numbered lists and bullet points help the reader see broad categories of information, make comparisons, or visualize sequences of events. They work just as well for the facts underlying a judicial opinion.

Like numbered lists and bullet points, headings create white space and offer signposts that help a busy reader navigate to a desired bit of text. Advocates commonly use headings in their filings, and the same technique can break up a judicial fact statement. The headings signal what is most important, or most memorable, about the facts.

Consider these three examples:

Benjamin Goldgar, *In Re Brent*

1. Jurisdiction
2. Background
   a. Attorney Compensation in Chapter 13
   b. Flat Fees in the Northern District of Illinois
   c. The Show Cause Orders
   d. The Show Cause Hearing
      i. Liou
      ii. Sukowicz

Michael Ponsor, *Angiodynamics, Inc. v. Biolitec, Inc.*

II. Factual Background
 A. The Parties.
 B. The Formation and Alleged Breach of the SDA.
 C. The Alleged Looting of Defendant BI.
 D. The Alleged Tortious Interference by Defendants BAG
 and Neuberger

Michael Kirby, *Green v. The Queen*

A fatal stabbing after a sexual advance
 The post mortem examination
 The course of the trial
 The decision of the Court of Criminal Appeal

Each of these examples offers a different way to lead the reader through the background that buttresses the legal analysis. Judge Goldgar follows the funnel pattern, starting with a broad context of fee petitions and narrowing to identify the two attorneys involved in the case. Judge Ponsor breaks down the fact section by major event. And Justice Kirby's headings could be chapter titles in a mystery novel.

In the end, fact statements are all about balance. They must reflect the record, yet they should also be much shorter and far more compelling. They must include enough background to orient the reader, yet even if the advocates have not done their homework, the court should avoid venturing into aimless and untested research. They should emphasize the facts that support their conclusion, yet they must still play fair with the losing side. They should remain faithful to the record, but they should also acknowledge that some facts are surprising, confusing, or conflicting.

In sum, the very best fact statements will have a voice. Like it or not, the court is a player in the narrative of every case, and the reader will appreciate a candid account of which facts stood out for you and why.

Practice Pointers for Fact Statements:

- Subtract all details—proper names and titles, calendar dates, times, street addresses, quantities and weights—that play no role in the analysis.
- When the parties don't provide enough information, make up the deficiency—within reason. Add well-known facts necessary to establish context, but avoid relying on facts that are unsupported or that are likely to be disputed. If you're wondering which side of the line a source falls on, consider how you'd react if a juror wanted to refer to it during deliberations.
- Emphasize the facts that are the most important to your reasoning. Treating them at length, add detailed descriptions, quote testimony, reproduce images, or otherwise give the reader a picture of the evidence. You can also de-emphasize facts by summarizing them in a sentence, using abstract words and conclusions.
- The court can function as character in the story who expresses a point of view. The court is a teacher, a guide, a resource to the reader. Don't be afraid to inject some personality into your factual account.
- Formatting devices can help the reader process complex facts. Use headings, subheadings, bullet points, and numbered paragraphs to draw the reader's attention to facts, to facilitate comparisons, and to highlight disputes.

PART 3

The Meat

The Legal Analysis

Overview: The Skeleton 81

Overview: In the Flesh 83

    Example: *Snyder v. Phelps* 83

        John Roberts, *Snyder v. Phelps* (Section II) 84

With You in Spirit: Paragraphs as Dialogues 97

        Shira Scheindlin, *United States v. Awadallah* 99

        Beverly McLachlin, *Schmeiser v. Monsanto* 101

        Marsha Berzon, *Minasyan v. Mukasey* 102

        Michael Ponsor, *United States v. Watts* 105

        Frank Easterbrook, *Matter of Sinclair* 106

        Antonin Scalia, *Scott v. Harris* 108

Order out of Chaos: Internal Organizational Devices 108

    A. Headings 108

        Shira Scheindlin, *New York Magazine v. Metropolitan Transit Authority* 109

        Beverly McLachlin, *Schmeiser v. Monsanto Canada Inc.* 110

        Lord Sumption, *Cox v. Ergo Versicherung AG* 111

    B. "Umbrella" Introductions 111

        Benjamin Goldgar, *In re Earley* 111

        Beverly McLachlin, *Seaboyer v. The Queen* 112

        Roger Traynor, *Drennan v. Star Paving Co.* 113

    C. Bulleted and Numbered Lists 114

        Antonin Scalia, *Scott v. Harris* 114

        D.P. Marshall, *Little Rock School Dist. v. North Little Rock School Dist.* 116

        Benjamin Goldgar, *In Re Brent* 117

Patrick Schiltz, *Shiraz Hookah, LLC v. City of Minneapolis* 118

Lord Sumption, *Prest v. Petrodel Resources Ltd.* 119

O. Rogeriee Thompson, *United States v. Seng Tan* 120

Me, Too: Analogizing 121

Jed Rakoff, *Garcia v. Bloomberg* 121

Benjamin Goldgar, *In re Brent* 122

D.P. Marshall, *Tucker v. Southwestern Energy Co.* 123

Jed Rakoff, *23-34 94th St. Grocery v. N.Y. City Bd.* 123

Patrick Schiltz, *Shiraz Hookah, LLC v. City of Minneapolis* 124

Patrick Schiltz, *Newton v. Walker* 125

Not Here, Not Now: Distinguishing 127

Patricia Wald, *Hubbard v. EPA* 127

Alex Kozinski, *Mattel v. MCA Records* 131

Shira Scheindlin, *New York Magazine v. Metropolitan Transit Authority* 132

Richard Posner, *Indiana Harbor Belt R.R. v. American Cyanamid Co.* 133

Learned Hand, *Cheney Bros. v. Doris Silk Corp.* 135

As an Aside: Parentheticals 136

Michael Ponsor, *Gatti v. Nat'l Union Fire Ins.* 136

Patricia Wald, *Steffan v. Perry*, dissenting 137

Shira Scheindlin, *Clark v. Perez* 137

John Roberts, *Messerschmidt v. Millender* 138

Michael Kirby, *Green v. The Queen*, dissenting 139

Diane Wood, *Tarpley v. Allen County, Indiana* 140

Lead 'Em On: Quoting without Tears 140

Frank Easterbrook, *In re Sinclair* 142

Alex Kozinski, *Mattel v. MCA Records* 143

Michael Kirby, *Green v. The Queen*, dissenting 144

Beverly McLachlin, *R. v. Keegstra*, dissenting 144

Antonin Scalia, *Scott v. Harris* 145

John Paul Stevens, *Scott v. Harris*, dissenting 146

Troubled Waters: The Footnoters' Dilemma 147

Antonin Scalia, *Sykes v. United States*, dissenting 148

Patricia Wald, *Steffan v. Perry*, dissenting 149

Michael Ponsor, *United States v. Watts* 150

Patrick Schiltz, *Newton v. Walker* 151

Ruth Bader Ginsburg, *United States v. Virginia* 152

Practice Pointers for the Analysis 153

Does a grand unifying theory apply to the organization of legal analysis?

Tips for advocates, such as "put your strongest points first," don't always work in judicial opinion-writing, and general advice such as "make an outline first" glosses over what such an outline should include. But that doesn't mean that anything goes. The main trait that makes judicial opinions easy to follow is that they are structured as more of a dialogue than a monologue: the best judicial writers preempt and then answer questions from an imaginary reader, and perhaps a skeptical one to boot. It's simply not enough to tell yourself that you're going to identify the issues, discuss the law, apply it to the facts, and then address any counterarguments. All judges do those four things, but with wildly varying results.

Simulating a dialogue with an imaginary reader can help resolve many common organizational problems, because it will prompt you to address points and counterpoints in the order that they're likely to arise in the reader's mind. To see how such a dialogue can work as an organizational device, let's begin with broad macro-structural techniques and then segue into the treatment of authorities and the other inner workings of legal analysis.

Overview: The Skeleton

Once you have settled on the result but before you begin writing, use these six questions to shape your legal analysis:

1) What logical questions might occur to a reader who is skeptical of your reasoning, and in what order? Answer those questions one at a time with just a sentence or two apiece.

2) Why should your answers be trusted? Under each answer, list the applicable authorities, facts, and reasons, and then explain the connection between each authority and each answer in your own words. Quote and copy sparingly at this juncture.

3) Is your answer to any question likely to prove controversial? If so, acknowledge all viable counterarguments ("To be sure," "Although it is true that," and so forth) and then explain why they should not prevail.

   You now have the makings of a first-rate analysis. The next steps are all cleanup.

4) What natural or logical divisions would make the analysis easier to navigate? Consider breaking down the overall structure by topic, by party, by motion, by claim, or by any other principle that grafts a beginning, middle, and end onto the analysis.

5) Use traditional outline structure (I, II, III; A, B, C), a modified outline structure, bullet points, headings and subheadings, or other visual cues to organize your analysis. If you or your court disfavor these devices and prefer either the uninterrupted-essay approach or the continually numbered-paragraphs approach, break up long paragraphs so that the analysis isn't overwhelming. And even if you number your paragraphs, consider adding some headings anyway.

6) Finally, add cues to help the reader navigate at the micro level within the sections. Start with a short "umbrella" paragraph previewing the entire analysis, also add a short "umbrella" paragraph at the start of each section, present old information before new, add transitions within and between paragraphs to show how your points connect to one another, and end each section with a short conclusion.

Overview: In the Flesh

Now let's consider how these six steps might look in practice. We'll begin with an example from the main analytical portion of a majority opinion by Chief Justice John Roberts. Roberts's legal analysis in *Snyder v. Phelps* is perfectly organized to lead the reader from broad legal principles through their application to facts—and to a conclusion that may be troubling for reasons both substantive (because Roberts appears to give a free pass to protestors at a funeral for a dead Marine, even though such conduct has since been outlawed in many states) and procedural (because Roberts overturns a jury verdict). Without clear and well-supported analysis, a skeptical reader might doubt the Court's conclusion, but the chief justice delivers.

Example: *Snyder v. Phelps*

Snyder v. Phelps is part of a long line of tough cases pitting freedom of expression against privacy rights. A group called the Westboro Baptist Church was vehemently opposed to homosexuality. It also made a habit of holding protests at sites sure to provoke controversy and attract media attention. At one of these protests, the group targeted the funeral of a young Marine fallen in Iraq. Although the group obeyed local ordinances requiring that they keep a certain distance from the funeral itself, they brandished such provocative signs as "God Hates Fags," "Priests Rape Boys," and "Thank God for Dead Soldiers."

The family members of the fallen soldier were outraged, and the soldier's father, Mr. Snyder, eventually prevailed on a common-law claim for intentional infliction of emotional distress. The jury awarded the family money damages, and the case wended its way to the U.S. Supreme Court, which eventually overturned the jury's award.

In crafting his legal analysis in support of this unpopular result, Chief Justice Roberts follows four guiding principles:

* Track a logical progression in the paragraph openers.
* Start paragraphs by referring to a point from the end of the previous paragraph.
* Preempt likely objections and concerns.
* Integrate key quotations from case law without burdening the reader with excess detail and regurgitated language.

The issue was whether the damage award to Mr. Snyder could withstand a freedom-of-expression challenge. The opening sentence of Roberts's opinion makes clear that he sees the plaintiff's burden as a heavy one. And by pivoting immediately to the First Amendment, Roberts hints that the defense will prevail:

John Roberts, *Snyder v. Phelps* (Section II)

To succeed on a claim for intentional infliction of emotional distress in Maryland, a plaintiff must demonstrate that the defendant intentionally or recklessly engaged in extreme and outrageous conduct that caused the plaintiff to suffer severe emotional distress. The Free Speech Clause of the First Amendment—"Congress shall make no law . . . abridging the freedom of speech"—can serve as a defense in state tort suits, including suits for intentional infliction of emotional distress.

With these two sentences, Roberts puts into the ring the two dueling principles that will duke it out for the rest of the opinion.

Now let's move on to Roberts's statement of the governing rule. The next paragraph begins by anticipating the reader's logical questions: *So which of these competing doctrines—compensating victims or free speech—will prevail? How will you decide whether the First*

Amendment will save the Westboro Baptist Church here? Roberts sets out a rule that will answer these questions: whether the speech is of public concern or of private concern:

> Whether the First Amendment prohibits holding Westboro liable for its speech in this case turns largely on whether that speech is of public or private concern, as determined by all the circumstances of the case. "[S]peech on 'matters of public concern' . . . is 'at the heart of the First Amendment's protection.'" The First Amendment reflects "a profound national commitment to the principle that debate on public issues should be uninhibited, robust, and wide-open." That is because "speech concerning public affairs is more than self-expression; it is the essence of self-government." Accordingly, "speech on public issues occupies the highest rung of the hierarchy of First Amendment values, and is entitled to special protection."*

A reader might next ask: *Why don't public speech and private speech enjoy the same protection?* Roberts explains:

> "'[N]ot all speech is of equal First Amendment importance,'" however, and where matters of purely private significance are at issue, First Amendment protections are often less rigorous. That is because restricting speech on purely private matters does not implicate the same constitutional

---

* Note three hallmark Roberts style traits: "To," not "in order to"; "must," not "is required to"; and "can," not "is able to." Not to mention the two-sentence paragraph.

Roberts uses "whether," not "whether or not," and "turns on," not "is contingent upon." He also merges short snippets of quotations and uses the elegant transitional phrase "That is because" to segue from self-expression to self-government.

> concerns as limiting speech on matters of public inter-
> est: "[T]here is no threat to the free and robust debate
> of public issues; there is no potential interference with a
> meaningful dialogue of ideas"; and the "threat of liability"
> does not pose the risk of "a reaction of self-censorship" on
> matters of public import.*

So the chief justice has drawn a line between rigorously protected speech on issues of public importance, on the one hand, and less protected speech on matters of purely private concern, on the other. The next paragraph answers two more related questions: *How do we determine what is public and what is private? And where on the dividing line will this case fall?* The topic sentence in the paragraph below admits that it is hard to categorize speech as either public or private, a concession that respects the lower court's decision while priming the reader for more:

> We noted a short time ago, in considering whether pub-
> lic employee speech addressed a matter of public concern,
> that "the boundaries of the public concern test are not well
> defined." Although that remains true today, we have articu-
> lated some guiding principles, principles that accord broad
> protection to speech to ensure that courts themselves do not
> become inadvertent censors.**

---

* I would prefer "when matters" to the legalistic "where matters," but for now, I'll let it go. Also note once again how Roberts merges short phrases from the case law into his final sentence.

** "Although," not "Despite the fact that" and "to ensure," not "in order to ensure." Also note "principles, principles that accord"—using a resumptive modifier that's more elegant (and clearer) than "principles, which accord" would have been.

Having declared that guiding principles govern, Roberts anticipates the reader's logical follow-up question: *Okay, then, so what are
they?* The next paragraph explains, beginning with public concern:

> Speech deals with matters of public concern when it can "be
> fairly considered as relating to any matter of political, social,
> or other concern to the community," or when it "is a subject of
> legitimate news interest; that is, a subject of general interest
> and of value and concern to the public[.]" The arguably "inappro-
> priate or controversial character of a statement is irrelevant to
> the question whether it deals with a matter of public concern."

So much for public concern, our reader thinks, *but what about the
other one, private concern?* Here is the chief justice's response:

> Our opinion in *Dun & Bradstreet,* on the other hand, provides
> an example of speech of only private concern. In that case
> we held, as a general matter, that information about a par-
> ticular individual's credit report "concerns no public issue."
> The content of the report, we explained, "was speech solely in
> the individual interest of the speaker and its specific business
> audience." That was confirmed by the fact that the particular
> report was sent to only five subscribers to the reporting ser-
> vice, who were bound not to disseminate it further. To cite
> another example, we concluded in *San Diego v. Roe* that, in
> the context of a government employer regulating the speech
> of its employees, videos of an employee engaging in sexually
> explicit acts did not address a public concern; the videos "did
> nothing to inform the public about any aspect of the [employ-
> ing agency's] functioning or operation."*

* Roberts puts "on the other hand" in the middle of the opening sentence to avoid
bogging down the start with "However." And to avoid cluttering up the discussion
of *San Diego v. Roe,* he replaces the name of the agency with "government employer."

Fine, says our reader. *But how do we know which side of the line we're on here?* Now Roberts morphs the public-private distinction into a "content, form, and context" test, which he helpfully characterizes as a "what, where, how" formulation:

> Deciding whether speech is of public or private concern requires us to examine the "content, form, and context'" of that speech," "'as revealed by the whole record.'" As in other First Amendment cases, the court is obliged "to "make an independent examination of the whole record" in order to make sure that "the judgment does not constitute a forbidden intrusion on the field of free expression." In considering content, form, and context, no factor is dispositive, and it is necessary to evaluate all the circumstances of the speech, including what was said, where it was said, and how it was said.

Having set out his three-element test, Roberts applies it to the facts of the case—facts that have so far been missing from the analysis. Again he anticipates the next logical question: *You've just said that to determine whether speech is public or private, we need to look at content, form, and context. Let's look first at content, or what was said. What are we looking for?*

> The "content" of Westboro's signs plainly relates to broad issues of interest to society at large, rather than matters of "purely private concern." The placards read "God Hates the USA/Thank God for 9/11," "America is Doomed," "Don't Pray for the USA," "Thank God for IEDs," "Fag Troops," "Semper Fi Fags," "God Hates Fags," "Maryland Taliban," "Fags Doom Nations," "Not Blessed Just Cursed," "Thank God for Dead Soldiers," "Pope in Hell," "Priests Rape Boys," "You're Going

> to Hell," and "God Hates You." While these messages may fall short of refined social or political commentary, the issues they highlight—the political and moral conduct of the United States and its citizens, the fate of our Nation, homosexuality in the military, and scandals involving the Catholic clergy—are matters of public import.*

Notice how Roberts uses the word "content" as a bridge transition that links the first sentence of this paragraph with the last sentence of the paragraph before. With typical understatement, he also concedes some bad facts here—the offensive signs—through the euphemism that they "may fall short of refined social or political commentary." And he deploys a pair of dashes to shift our attention away from the awful signs and toward the far loftier-sounding anodyne inquiries that Roberts suggests the signs reflect.

Yet Roberts knows that he can't make the signs disappear. *Wait,* says the reader. *Some of those signs sure sound ugly and personal to me—especially because they were brandished at a funeral. How can speaking to mourners at my loved one's funeral be "public" if speaking to banks reading my credit report is "private"?*

Roberts is armed with a response:

> The signs certainly convey Westboro's position on those issues, in a manner designed, unlike the private speech in *Dun & Bradstreet,* to reach as broad a public audience as possible. And even if a few of the signs—such as "You're Going to Hell" and "God Hates You"—were viewed as containing messages related to Matthew Snyder or the Snyders specifically, that

---

* Because "matters" is so far from "relates," I would suggest repeating "to" before "matters" for parallelism and clarity purposes.

> would not change the fact that the overall thrust and dominant theme of Westboro's demonstration spoke to broader public issues.

So what matters, Roberts explains to us naysayers, is the intent behind the signs, not the text of the signs themselves: a "public" message is simply one that seeks a broad audience. Stylistically, Roberts also downplays the Snyders' pain with the passive construction "were viewed as." It's almost as if Roberts is saying that the funeral protest had nothing to do with the Snyders.

But our skeptical reader remains unconvinced, wondering if Roberts is giving Westboro too much credit. *Wait, you also said that "context" matters. How you can divorce the comments about God and the military from the context of a funeral for a dead soldier? Doesn't the context make it private?* Roberts doesn't think so:

> Apart from the content of Westboro's signs, Snyder contends that the "context" of the speech—its connection with his son's funeral—makes the speech a matter of private rather than public concern. The fact that Westboro spoke in connection with a funeral, however, cannot by itself transform the nature of Westboro's speech. Westboro's signs, displayed on public land next to a public street, reflect the fact that the church finds much to condemn in modern society. Its speech is "fairly characterized as constituting speech on a matter of public concern," and the funeral setting does not alter that conclusion.

This particular paragraph borders on being circular: Roberts appears to suggest that as long as the "content" passes muster, the "context" will, too. By now, in fact, many readers will be frustrated, especially if they know that this isn't Westboro's first rodeo. *When Westboro has deliberately chosen a context and form of communication that is cruel to grieving families, why should it be allowed to cloak itself in the First Amendment?* Roberts responds:

> Snyder argues that the church members in fact mounted a personal attack on Snyder and his family, and then attempted to "immunize their conduct by claiming that they were actually protesting the United States' tolerance of homosexuality or the supposed evils of the Catholic Church." We are not concerned in this case that Westboro's speech on public matters was in any way contrived to insulate speech on a private matter from liability. Westboro had been actively engaged in speaking on the subjects addressed in its picketing long before it became aware of Matthew Snyder, and there can be no serious claim that Westboro's picketing did not represent its "honestly believed" views on public issues. There was no pre-existing relationship or conflict between Westboro and Snyder that might suggest Westboro's speech on public matters was intended to mask an attack on Snyder over a private matter. Contrast *Connick, supra,* (finding public employee speech a matter of private concern when it was "no coincidence that [the speech] followed upon the heels of [a] transfer notice" affecting the employee).*

Roberts knows that his conclusion will be unpopular, and he expects more reader resistance. *Even if you give Westboro a pass on the signs, how can you let it get away with purposely choosing the venue of a young person's funeral just to get more publicity?* To the contrary,

---

* Note the clean and crisp use of a parenthetical to distinguish *Connick*. Roberts follows all the rules here: participle up front, the word "because" or "when," and then why the case cited proves the preceding point true.

Roberts suggests, the desire to seek publicity, even if unseemly, affords speech *more* protection, not less:

> Snyder goes on to argue that Westboro's speech should be afforded less than full First Amendment protection "not only because of the words" but also because the church members exploited the funeral "as a platform to bring their message to a broader audience." There is no doubt that Westboro chose to stage its picketing at the Naval Academy, the Maryland State House, and Matthew Snyder's funeral to increase publicity for its views and because of the relation between those sites and its views—in the case of the military funeral, because Westboro believes that God is killing American soldiers as punishment for the Nation's sinful policies.

So far the analysis has been relentlessly logical, if not steely. A reader might wonder if Roberts has a heart. Of course, it's an open question whether judges should stray from doctrinal analysis and acknowledge their own discomfort. Consciously or not, Roberts does emote a bit in the next paragraph—"hurtful," "anguish," "incalculable grief"—and that makes both him and the Court sound humane. But before you get too excited, he pivots right back to doctrine, diverting your attention to the public streets where the protest was staged:

> Westboro's choice to convey its views in conjunction with Matthew Snyder's funeral made the expression of those views particularly hurtful to many, especially to Matthew's father. The record makes clear that the applicable legal term— "emotional distress"—fails to capture fully the anguish Westboro's choice added to Mr. Snyder's already incalculable grief. But Westboro conducted its picketing peacefully on matters of public concern at a public place adjacent to a public street. Such space occupies a "special position in terms of First Amendment protection." "[W]e have repeatedly referred to

public streets as the archetype of a traditional public forum," noting that "'[t]ime out of mind' public streets and sidewalks have been used for public assembly and debate."

Note that this last paragraph echoes the first two paragraphs that began Roberts's analysis: the First Amendment's special treatment of public speech trumps state tort law. In other words, Roberts drops a hint at the start, and now makes explicit, that emotional distress—and sometimes, yes, anguish—are the price we pay for freedom of speech.

But our restless reader is perhaps left cold by these homilies. *So you're saying our hands are tied? Not even funerals are sacrosanct anymore?* Perhaps wanting to provide a way out, Roberts next flirts with giving advice to the legislative branch and also reassures the reader that the law is evolving:

That said, "[e]ven protected speech is not equally permissible in all places and at all times." Westboro's choice of where and when to conduct its picketing is not beyond the Government's regulatory reach—it is "subject to reasonable time, place, or manner restrictions" that are consistent with the standards announced in this Court's precedents. Maryland now has a law imposing restrictions on funeral picketing, as do 43 other States and the Federal Government. To the extent these laws are content neutral, they raise very different questions from the tort verdict at issue in this case. Maryland's law, however, was not in effect at the time of the events at issue here, so we have no occasion to consider how it might apply to facts such as those before us, or whether it or other similar regulations are constitutional.*

---

* "Now," not "currently." "However" is inside the sentence, not at the beginning. "So we," not "; therefore, we." And note the nice parallel construction Roberts creates with "how it might apply. . . or whether it. . . ." But he also makes a minor error: the questions the laws raise are not "very different . . . from the tort verdict at issue." He means "raises very different questions than does the tort verdict at issue" or "very different questions from those raised by the tort verdict at issue."

Then Roberts even offers a sort of how-to-ban-funeral-picketing guide. The next paragraph is aimed at astute readers of the Court's precedent, who might think that they've trapped the chief justice in an inconsistency: *If you can ban picketing at a house or an abortion clinic, why not at a funeral?*

> We have identified a few limited situations where the location of targeted picketing can be regulated under provisions that the Court has determined to be content neutral. In *Frisby*, for example, we upheld a ban on such picketing "before or about" a particular residence. In *Madsen v. Women's Health Center, Inc.*, we approved an injunction requiring a buffer zone between protesters and an abortion clinic entrance. The facts here are obviously quite different, both with respect to the activity being regulated and the means of restricting those activities.*

A reader might ask, *Exactly how is funeral picketing "obviously quite different" from picketing homes or abortion clinics?* In the next paragraph, Roberts makes his case:

> Simply put, the church members had the right to be where they were. Westboro alerted local authorities to its funeral protest and fully complied with police guidance on where the picketing could be staged. The picketing was conducted under police supervision some 1,000 feet from the church, out of the sight of those at the church. The protest was not unruly; there was no shouting, profanity, or violence.**

* Another minor glitch here: switch "both" with "with respect to" to fix the faulty parallel.

** Note the taut and speedy style, mostly from all the one-syllable words: "had the right to be where they were," "out of the sight of those at the church."

So you're saying that you can be as cruel to others as you see fit, as long as you don't shout, shove, or swear? Roberts himself might be uncomfortable with the signs, but now he wants to make his skeptical readers—who likely align themselves with the good guy here—squirm in their chairs as well. The truth, he suggests, is that Westboro's critics here have no problem with demonstrations near funerals as long as they approve of what the demonstrators have to say:

> The record confirms that any distress occasioned by Westboro's picketing turned on the content and viewpoint of the message conveyed, rather than any interference with the funeral itself. A group of parishioners standing at the very spot where Westboro stood, holding signs that said "God Bless America" and "God Loves You," would not have been subjected to liability. It was what Westboro said that exposed it to tort damages.

Okay, says the skeptical reader, *I see your point about content, but I still just can't accept this result. Why does Westboro get every doubt resolved in its favor?* Roberts's response: because public speech gets special protection.

> Given that Westboro's speech was at a public place on a matter of public concern, that speech is entitled to "special protection" under the First Amendment. Such speech cannot be restricted simply because it is upsetting or arouses contempt. "If there is a bedrock principle underlying the First Amendment, it is that the government may not prohibit the expression of an idea simply because society finds the idea itself offensive or disagreeable." Indeed, "the point of all speech protection . . . is to shield just those choices of content that in someone's eyes are misguided, or even hurtful."

Are you sure? asks our reader. *We're talking about a jury verdict here. We all know that a lot of bad conduct can fit under the big umbrella of "infliction of emotional distress." If a jury found Westboro liable on that ground, why not just leave it alone?* So the next paragraph responds to concerns about casting a jury verdict aside so lightly, and then suggests that a jury can't be a dispassionate decision-maker in the face of ugly speech:

> The jury here was instructed that it could hold Westboro liable for intentional infliction of emotional distress based on a finding that Westboro's picketing was "outrageous." "Outrageousness," however, is a highly malleable standard with "an inherent subjectiveness about it which would allow a jury to impose liability on the basis of the jurors' tastes or views, or perhaps on the basis of their dislike of a particular expression." In a case such as this, a jury is "unlikely to be neutral with respect to the content of [the] speech," posing "a real danger of becoming an instrument for the suppression of . . . 'vehement, caustic, and sometimes unpleasan[t]'" expression. Such a risk is unacceptable; "in public debate [we] must tolerate insulting, and even outrageous, speech in order to provide adequate 'breathing space' to the freedoms protected by the First Amendment." What Westboro said, in the whole context of how and where it chose to say it, is entitled to "special protection" under the First Amendment, and that protection cannot be overcome by a jury finding that the picketing was outrageous.

And now, Roberts's short, tight, logically progressive sentences have marched to their unappealing but inevitable destination:

> For all these reasons, the jury verdict imposing tort liability on Westboro for intentional infliction of emotional distress must be set aside.

Roberts's incredibly economical and disciplined approach to structure is rare among American judges—and perhaps even rarer elsewhere these days. Whether or not you agree with the chief justice on the merits, he follows every organizational precept that so many judges can rattle off by heart but that so few follow in practice:

- Keep most paragraphs short.
- Start paragraphs with a central point that the rest of the paragraph develops.
- Make sure that those paragraph openers follow logically from one to the next.
- Cite only enough authorities to prove your point.
- Quote sparingly and thoughtfully.
- Transition smoothly within paragraphs and between them.

Like a lot of writing advice, these mantras are easy to intone but hard to follow. If you look at what the world's judges do, rather than what they say they do (or, for that matter, what they say attorneys should do), you'll see that opinions are getting longer and more disjointed by the day, particularly in courts that favor isolated numbered paragraphs.

So with the Roberts model as our guide, let's break down the structure conundrum into specific techniques for organizing legal analysis in a reader-friendly way.

With You in Spirit: Paragraphs as Dialogues

The "With You in Spirit" technique helps avoid the problem of focusing each paragraph on an out-of-nowhere summary of a case, with no hint of what question the case answers, as in the all-too-typical examples below. Look at some opening sentences of paragraphs in a random but representative judicial opinion:

> In *Yearsley*, the Supreme Court considered whether a private contractor that was building river dikes at the direction of the United States Army Corps of Engineers could be held liable for a "taking"....
>
> In *Ackerson*, the Army Corps of Engineers contracted with defendant contractors to dredge the Mississippi River....
>
> In *Gomez*, the District Court for the Central District of California granted a government contractor's motion for summary judgment, ...
>
> [The defendant] also cites to the Supreme Court decision in *Filarsky v. Delia*....

Before launching into the paragraphs above, the opinion tells us that *Yearsley, Ackerson, Gomez*, and *Filarsky* are not "directly on point" for the issues being addressing. But can you tell from any of these opening sentences why these cases aren't relevant? Probably not, because the reasons are buried at the end of each paragraph. Had the author's opening sentences anticipated a reader's likely questions–*Why are you talking about this case? Why isn't each case on point?*—the paragraphs would flow better and the analysis would gel.

Advocates who enjoy oral argument often relish the chance to engage the court in a conversation about its doubts and concerns. As I suggested above, a good opinion writer should follow their lead: imagine talking to a reader—and not necessarily one of the parties—while predicting and then answering questions.

That's just what trial judge Shira Scheindlin does in our next example. The case involved an arrest warrant issued to secure a witness for grand jury testimony about one of the men who hijacked Flight 77 and flew it into the Pentagon on September 11, 2001.

Notice how Judge Scheindlin anticipates and answers likely reader questions: *Under what circumstances can a grand jury witness be arrested? How sure must a court be that the witness is material, and that it may be impracticable to secure the witness later? How can the probable cause standard be met in the grand jury context where everything is secret? If the burden is so low, isn't it odd that the statute's requirements haven't been met here?*

Shira Scheindlin, *United States v. Awadallah*

Assuming, *arguendo*, that the material witness statute applies to grand jury witnesses, the question for the Court is whether Awadallah was appropriately detained in accordance with the requirements of that statute. The statute sets forth two explicit requirements for ordering the arrest of a material witness: (1) "the testimony of [the] person is material" and (2) "it is shown that it may become impracticable to secure the presence of the person by subpoena."

[The material witness statute] is silent as to what standard a court should use to decide whether "the testimony of [the] person is material" and "whether "it may become impracticable to secure the presence of the person by subpoena." One federal court has suggested that the standard should be "probable cause to believe" that these conditions are met. . . . [F]or the limited purpose of determining whether the arrest warrant was improvidently issued, I shall apply the probable cause standard.

The materiality requirement is problematic in a grand jury context, which is, by definition, secret. Nonetheless, because there is no real way for a court to assess whether the testimony of a person is "material" to a grand jury proceeding, I shall accept the view of the *Bacon* court that "a mere statement by a responsible official, such as the United States Attorney, is sufficient to satisfy [the materiality prong]."

In this case however, the affidavit fails to comply even with this requirement because it was submitted by Agent Plunkett based solely upon his personal knowledge. Plunkett may have been able to assess the materiality of Awadallah's knowledge to the FBI's investigation. But he could not have made an informed judgment about the materiality of Awadallah's testimony to the grand jury's investigation as he was never present in the grand jury. . . .

The second prong also presents a serious problem. Plunkett's affidavit, submitted in support of the arrest warrant application, offered the court four reasons to conclude that "it may become impracticable to secure [Adwallah's] presence . . . by subpoena." . . . [His] statements are misleading.
. . .

If the misleading information had been removed and the omitted information disclosed, it is overwhelmingly likely that the court would have found that Awadallah's presence at the grand jury could have been secured by a subpoena.*

The next example comes from a patent-infringement case before the Supreme Court of Canada involving patented plant genes and cells. After finding that the trial court correctly held that the respondent had infringed patents belonging to Plaintiff Monsanto, Chief Justice Beverly McLachlin predicts readers' questions about the remedy: *What remedies are available? What is an accounting of profits, and how is it measured? If the trial court awarded the right type of remedy, why isn't that remedy appropriate?*

---

* Change "Assuming, arguendo, that" at the beginning to "Even if."

Beverly McLachlin, *Schmeiser v. Monsanto*

The *Patent Act* permits two alternative types of remedy: damages and an accounting of profits. Damages represent the inventor's loss, which may include the patent holder's lost profits from sales or lost royalty payments. An accounting of profits, by contrast, is measured by the profits made by the infringer, rather than the amount lost by the inventor. Here, damages are not available, in view of Monsanto's election to seek an accounting of profits.

It is settled law that the inventor is only entitled to that portion of the infringer's profit which is causally attributable to the invention. This is consistent with the general law on awarding non-punitive remedies: "[I]t is essential that the losses made good are only those which, on a common sense view of causation, were caused by the breach."

The preferred means of calculating an accounting of profits is what has been termed the value-based or "differential profit" approach, where profits are allocated according to the value contributed to the defendant's wares by the patent. A comparison is to be made between the defendant's profit attributable to the invention and his profit had he used the best non-infringing option.

The difficulty with the trial judge's award is that it does not identify any causal connection between the profits the appellants were found to have earned through growing Roundup Ready Canola and the invention. On the facts found, the appellants made no profits *as a result of the invention*.

Although the examples above anticipate legal questions that arise in most cases—*What is the general rule? How does it operate in practice? What does it mean in this case?*—predicting reader questions is all the more important when you're addressing an issue with spare or conflicting precedent, relying heavily on policy arguments, or reaching a decision that many will find counterintuitive or distasteful.

The next two examples illustrate that point. In the first, Ninth Circuit Judge Berzon confronted her own court's recent precedent holding that a one-year filing period equaled 365 days. So what to do with an asylum petition filed on Day 366? An immigration judge and the Board of Immigration Appeals had denied the petition, but Berzon found it timely. She explains herself by anticipating questions from a skeptical reader: *Why aren't you deferring to the agency's reading of the statute? If the statute says "one year," why isn't that 365 days? What support is there in the law for your interpretation? Why doesn't your own precedent control?*

Marsha Berzon, *Minasyan v. Mukasey*

We review the denial of a motion for reconsideration for abuse of discretion. The [Board of Immigration Appeals] abuses its discretion if its decision "is 'arbitrary, irrational, or contrary to law.'" Where, as here, the BIA bases its decision on a "purely legal question [] concerning the meaning of the immigration laws," we review the BIA's decision de novo.

We conclude that the BIA abused its discretion in this case, as its interpretation of the one-year period for filing an asylum application runs directly counter to the plain meaning of the statute. Section 208 of the INA provides that an alien seeking asylum must demonstrate "by clear and convincing evidence that the application has been filed *within one year after the date* of the alien's arrival in the United States." The parties agree that Minasyan arrived in the United States on April 9, 2001. He was therefore required to file an application for asylum within one year after that date—that is, not counting that date. The first day of the one-year filing period was thus April 10, 2001, meaning that the application filed by Minasyan on April 9, 2002—the 365th day after April 9, 2001—was timely.

This reading of the statutory text accords with common legal usage. Both the Federal Rules of Civil and Appellate Procedure use a similar "within x days after" formulation to establish filing deadlines for federal litigants. . . . If a defendant was served with a summons and complaint on April 9th and the Rules provided him with 20 days after that date to serve an answer, for example, the parties would understand that the answer was due on April 29th—the twentieth day after April 9th, with April 9th itself excluded from that count. Similarly, if a defendant was served with a summons and complaint on April 9th and the Rules provided him with one year after that date to serve an answer, the parties would understand that the answer was due on April 9th of the following year—the 365th day after April 9th, with the date of service excluded from that count. The Government has not provided us with any reason to calculate the statutory deadline for filing an asylum application differently.

Our decision in _Lagandaon_ is not only not to the contrary, but in fact supports our conclusion. _Lagandaon_ addressed the separate question "whether the period beginning May 14, 1987, and ending May 13, 1997," constituted "a continuous period of not less than 10 years" for purposes of cancellation of removal under 8 U.S.C. § 1229b(b)(1). We held that it did, because "a year runs from one date to the prior date in the next year—365 days, the equivalent of the period from January 1 to December 31."

In _Lagandaon_, the date upon which the statutory time period began to run was not at issue. The statute did not use the "within x days after" formulation to specify that the date of arrival was to be left out of the calculation, and the parties agreed that ten years of continuous presence began on the day that Lagandaon arrived in the country. In Minasyan's case, by contrast, the statute specifically provides that the one-year period for filing an asylum application commences after the date of arrival, meaning that his date of arrival does not count as "day one" for purposes of the filing deadline. This difference in the statutory language makes perfect sense, as the year-long periods serve different purposes—in the continuous presence context, to measure the length of an alien's connection to this country; in the various time deadline contexts, to give an individual a certain clearly calculable amount of time to accomplish a certain task.

At the same time, we do apply here *Lagandaon*'s common-sense conclusion that one year equals 365 days, the "one year" in this case extending from April 10, 2001, to April 9, 2002. Were we instead to have accepted the INS's position in *Lagandaon*, Minasyan's deadline would have been April 10, 2002, and he would have had a day to spare. Instead, he barely squeezed in under the wire.

In short, our decision in *Lagandaon* simply does not address the question of when a one-year statutory filing deadline begins to run, particularly when it is specified as beginning the day "after" the event that triggers the deadline. Both the [Immigration Judge] and the BIA mistook the plain meaning of the statute by including Minasyan's date of arrival in their calculation of the one-year period for filing asylum claims. Nothing in *Lagandaon* supports that miscalculation. To the contrary, once "day one" of the filing period is properly established as April 10, 2001, *Lagandaon*'s definition of a year as running "from one date to the prior date in the next year" confirms that Minasyan's application, filed on April 9, 2002, was just on time.

In the second example, from an opinion we first met in the *Op-Ed* section of Part 1, trial judge Michael Ponsor faced a question that his reviewing circuit hadn't addressed: whether the Fair Sentencing Act, which lowered penalties for crack-cocaine offenders, was retroactive. Lower courts were divided on the issue, and policy arguments had to fill the holes left by the gaping precedent.

Judge Ponsor begins his opinion by describing the history of mandatory minimums for drug crimes, the racial injustice these minimums perpetuated, and other decisions finding that the Fair Sentencing Act was not retroactive. Contradicting those decisions, Ponsor appears to preempt the reader's worries: *I understand your policy arguments, but what does the First Circuit say about this? Well, if the First Circuit hasn't addressed the issue, is there any case on your side? OK, there are courts that agree with you. But have any courts disagreed?*

Michael Ponsor, *United States v. Watts*

No guidance has yet issued from the First Circuit on the [Fair Sentencing Act's] applicability either to sentenced defendants, or to those awaiting sentencing. Decisions coming from the district courts in the First Circuit are so far in agreement with the decisions of other courts of appeals that the FSA is inapplicable to defendants who were *sentenced* prior to . . . the effective date of the statute.

With regard to defendants appearing for sentencing, however, U.S. District Judge Brock Hornby of the District of Maine has held that the statutory amendments contained in the FSA are applicable to defendants who committed their crimes prior to its passage but are appearing for sentencing after its effective date. *United States v. Douglas* ("[A] defendant not yet sentenced on November 1, 2010, is to be sentenced under the amended Guidelines, and the Fair

> Sentencing Act's altered mandatory minimums apply to such a defendant as well.").
>
> **Subsequent decisions issued by a number of district judges around the country have agreed with Judge Hornby's reasoning.** In addition, a number of judges from this district have followed *Douglas* in unreported decisions. . . .
>
> **Admittedly, some district judges have taken a different view. . . .**
>
> A careful examination of the law makes clear that Judge Hornby's reasoning in *Douglas* not only avoids perpetuating the injustice that the FSA was intended to remedy but satisfies the demands of the law as well.*

Anticipating reader questions in the order they're likely to occur is a great way both to organize an opinion and to ensure that you've tagged all the bases when reaching a decision that's likely to prove controversial.

In the two unusual examples below, the courts don't just imagine a reader's likely questions. They spell them out for all to see.

The first is from an opinion by Judge Easterbrook about a bankruptcy statute that prevented farmers from converting chapter 11 bankruptcy petitions to chapter 12, even though the legislative conference report suggested that they could. He frames his discussion around the questions he expects from lawyer-readers and from the lower courts alike:

> **Frank Easterbrook, *Matter of Sinclair***
>
> **Which prevails in the event of conflict, the statute or its legislative history?** The statute was enacted, the report just

---

* Note the effective use of "Admittedly" to address counterexamples head on. But change "with regard to defendants" to "for defendants."

the staff's explanation. Congress votes on the text of the bill, and the President signed that text. Committee reports help courts understand the law, but this report contradicts rather than explains the text. So the statute must prevail. Such is the holding of *In re Erickson Partnership*.

Yet the advice from the Supreme Court about how to deal with our situation seems scarcely more harmonious than the advice from the legislature. The reports teem with statements such as: "When we find the terms of a statute unambiguous, judicial inquiry is complete[.]" Less frequently, yet with equal conviction, the Court writes: "When aid to the construction of the meaning of words, as used in the statute, is available, there certainly can be no 'rule of law' which forbids its use, however clear the words may appear on 'superficial examination.'" Some cases boldly stake out a middle ground, saying, for example: "only the most extraordinary showing of contrary intentions from [the legislative history] would justify a limitation on the 'plain meaning' of the statutory language." This implies that once in a blue moon the legislative history trumps the statute (as opposed to affording a basis for its interpretation) but does not help locate such strange astronomical phenomena. These lines of cases have coexisted for a century, and many cases contain statements associated with two or even all three of them, not recognizing the tension.

What's a court to do? The answer lies in distinguishing among uses of legislative history. . . .

And below, in a police-chase case, Justice Scalia opts for a less pedagogical and more rhetorical approach, playing the role of a skeptical reader (including, perhaps, the losing party himself), and then putting that reader in his place:

Antonin Scalia, *Scott v. Harris*

But wait, says respondent: Couldn't the innocent public equally have been protected, and the tragic accident entirely avoided, if the police had simply ceased their pursuit? We think the police need not have taken that chance and hoped for the best. Whereas Scott's action—ramming respondent off the road—was *certain* to eliminate the risk that respondent posed to the public, ceasing pursuit was not.

Order out of Chaos: Internal Organizational Devices

Let's assume that you've now worked out the broad strokes of the legal analysis at the macro level, imagining the overarching structure as more of a question-and-answer dialogue than a stream-of-consciousness monologue. So what can you do to impose order at the micro level as well? Consider these three strategies: adding headings and subheadings, using "umbrella" passages that preview analysis and prep the reader, and numbering the reasons that support your conclusion.

A. Headings

Beyond a basic three-point structure such as "Background," "Discussion/Analysis," and "Conclusion," most opinions have no internal headings. Some judges, such as Judge Posner, shun headings as a matter of principle. His approach offers the advantage of a cohesive, essay-like presentation and works especially well for short opinions. But unless the judge is an extraordinarily disciplined writer, if the analysis goes on uninterrupted for more than just a few pages, the reader can drown in an unbroken and intimidating sea of text. That's why headings are often helpful.

Some judges sit on the other side of the fence, peppering their opinions with full sentence-length substantive headings, much like those in good advocacy filings or good newspaper headlines, for that matter. Such headings and subheadings allow the reader to glean the logic of the opinion through a quick scan. They do take time to draft and edit, making them better suited for complex, dispositive, or high-profile opinions than for simple evidentiary or trial motions.

Below, trial judge Shira Scheindlin interplays phrases, questions, and statements in her headings as she considers—after the introduction we saw in Part 1—whether *New York Magazine* can state a constitutional claim against former New York Mayor Rudolph Giuliani for removing its satirical ads from public buses.

Shira Scheindlin, *New York Magazine v. Metropolitan Transit Authority*

III. Section 1983 Constitutional Claim

A. *Elements of a Section 1983 Claim*

B. *Is a Preliminary Injunction Warranted?*

C. *Is Plaintiff's Speech Protected by the First Amendment?*
  1. *Is the Ad in Issue Commercial Speech?*
  2. *The Standard for Protecting Commercial Speech*

D. *Is the Exterior of a City Bus a Public Forum, a Designated* Public Forum, a Limited Public Forum or a Non-public Forum?

E. *The Exclusion of the Ad*

F. *Does Section 50 Cover the Use of "Rudy" in the Ad in Issue?*
  1. *The Purpose of the "Right of Publicity"*
  2. *The Judicial Exceptions to the Right of Publicity*

> a. *Incidental Use Exception*
> b. *Public Interest/Newsworthy Exception*
> c. *The Incidental Use and Public Interest Exceptions Applied*
> 3. *Summary*
> G. *Balance of Public Interests*
> H. *A Preliminary Injunction Is Warranted*

Deciding whether to use questions rather than conclusions is a bit like deciding whether to tell the reader the outcome of the case in the introduction: there's no right answer.

Here's a variation on the interrogatory theme by Canada's Chief Justice McLachlin:

> **Beverly McLachlin, *Schmeiser v. Monsanto Canada Inc.***
>
> A. The Patent: Its Scope and Validity
> B. Did Schmeiser "Make" or "Construct" the Patented Gene and Cell, Thus Infringing the Patent?
> C. Did Schmeiser "Use" the Patented Gene or Cell, Thus Infringing the Patent?
>   (1) The Law on "Use"
>   (2) Application of the Law
> D. Remedy

The middle ground is to sprinkle in brief, topical, phrase-length headings that break the text into chunks. These short headers are easy to draft and make the opinion easy to navigate, but they are not persuasive or even particularly substantive. Phrase-like headings thus work best for complex opinions written under time pressure.

A short-and-sweet approach is particularly popular with the U.K. Supreme Court, as you can see in the following headings from a judgment penned by Lord Sumption:

> **Lord Sumption, *Cox v. Ergo Versicherung AG***
>
> German and English law
>   Choice of law: the legal framework
>   Procedure or substance?
>   Overriding effect of English law
>   Extra-territorial application
>   Mandatory rules

To sum up, headings and subheadings are by no means necessary, but nor should you overhype the virtues of an essay-like unbroken presentation. Readers need our help when they scan for cues about which parts of the opinion matter most. Although short phrase-like headings have aesthetic value, headings that form complete thoughts—whether declarative or interrogatory—are probably the best organizational device. And given that drafting these longer headings can help you stick to the broad strokes of your analysis, they are well worth your time as a writer as well.

B. "Umbrella" Introductions

Another way to orient the reader is through an "umbrella" paragraph, or mini-introduction, at the beginning of each longer section of analysis. Here, Bankruptcy Judge Goldgar previews the reasoning he uses—and also the reasoning he rejects—before delving into the analytical nitty-gritty:

> **Benjamin Goldgar, *In re Earley***
>
> Earley's plan properly treats Triad's claim as unsecured, but not because *Hunt* controls the issue. It does not. Triad's claim is unsecured because of the nature of Triad's lien and

the interplay between the [Illinois Wage Deduction Act] and the automatic stay under the Bankruptcy Code, 11 U.S.C. § 362(a). Triad's objection will therefore be overruled and its motion to dismiss denied.

And in the umbrella paragraph below, Chief Justice McLachlin narrows a dispute by first highlighting a point of agreement. To preview coming attractions, she juxtaposes—though she does not resolve—the parties' views on whether rape-shield statutes infringe a criminal defendant's rights. Finally, and helpfully, she frames the two questions that will inform the legal analysis to follow:

Beverly McLachlin, *Seaboyer v. The Queen*

All the parties agree that the right to a fair trial—one which permits the trier of fact to get at the truth and properly and fairly dispose of the case—is a principle of fundamental justice. Nor is there any dispute that encouraging reporting of sexual offences and protection of the complainant's privacy are legitimate goals provided they do not interfere with the primary objective of a fair trial. Where the parties part company is on the issue of whether ss. 276 and 277 of the *Criminal Code* in fact infringe the right to a fair trial. The supporters of the legislation urge that it furthers the right to a fair trial by eliminating evidence of little or no worth and considerable prejudice. The appellants, on the other hand, say that the legislation goes too far and in fact eliminates relevant evidence which should be admitted notwithstanding the possibility of prejudice.

This raises two questions. First, what are the fundamental principles governing the right to introduce relevant defence evidence which may also be prejudicial? Second, does the legislation infringe these principles?*

And here's a mini-introduction from California Supreme Court Justice Roger Traynor. Dropped at the very start of the legal analysis, his introduction summarizes the facts, previews the parties' arguments, and tees up the issue in interrogatory form:

Roger Traynor, *Drennan v. Star Paving Co.*

Defendant contends that there was no enforceable contract between the parties on the ground that it made a revocable offer and revoked it before plaintiff communicated his acceptance to defendant. There is no evidence that defendant offered to make its bid irrevocable in exchange for plaintiff's use of its figures in computing his bid. Nor is there evidence that would warrant interpreting plaintiff's use of defendant's bid as the acceptance thereof, binding plaintiff, on condition he received the main contract, to award the subcontract to defendant. In sum, there was neither an option supported by consideration nor a bilateral contract binding on both parties.

Plaintiff contends, however, that he relied to his detriment on defendant's offer and that defendant must therefore

---

* I generally caution against using "This" before a verb, as in "This raises" in the last paragraph. This what? On closer analysis, Chief Justice McLachlin is apparently referring to the broader debate between the appellants and the legislation's supporters, but at first it seems as though she's talking just about the possibility of prejudice alone. Simply adding the word "debate" could have cleared things up: "This debate raises. . . ."

> answer in damages for its refusal to perform. Thus the question is squarely presented: Did plaintiff's reliance make defendant's offer irrevocable?

These short "umbrella" passages help the reader digest what's already been presented and then fit it into a framework that will help process what's to come. The best examples summarize each party's arguments and then highlight the question that the court needs to decide next.

C. Bulleted and Numbered Lists

A third helpful organizational technique is to use numbered or bullet-pointed lists of reasons. Do you remember the excerpt above in which Justice Scalia asked whether the police should have stopped a pursuit? He answered his own question "no," suggesting that calling off the pursuit would have been too risky to other drivers. But then Justice Scalia kept going, sounding off two numbered reasons he's right:

Antonin Scalia, *Scott v. Harris*

But wait, says respondent: Couldn't the innocent public equally have been protected, and the tragic accident entirely avoided, if the police had simply ceased their pursuit? We think the police need not have taken that chance and hoped for the best. Whereas Scott's action—ramming respondent off the road—was *certain* to eliminate the risk that respondent posed to the public, ceasing pursuit was not. **First** of all, there would have been no way to convey convincingly to respondent that the chase was off, and that he was free to go. Had respondent looked in his rearview mirror and seen the police cars deactivate their flashing lights and turn around, he would have had no idea whether they were truly letting him get away, or simply devising a new strategy for capture. Perhaps the police knew a shortcut he didn't know, and would reappear down the road to intercept him; or perhaps they were setting up a roadblock in his path. Given such uncertainty, respondent might have been just as likely to respond by continuing to drive recklessly as by slowing down and wiping his brow.

Second, we are loath to lay down a rule requiring the police to allow fleeing suspects to get away whenever they drive *so recklessly* that they put other people's lives in danger. It is obvious the perverse incentives such a rule would create: Every fleeing motorist would know that escape is within his grasp, if only he accelerates to 90 miles per hour, crosses the double-yellow line a few times, and runs a few red lights. The Constitution assuredly does not impose this invitation to impunity-earned-by-recklessness.*

Just as readers' likely questions should govern the overarching analysis, so should such questions drive the microanalysis within subsections and paragraphs. It's just that at the micro level, numbered reasons should answer a single question—"Why should I believe you on that point?"—in discrete ways.

Take the example below. Trial judge D.P. Marshall starts each paragraph with a numbered reason explaining something that might

---

* Note the contractions and the strings of almost all one-syllable words: "We think the police need not have taken that chance and hoped for the best." And the alliteration: "We are loath to lay down a rule." And the evocative example of the 90-mile-an-hour, double-yellow-line-crossing, red-light running motorist. And finally, Scalia's trademark hyphenated compound: "impunity-earned-by-recklessness." I will discuss this Scalia hallmark in more detail in Part 4.

surprise many readers: charter schools have done little to decrease desegregation in Little Rock:

D.P. Marshall, *Little Rock School Dist. v. North Little Rock School Dist.*

First consider the numbers. They are undisputed. From the 2005-2006 school year until the 2010-2011 school year, 324 students transferred from the stipulation magnets to open-enrollment charter schools in Pulaski County. . . . During the same period, 109 students transferred the other way . . . .

Second, consider the stipulation magnet schools. Depositions given by principals from three of them are in the record. Each principal was asked how his or her school was performing. Each testified that his or her school was functioning well. . . .

Third, consider M-to-M [majority-to-minority] transfers. Here again, the numbers are undisputed. During the relevant six-year period, a total of 20 M-to-M students transferred from [Little Rock School District] to an open-enrollment charter school. . . .

Fourth, consider the intradistrict desegregation situation for each of the three Pulaski County districts. [Little Rock School District] has been completely unitary since 2007 . . . . [Northern Little Rock School District] is completely unitary. [Pulaski County Special School District] still has work to do in nine areas. . . .

Fifth, and finally, it bears mention that the Charter Schools Act is not silent about desegregation. The Act requires all parties to consider "the potential impact" of a charter application on school districts' efforts "to comply with court orders and statutory obligations to create and maintain a unitary system of desegregated public schools."

Note, too, the unorthodox yet highly effective technique of speaking directly to the reader in the second person: "consider," "consider," "consider," and "consider." Though switching to "it bears mention" in the fifth reason does mar the pattern a bit.

Numbered reasons can also let the losing party know that all of its arguments have been considered—even if they are ultimately rejected. Here, for example, Bankruptcy Judge Goldgar uses numbering to shoot down the defenses of a lawyer facing sanctions for allegedly hiding changes to his standard fee agreement:

Benjamin Goldgar, *In Re Brent*

[Respondent's] assertions will not wash. **First, they are factually inaccurate.** As discussed earlier, Liou did not use the [Model Retention Agreement] with the addendum "openly," in the sense that he started attaching them to his Rule 2016(b) statements, until mid-2009. But even if Liou had always filed the MRA and addendum with his Rule 2016(b) statements, it would not absolve him of the misstatements in his fee applications—to which the MRA was rarely attached and the addendum never attached. . . .

Second, Liou's assertions are legally irrelevant. Again, an attorney's Rule 9011 obligations are non-delegable. An attorney has a personal responsibility to ensure he tells the court the truth. So it makes no difference that no one pointed out to Liou he was being less than truthful. . . .

Finally, Liou contends that the court's General Order 11–2 issued in March 2011 confirms the reasonableness of his belief that his statements were true. According to Liou, the General Order imposed a new prohibition, demonstrating that the court itself "did not come to the conclusion" Liou's conduct was impermissible until recently.

Liou could not be more mistaken. Some amendments to statutes and rules clarify rather than change existing law. . . .

And below, trial judge Patrick Schiltz was called on to decide whether a hookah shop had stated an equal-protection claim based on an ordinance that outlawed in-store tobacco sampling. He starts each paragraph with a numbered reason that the complaint states a claim:

Patrick Schiltz, *Shiraz Hookah, LLC v. City of Minneapolis*

According to the City, Shiraz has failed to allege that it is similarly situated to a cigar shop because Shiraz has not alleged that cigar shops, like hookah shops, provide devices for sampling tobacco or that cigar shops, like hookah shops, derive most of their revenue from onsite tobacco sampling.

The City's argument is misplaced for two reasons:

First, the City's argument—although presented as an attack on the adequacy of Shiraz's complaint—is, in fact, a defense on the merits to Shiraz's equal-protection claim. Shiraz has adequately pleaded that its equal-protection rights were violated because, even though cigar shops also sell tobacco for onsite sampling, it is treated worse under the Ordinance than cigar shops. The City's argument that hookah shops such as Shiraz derive most of their revenue from onsite tobacco sampling, while cigar shops do not, may provide a rational basis for the difference in treatment. But that is an argument that goes to the merits of Shiraz's equal-protection claim.

Second, Shiraz seeks to protect both its equal-protection rights *and* the equal-protection rights of its customers. As to its customers' equal protection claims, Shiraz alleges that the Ordinance disproportionately burdens hookah smokers vis-à-vis cigar smokers. The proper inquiry, as far as Shiraz's customers are concerned, is not whether hookah shops are similarly situated to cigar shops, but whether hookah smokers are similarly situated to cigar smokers. The City has not pointed to a material difference between those two groups.

And over in the United Kingdom, Lord Sumption explains step by step why a lower court erred in ordering a husband's corporate assets transferred to his ex-wife:

Lord Sumption, *Prest v. Petrodel Resources Ltd.*

In the first place, it is axiomatic that general words in a statute are not to be read in a way which "would overthrow fundamental principles, infringe rights, or depart from the general system of law, without expressing its intention with irresistible clearness". The words are those of Lord Atkin in *Nokes v Doncaster Amalgamated Collieries Ltd*, but the principle is very familiar and has been restated by the courts in many contexts and at every level. . . . **Secondly,** a transfer of this kind will ordinarily be unnecessary for the purpose of achieving a fair distribution of the assets of the marriage. Where assets belong to a company owned by one party to the marriage, the proper claims of the other can ordinarily be satisfied by directing the transfer of the shares. . . . **Third,** so far as a party to matrimonial proceedings deliberately attempts to frustrate the exercise of the court's ancillary powers by disposing of assets, section 37 provides for the setting aside of those dispositions in certain circumstances. . . .*

---

* Lord Sumption's shift between "secondly" and "third" is an unusual combination of British English and American English. Perhaps he's angling for a nomination to the U.S. Supreme Court?

Finally, if systematic numbering is a bit too militaristic for your tastes, take a look at First Circuit Judge Thompson's opinion dismantling a convicted defendant's argument that there wasn't enough evidence at trial to convict her of money laundering:

O. Rogeriee Thompson, *United States v. Seng Tan*

For starters, Tan argues that the underlying illegal activity here was mail fraud "for sending checks" to some of the persons cheated by the scammers. Oversimplifying slightly, the essential elements for mail fraud are a scheme to defraud that involves a use of the mail for the purpose of furthering the scheme.

Jumping off from there, Tan says that a dividend payment cannot constitute criminally-derived proceeds—only getting "money can result in a proceed," she says. And so, she claims, "sending mail cannot form the predicate convictions from which money laundering proceeds can be derived."

Tan is wrong on a couple of levels. For one thing, her description of the record is not quite right. . . .

Tan does no better with her next attack—one that takes aim at her conviction on a money-laundering count involving a $255,090 check, dated December 10, 2004, written on a [company] account and payable to a Caesars casino.

Thompson teeters on the colloquial end of the style spectrum, but her prose is refreshing, even when it comes to the way she counts!

So now we've developed a plan for the broad paragraph openers and for internally numbered lists of reasons. The next step is to develop effective ways to incorporate authorities and counter-authorities within the paragraphs themselves. Let's turn in that regard to analogizing, distinguishing, and using footnotes—both the "whether" and the "how."

Me, Too: Analogizing

The key to analogizing authorities is to avoid two temptations: First, the temptation to declare that an authority applies without ferreting out the key facts that link the case you're citing with the one you're adjudicating. And second, on the other extreme, the temptation to regurgitate facts and quotes from an authority without introduction or explanation, forcing the reader to do all the analytical work in your stead.

There's a better way. Take the excerpt below, in which trial judge Jed Rakoff considers whether police officers could have reasonably believed that an officer's instructions delivered through a bullhorn gave Occupy Wall Street protestors fair warning that they could be arrested for marching in the streets. After identifying the key disputed facts, Judge Rakoff focuses on a case called *Vodak*, one that also involved commands given through a police bullhorn. Watch how he merges in a snippet from *Vodak*'s most apt language:

Jed Rakoff, *Garcia v. Bloomberg*

The marchers . . . relied on the police officers' commands in order to determine how they could legally proceed.

Under these circumstances, a reasonable officer would have understood that it was incumbent on the police to clearly warn the demonstrators that they must not proceed onto the Brooklyn Bridge's vehicular roadway. While, initially, the police officers congregated at the entrance to the bridge's vehicular roadway, thus effectively blocking the demonstrators from proceeding further, the officers then turned and started walking away from the demonstrators and onto the roadway—an implicit invitation to follow. While the demonstrators might have inferred otherwise if they had heard the bull-horn message, no reasonable officer could imagine, in these circumstances, that this warning was heard by more than a small fraction of the gathered multitude. **Here, as in *Vodak*, a single bull horn was "no mechanism ... for conveying a command" to the hundreds, if not thousands, of demonstrators present.** Indeed, the plaintiffs' video shows what should have been obvious to any reasonable officer, namely, that the surrounding clamor interfered with the ability of demonstrators as few as fifteen feet away from the bull horn to understand the officer's instructions.*

Below, in excerpts from the disciplinary proceeding we have seen in Parts 1 and 2, Bankruptcy Judge Goldgar uses a similar snippet-merging technique to rebut a lawyer's insistence that his conduct was ethical mainly because he had consulted counsel about it:

Benjamin Goldgar, *In re Brent*

Although consultation with counsel may be "an important step" in making a reasonable inquiry, "no amount of outside advice" can excuse a statement a reasonable lawyer should know is false and misleading.

---

* The paragraph would have been even stronger without the word "while." The first time "while" is used, it's not clear whether the judge means "while" as in time or "while" as in "although." ("While, initially, the police officers congregated at the entrance.") And the second time it's used, he definitely means "although". ("While the demonstrators might have [avoided the bridge] if they had heard the bull-horn message, no reasonable officer could imagine... that the warning was heard"). It's better to use "while" only for time, and to use "although" or "even though" for subordination. "Initially" should also have preceded "congregated" to set up a closer parallel with "then turned." And finally, consider cutting "namely" toward the end—and elsewhere. A colon or dash is more elegant and effective.

The authorities you analogize need not be cases, of course. The same principles apply to secondary authorities. Here, for example, trial judge D.P. Marshall quotes snippets from the Second Restatement of Torts to show that if a fracking company polluted a landowner's air, it would be trespassing under Arkansas law:

> **D.P. Marshall, *Tucker v. Southwestern Energy Co.***
>
> But the legal principles at work, *e.g.*, RESTATEMENT (SECOND) OF TORTS § 158, support the trespass claim. Noxious substances are entering the air right above the Berrys' land and remaining there long enough to be detected before the wind moves them on. No one is removing the substances; the wind is. If it is an actionable trespass to "to fly an advertising kite or balloon through the air above [the Berrys' land]," then sending noxious chemicals their way is a trespass too.

So far, we've seen ways to analogize effectively by asserting that the case cited and the case before the court are two peas in a pod. But sometimes a judge might want to go bold, suggesting that the case cited applies to the current dispute even more than it applied to the cited case itself! Here, for example, Judge Rakoff cites a case striking down a public-health regulation to claim that the regulation now before the court should be struck down with even more gusto:

> **Jed Rakoff, *23-34 94th St. Grocery v. N.Y. City Bd.***
>
> Under *Vango Media*, a local regulation with even an indirect relationship to cigarette advertising (or here, promotion) is nonetheless pre-empted by the Labeling Act if it "imposes conditions" that "substantially impact[]" such advertising (or, here again, promotion).

Here, the provision of Article 181.19 calling for tobacco retailers to post a large anti-smoking sign wherever "tobacco products are displayed" plainly imposes conditions on the promotion of cigarettes—indeed, **in a far more direct way than the New York City regulation** (requiring taxis to display one public health message for every four tobacco advertisements) that was found to be preempted in *Vango Media*.

In *Point Made*, my book for advocates, I call this technique *One Up*. It's a slightly cocky move: "I've got a case that's even better for me than it was for them." In the *One Up* example from Judge Schiltz below, he suggests just that: the complaint before me is even less adequate than the inadequate one I cite.

Patrick Schiltz, *Shiraz Hookah, LLC v. City of Minneapolis*

Like the complaint filed in *Friends of Lake View*, the complaint filed by Shiraz in this case fails to allege sufficient facts to trigger application of strict scrutiny. Shiraz's naked allegation that the "ordinance is plainly discriminatory on the basis of race and national origin," is conclusory and therefore "not entitled to the assumption of truth." Shiraz does allege facts that, if true, establish disproportionate *impact* on persons of Middle Eastern and African origin. But, again, disproportionate impact does not establish discriminatory purpose, even if the legislative body was aware of the likely impact. **In fact, Shiraz's complaint presents a weaker case for strict scrutiny than the complaint in *Friends of Lake View*, because Shiraz does not even allege that the City knew that the Ordinance would disproportionately burden members of**

> a suspect class, let alone facts that permit the inference
> that the City acted for the *purpose* of burdening those
> individuals.*

Schiltz shows his analogizing chops once again in a Fourth
Amendment excessive-force case. Here he extracts the essence of
two earlier cases, insisting that if police tasering was bad there, it's
even worse here:

Patrick Schiltz, *Newton v. Walker*

The facts of this case are **essentially indistinguishable**
from two other recent Eighth Circuit cases: *Brown v. City of
Golden Valley*, and *Shekleton v. Eichenberger*. **In both *Brown*
and *Shekleton*, an officer tasered a nonviolent, nonresist-
ing plaintiff who was suspected of a minor crime.** In both
cases, the Eighth Circuit held that the officer was not entitled
to qualified immunity:

> At the time Zarrett deployed his Taser and arrested
> Sandra, the law was sufficiently clear to inform a rea-
> sonable officer that it was unlawful to Taser a nonvio-
> lent, suspected misdemeanant who was not fleeing or
> resisting arrest, who posed little to no threat to anyone's
> safety, and whose only noncompliance with the officer's
> commands was to disobey two orders to end her phone
> call to a 911 operator.

Brown, 574 F.3d at 499; *see also Shekleton*, 677 F.3d at 367
(noting that, in *Brown*, "we determined that the general law

---

* Note the effective use of a comma to set off the long "because" clause.

> prohibiting excessive force in place at the time of the inci-
> dent was sufficient to inform an officer that use of his taser
> on a nonfleeing, nonviolent suspected misdemeanant was
> unreasonable, even though we did not have a case specifically
> addressing officer taser use prior to the incident").
>
> **Like this case, both _Brown_ and _Shekleton_ involved inci-
> dents that occurred before the Eighth Circuit issued its
> decision in _Chambers_. Thus,** a reasonable officer in Walker's
> position—**like a reasonable officer in the position of the
> officers in _Brown_ and _Shekleton_**—should have known that
> tasering a nonviolent, nonresisting suspected misdemeanant
> violates the Fourth Amendment. Indeed, the Eighth Circuit's
> decision in _Brown_ predated Walker's tasering of Newton. **Thus,
> it would have been _clearer_ to a reasonable officer in Walker's
> position than it would have been to a reasonable officer in the
> position of the officer in _Brown_ that tasering a nonviolent,
> nonresisting suspected misdemeanant violates the Fourth
> Amendment.** Walker is not entitled to qualified immunity.*

Schiltz's summary of _Brown_ and _Shekleton_ strikes at the key
points of similarity with the current case. In the process, he glosses
over the fact that _Brown_ and _Shekleton_ cannot readily be reconciled
with _Chambers_—a diplomatic move for a lower-court judge when a
higher court's precedents conflict!

The bottom line: analogizing works best when it's spare and
focused. Avoid quoting and regurgitating unrelated facts, focus
like a laser beam on the key points of similarity, and merge short
snippets from the cited authorities into your own discussion of the
case before you, but without unfairly taking those snippets out of
context.

---

* I'm not thrilled that two out of three sentences begin with "thus."

Not Here, Not Now: Distinguishing

As with analogizing, the trick here is to avoid getting bogged down as you highlight the key points of difference. As always, less is more, but you do not want to dismiss counter-authorities too glibly.

Let's start with some default models. In a case about whether the United States could assert sovereign immunity if a federal employee sues for back pay, former D.C. Circuit Chief Judge Wald distinguished the plaintiff's cited authorities in three effective ways.

The first two discussions are short: she simply explains why the authorities—a common-law case and a reference to legislative history—don't support the losing party's point. The case doesn't apply because it was about suing the wrong defendant, not about back pay. Nor does the legislative history shed light on the back-pay issue, because it was really about how the government can skirt lawsuits even after it has waived sovereign immunity:

Patricia Wald, *Hubbard v. EPA*

The other references highlighted by Hubbard are even more tangential. Hubbard notes that the facts of *Gnotta v. United States*, a government employment case, were specifically discussed at the 1970 hearing [on amending 5 U.S.C. § 702]. But neither *Gnotta* nor the discussion of it at the hearings dealt with back pay. The sovereign immunity problem in *Gnotta* involved a federal employee who could not obtain any form of relief because he had chosen the wrong defendants to sue.

Hubbard also cites references to "federal employment" in discussions relating to the removal of the amount in controversy requirement, a statutory change separate from the waiver of sovereign immunity but which was also accomplished through the 1976 amendments. That reference merely demonstrates that Congress understood that where

> sovereign immunity was waived, there was still a barrier to federal court jurisdiction if the employee's loss was not quantifiable or did not exceed $10,000. The mention of federal employment in that context tells us zero about Congress' intent to expand the scope of immunity for back pay.*

Wald offers a helpful and economical formula here: *Party cites X. But X did not deal with Y. And Party cites A. But A merely shows B.*

Of course, not all adverse authorities lend themselves to a disappearing act. The third authority that Judge Wald faces, a Supreme Court case called *Bowen v. Massachusetts* that is at first blush right on point, demands more attention and a slower pace. Suddenly Wald's tone is less cocksure and her analysis more painstaking. Wald's starting point is the plaintiff's rendition of the holding. Then she moves on to her own alternative view, zooming in on a close read of the language in question. She eventually neutralizes that language in three swipes: (1) she relegates it to "dicta," (2) she claims that it is less ambiguous than it appears in the context of the rest of the opinion and its internal authorities, and (3) she appeals to common sense, arguing that if the Supreme Court had wanted to adopt the plaintiff's reading, it would have said so:

> *Bowen v. Massachusetts* does not resuscitate Hubbard's claim. Before *Bowen*, courts consistently found that back pay was not among the types of relief for which § 702 waived sovereign immunity. Hubbard argues that *Bowen* changed all that. We do not find that to be true.

---

* Note her use of "That reference" rather than the bureaucratic "Such reference" as well as her almost jarringly colloquial phrase "tell us zero about" when she discusses congressional intent.

As already noted, in *Bowen* the Supreme Court emphasized that § 702's reference to "other than money damages" invoked the distinction between "damages" which are "'sum[s] of money used as compensatory relief'" and "specific remedies" which "'are not substitute remedies at all, but attempt to give the plaintiff the very thing to which he was entitled.'" Applying that dichotomy to the case in front of it, the Court determined that Massachusetts' suit to enforce a statutory *entitlement* to receive withheld federal grant-in-aid money was a suit for specific relief. The fact that the entitlement Massachusetts sought to enforce was a cash allotment did not alter this conclusion: "The State's suit . . . is not a suit seeking money in *compensation* for the damage sustained by the failure of the Federal Government to pay as mandated; rather, it is a suit seeking to enforce the statutory mandate itself, which happens to be one for the payment of money."

. . .

Hubbard ultimately bases his case on one line of dicta in *Bowen* possibly suggesting that back pay may be specific relief. In a background paragraph explaining the difference between specific and compensatory relief, the Court said:

> Our cases have long recognized the distinction between an action at law for damages—which are intended to provide a victim with monetary compensation for an injury to his person, property, or reputation—and an equitable action for specific relief—which may include an order providing for the reinstatement of an employee with back pay, or for the recovery of specific property or monies, ejectment from land, or injunction either directing or restraining the defendant officer's actions.

Viewed in isolation, it is ambiguous whether the sentence was labelling back pay itself as specific relief, or merely making the unremarkable point that back pay often accompanies an award of reinstatement, which itself is unquestionably a form of specific relief. In the context of the entire opinion, however, we believe that the single reference cannot shoulder the burden of demonstrating that the Court intended to mandate an about-face on the hornbook view of back pay as damages as well as the decisions of all courts up to that point that back pay was not a form of specific relief for § 702 purposes but, rather, a form of compensatory damages. *Bowen* itself relies on *Dobbs on Remedies* for the distinction between specific and compensatory relief. Further, *Bowen* specifically refers to the Back Pay Act as a law that provides *compensatory* relief. *See Bowen* (referring to the Back Pay Act and other statutes as laws which "attempt to compensate a particular class of persons for past injuries or labors"). In the end, we cannot rest a general waiver of sovereign immunity as to back pay for federal employees on a single, ambiguous phrase in a background, descriptive portion of the *Bowen* opinion. We believe that the Court would have given us more explicit guidance than that had it intended to overturn both the common law understanding of back pay as well as lower courts' decade-long interpretation of § 702 as barring back pay relief.*

---

* First, as Strunk & White advise in *The Elements of Style*, recast "the fact that" sentences. So rather than "The fact that the entitlement Massachusetts sought to enforce was a cash allotment did not alter this conclusion," try "This conclusion did not change merely because the entitlement that Massachusetts sought to enforce was a cash allotment." Eliminating "the fact that" would also help improve the flow by moving "this conclusion" closer to the previous sentence, which was about that conclusion. Second, in the quotation from the Supreme Court, it's indeed helpful to use semicolons to sharpen contrasts, but cut the "rather" or "however" when you do. So "The State's suit is not a suit seeking X; it is a suit seeking Y." No "rather"—it ruins the parallel structure, a bit like writing "To err is human; however, to forgive is divine." (See Part 4 for more on this.) The same is true of Judge

As Judge Wald shows in her nuanced treatment of *Bowen*, judges, like advocates, should avoid simply announcing that a case is "distinguishable" and then start reciting the facts. It's better to identify the main point of distinction up front.

That's precisely what Ninth Circuit Judge Kozinski does below. In an intellectual-property dispute involving a song that references Barbie dolls and that thus implicates the Barbie trademark, he needs to distinguish a binding case known as *Dr. Seuss*. That case was a copyright-infringement dispute over a parody of the O.J. Simpson trial in which the authors inserted words and images from *The Cat and the Hat*. But rather than begin by writing that "*Dr. Seuss* is distinguishable," Kozinski anchors his analysis on the core doctrinal contrast, a contrast between referencing a trademarked product to mock the product itself and referencing a trademarked product to mock something else. Then and only then does he claim that *Dr. Seuss* is distinguishable:

Alex Kozinski, *Mattel v. MCA Records*

The song ["Barbie Girl"] does not rely on the Barbie mark to poke fun at another subject but targets Barbie herself. This case is therefore distinguishable from *Dr. Seuss*, where we held that the book *The Cat NOT in the Hat!* borrowed Dr. Seuss's trademarks and lyrics to get attention rather than to mock *The Cat in the Hat!* The defendant's use of the

---

Wald's own formulation in the next paragraph: "Hubbard's basic claim is not for enforcement of any legal mandate that the EPA pay him a sum of money; rather, it is to force the EPA to offer him the job it denied him." Once again, the "rather" mars the parallelism, but so does the contrast between "for enforcement" and "to force." Here's a revision: "The point of Hubbard's claim is not to enforce a legal mandate that the EPA pay him a sum of money; it is to force the EPA to offer him the job that it denied him." Third, watch for dangling modifiers in phrases like "Viewed in isolation, it is ambiguous whether the sentence. . . ." The "sentence" is what's viewed in isolation, not the dummy-subject "it." And finally, "both" at the end of the passage—in fact, "both" anywhere—takes "and," not "as well as."

Dr. Seuss trademarks and copyrighted works had "no critical bearing on the substance or style of" *The Cat in the Hat!*, and therefore could not claim First Amendment protection. *Dr. Seuss* recognized that, where an artistic work targets the original and does not merely borrow another's property to get attention, First Amendment interests weigh more heavily in the balance.

Turning from Barbie dolls to political satire, let's consider a strong trial example.

As we saw above, trial judge Shira Scheindlin was tasked with considering whether a magazine ad was political speech when it touted the magazine as "possibly the only good thing in New York that Rudy [Giuliani] hasn't taken credit for." Below, she distinguishes the ad from a previous case in which *Penthouse* had portrayed 1984 presidential candidate Walter Mondale as a stripper basking in female lust because of his support for the Equal Rights Amendment:

Shira Scheindlin, *New York Magazine v. Metropolitan Transit Authority*

The *Penthouse* case is surely factually similar to this one. Yet, there are certain distinguishing features that permit me to reach a different conclusion here. The most important distinction is that **the speech in the Penthouse ad is a comment about a political position** Vice-President Mondale was taking in the then current Presidential campaign: to wit, support for the ERA. **By contrast, the speech in the Ad in issue is merely a comment on the political style of the Mayor.** The Mondale caricature, appearing in any medium, would undoubtedly be viewed as political speech. The N.Y. Magazine Ad, wherever it appeared, would be viewed as promoting

> N.Y. Magazine. The Penthouse ad is surely protected political speech; the N.Y. Magazine Ad falls in a grey area.

The strong contrast that Scheindlin draws between political positions and political style is helpful and persuasive.*

Of course, judges often have to distinguish not a single case but an entire line of cases—sometimes in one fell swoop, and other times piecemeal.

Below, Judge Posner tackles a line of cases all at once, and all on the same grounds. In this dispute over a toxin that had leaked from a railroad car, Posner asserts that differences between shippers and carriers and between manufacturers and transporters make all the difference in the world:

> ### Richard Posner, *Indiana Harbor Belt R.R. v. American Cyanamid Co.*
>
> The difference between shipper and carrier points to a deep flaw in the plaintiff's case. Unlike *Guille*, and unlike *Siegler*, and unlike the storage cases, beginning with *Rylands* itself, here it is not the actors—that is, the transporters of acrylonitrile and other chemicals—but the manufacturers, who are sought to be held strictly liable. *Cf. City of Bloomington v. Westinghouse Elec. Corp.*, 891 F.2d at 615–16. A shipper can in the bill of lading designate the route of his shipment if he likes, but is it realistic to suppose that shippers will become students of railroading in order to lay out the safest route by which to ship their goods? Anyway, rerouting is no panacea.

---

* I'd cut down on the meta-commentary in the first two sentences and boil the whole thing down to something like "Although *Penthouse* appears to have similar facts" it is different in key ways." Or better yet, just start with "Although *Penthouse* appears to have similar facts" and then jump to "the speech in the Penthouse ad."

Often it will increase the length of the journey, or compel the use of poorer track, or both. When this happens, the probability of an accident is increased, even if the consequences of an accident if one occurs are reduced; so the expected accident cost, being the product of the probability of an accident and the harm if the accident occurs, may rise. It is easy to see how the accident in this case might have been prevented at reasonable cost by greater care on the part of those who handled the tank car of acrylonitrile. It is difficult to see how it might have been prevented at reasonable cost by a change in the activity of transporting the chemical. This is therefore not an apt case for strict liability.*

Speaking of Learned Hand, he's the source of our final distinguished example of distinguishing. Whereas Judge Posner had the luxury of distinguishing a string of cases all on the same grounds, in the example below, Hand faces a thornier problem: he needed to dispense with several cases, each with its own point of distinction.

In *Cheney Bros. v. Doris Silk Corp.*, a case we visited in Part 1, the plaintiff silk manufacturer alleged that the defendant had copied one of its silk designs and then undercut the plaintiff's prices. The plaintiff sought to prevent the defendant from selling the copied silk design, but it was neither patented nor protected by copyright. In disposing of the plaintiff's cases, Hand resists the temptation

---

* Even in something as staid as common-law case distinction, you can see plenty of vintage Posner here: the conversational tone, the quips like "Anyway, rerouting is no panacea," the contrasts between "it is easy to see" and "it is difficult to see," the light word choices like "when" and "so" and "handled," and even the pseudo-rhetorical question and the pair of em dashes. Not to mention the dose of law and economics, of course, and the reference to Learned Hand's famous formula in *United States v. Carroll Towing Co.*

to get bogged down in long paragraphs distinguishing each case one at a time. Instead, he distinguishes ten cases in a single, swift paragraph:

Learned Hand, *Cheney Bros. v. Doris Silk Corp.*

The other cases are easily distinguishable. *Board of Trade v. Christie* went upon the fact that the defendants had procured their information through a breach of contract between the plaintiff and its subscribers, or some surreptitious and dishonest conduct. *Hunt v. N.Y. Cotton Exchange* was another instance of the same kind. There is, indeed, language in *National Tel. News Co. v. West Un. Tel. Co.* which goes further, but we take it that the authoritative statement of the doctrine must be found in *Board of Trade v. Christie*. Though the limitations there imposed have indeed been extended in *International News Service v. Associated Press*, they still comprise no more than cases involving news and perhaps market quotations. *Prest-O-Lite v. Bogen* and *Prest-O-Lite v. Davis* were cases of passing off. In [four other cases], again, either there was a breach of contract between the plaintiff and its subscriber, or the defendant had dishonestly procured the information. They are like *Board of Trade v. Christie*.

Hand gets right to the key distinguishing feature of each case. Unlike the case here, Hand tells us, *Christie* and *Hunt* involved dishonesty, *National Television News Co.* is not binding and is trumped by binding precedent, *International News Service* is about a different industry, the *Prest-O-Lite* cases involved trademark infringement, and the final four cases were like the first two cases involving dishonesty. Phew! It would be hard to top this excerpt when it comes to economical and compact distinguishing.

Sometimes, distinguishing a case is simple (that's California and this is New York; that's a manufacturer and this is a distributor). And other times, as with Wald's treatment of *Bowen*, life is messier. But a great judge will always keep the reader in mind, minimizing both regurgitation and conclusory reasoning and leading with clear points of distinction instead.

As an Aside: Parentheticals

Parentheticals can be highly effective tools for synthesizing authorities and lines of authorities. Helpful parentheticals buttress the analysis and immerse readers in key nuggets from cited decisions. But just including your thoughts about a case haphazardly won't make your readers' lives any easier, and it may actually slow your readers down.

A few guidelines before we peek at some picture-perfect parentheticals.

Don't: Simply jot down observations about an authority and then enclose them inside parentheses (or inside brackets, for you British English types).

Do: Make your parentheticals parallel and easy to follow by starting them with participles reflecting what the target court did.

Trial judge Michael Ponsor uses a textbook parenthetical in this next example. Notice that he leads with a participle indicating what the court did ("upholding . . . ") and then describes the key facts ("where . . ."):

Michael Ponsor, *Gatti v. Nat'l Union Fire Ins.*

If the court were to conclude that these claims arise out of the same nucleus of facts, then the claims are precluded under the doctrine of *res judicata*. *Stewart v. U.S. Bancorp*, 297 F.3d 953 (9th Cir. 2002) (**upholding** the district court's dismissal based on *res judicata* of a new complaint alleging ERISA violations **where** the earlier complaint arising out of "same nucleus of facts" had been dismissed because the state contract claims were preempted by ERISA).

Of course, parallel parentheticals are particularly potent when you have a string of cites supporting the same proposition. Here, former D.C. Circuit Chief Judge Wald uses parallel parentheticals to string together several authorities supporting her position:

Patricia Wald, *Steffan v. Perry*, dissenting

Indeed, the Supreme Court's decisions indicate that the government may *neither* punish *nor* make "employment decisions" solely on the basis of citizens' political affiliations or membership in "subversive organizations." *See Elrod v. Burns*, 427 US. 347, 372-73, 96 S.Ct. 2673, 2689, 49 L.Ed.2d 547 (1976) (**prohibiting** dismissal of non-policymaking county employees based on political affiliation); *Elfbrandt v. Russel*, 384 U.S. 11, 17-19, 96 S.Ct. 1238, 1241-42, 16 L.Ed.2d 321 (1966) (**invalidating** law denying employment on grounds of membership in subversive organization). *Cf. Meinhold*, 34 F.3d at 1478 (**pointing out** "the constitutionally significant danger of making status a surrogate for prohibited conduct").

Trial judge Shira Scheindlin uses a similar strategy in a footnote dispensing with the State of New York's contention that laches could bar challenges to criminal convictions:

Shira Scheindlin, *Clark v. Perez*

[169] *See People v. Reed*, 709 N.Y.S.2d 764, 765 (4th Dep't 200) (**concluding** that the lower court had "erred in denying defendant's motion on the ground that it was barred by the

> doctrine of laches" and vacating sentence of defendant, who was convicted in 1954); *People v. Kirkland*, 781 N.Y.S.2d 627 (Sup.Ct. Kings Co.2003) (**conducting** an in depth analysis and **concluding that** "[e]ven if this court is not bound by [the] *Reed* decision, the court would hold that as a matter of law, laches does not apply to motions to vacate a judgment"); *People v. Bell*, 689 N.Y.S.2d 259 (Sup.Ct.N.Y.Co.1998) (**refusing** to dismiss a section 440.10 motion on the basis of laches although convictions occurred over twenty-three years earlier).

In addition to using great parallel participles, Wald and Scheindlin also use another popular parenthetical technique: combining a leading participle with a quote from the cited material. Chief Justice John Roberts does the same below in a case challenging the constitutionality of a search warrant:

> ### John Roberts, *Messerschmidt v. Millender*
>
> It would therefore not have been unreasonable—based on the facts set out in the affidavit—for an officer to believe that evidence regarding Bowen's gang affiliation would prove helpful in prosecuting him for the attack on Kelly. See *Warden, Md. Penitentiary v. Hayden*, 387 U.S. 294, 307, 87 S.Ct. 1642, 18 L.Ed.2d 782 (1967) (**holding** that the Fourth Amendment allows a search for evidence when there is **"probable cause . . . to believe that the evidence sought will aid in a particular apprehension or conviction"**).*

---

* I prefer his "when" here to the legalistic and nonstandard "where" I often see elsewhere.

The leading participle isn't always needed when you want to highlight quoted material. Although it's often better to use your own words to introduce or describe a cited authority, don't be afraid to let a single-sentence quotation speak for itself. In the next example, Justice Michael Kirby uses such a technique in a footnote to highlight the long history of the "ordinary man" standard in Australian provocation decisions:

Michael Kirby, *Green v. The Queen*,
dissenting

207 See for example Dixon J in *Packett v The King* [1937] HCA 53; (1937) 58 CLR 190 at 217-218 ("**At common law the test of provocation is ... whether it would suffice to deprive a reasonable man *in his situation* of self-control**"); Windeyer J in *Parker v The Queen* [1963] HCA 14; (1963) 111 CLR 610 at 655 ("**[T]he matter must be considered from the standpoint of the mind of an ordinary man *in the circumstances*"**) and Brennan, Deane, Dawson and Gaudron JJ in *Masciantonio v The Queen* [1995] HCA 67; (1995) 183 CLR 58 at 69 ("**Whether an ordinary person could have reacted in the way in which the appellant did [might depend on whether] the provocation offered by the deceased was, *in the circumstances in which the appellant found himself,* of a high degree.**") (emphasis added in each case)

And here, Seventh Circuit Judge Wood does the same in a case in which an inmate alleged that his free-exercise rights were violated when he was prohibited from using his own Bible but was allowed to use the jail's Bible. Although Judge Wood ultimately dismissed the inmate's claims, she uses a single-sentence quotation to concede the merit in his argument so that she can move on to its shortcomings next:

Diane Wood, *Tarpley v. Allen County, Indiana*

Tarpley is correct that his right freely to exercise his religion does not evaporate entirely when he enters a jail. *See Cruz v. Beto*, 405 U.S. 319, 322 n. 2, 92 S.Ct. 1079, 31 L.Ed.2d 263 (1972) (**"reasonable opportunities must be afforded to all prisoners to exercise the religious freedom guaranteed by the First and Fourteenth Amendments without fear of penalty"**). On the other hand, the Allen County defendants are equally correct that his right is not unfettered.

When parentheticals are thoughtful and effective, they allow you to marshal authorities with spare and focused language. The key is to stick to parallel form and to cite only essential facts.

Lead 'Em On: Quoting without Tears

Whether you're a judge, advocate, or journalist, stringing together quotations is not "writing." A surgical strike with lean quoted language will often beat a bulky block quotation bursting all over the page. And yet sometimes, when binding precedent is worded just right, even an economical judge will want to preserve the language in the original court's own words. Here's how to navigate these block-quote minefields.

For starters, don't just dump the quote and run. Introduce a long quote the way you would introduce a stranger to a friend—by telling the friend about what they have in common, and why this new person might be interesting to get to know. Unconsciously or not, many judges (like many lawyers) use block quotes not to buttress the analysis, but to replace it. Here for example, one judge simply strings together three long quotes, each time with the equivalent of "As remarked/discussed by so-and-so":

> This court has recognized the existence of a presumption concerning joint liability of the parties for debts that were accumulated from joint property. . . . **The remarks of [] are relevant to this issue:**
>
> > "It seems to me that justice demands and logic dictates that one spouse cannot and should not be only the beneficiary from the partnership with the other spouse in the family assets, without also bearing the burden of the debts that were incurred . . . "
>
> **This was also discussed by []:**
>
> > "It may be argued that whenever one of the spouses benefits from the work of the other spouse, why should he be a partner only in profits, while the other spouse is solely liable for losses and expenses? . . ."
>
> **The principles of the rule were discussed by []:**
>
> > "The presumption of joint liability for debts supplements the presumption of joint ownership of assets. . . ."
>
> Thus we see that the presumption of joint liability for debts is a corresponding and supplementary presumption to the presumption of joint ownership of rights . . . .

There's a better way. Take this example from Judge Easterbrook. He makes a point about statutory interpretation and quotes Justice Holmes in support. But rather than just reproduce Holmes's quote into the text after a vacuous lead-in like "As Justice Holmes has put it," Easterbrook situates the quote for the reader, explaining why Holmes is in his camp:

Frank Easterbrook, *In re Sinclair*

Statutes are law, not evidence of law. References to "intent" in judicial opinions do not imply that legislators' motives and beliefs, as opposed to their public acts, establish the norms to which all others must conform. "Original meaning" rather than "intent" frequently captures the interpretive task more precisely, reminding us that it is the work of the political branches (the "meaning") rather than of the courts that matters, and that their work acquires its meaning when enacted ("originally"). Revisionist history may be revelatory; revisionist judging is simply unfaithful to the enterprise. **Justice Holmes made the point when denouncing a claim that judges should give weight to the intent of a document's authors:**

> [A statute] does not disclose one meaning conclusively according to the laws of language. Thereupon we ask, not what this man meant, but what those words would mean in the mouth of a normal speaker of English, using them in the circumstances in which they were used. . . . But the normal speaker of English is merely a special variety, a literary form, so to speak, of our old friend the prudent man. He is external to the particular writer, and a reference to him as the criterion is simply another instance of the externality of the law. . . . We do not inquire what the legislature meant; we ask only what the statute means.

Note how the end of the quotation echoes the lead-in. The cuts and ellipses in this example, by the way, are Easterbrook's, not mine: especially in a long quote, every sentence should count.

Sometimes you can go even further in recasting the language that you're about to share. Take the example below from Judge Kozinski. He argues that titles don't necessarily speak to the origin of a work—a point that another court of appeals had already addressed. He offers two hypothetical illustrations, and then segues to the block quote from his counterpart court through a pithy summary sentence all his own:

Alex Kozinski, *Mattel v. MCA Records*

A title is designed to catch the eye and to promote the value of the underlying work. Consumers expect a title to communicate a message about the book or movie, but they do not expect it to identify the publisher or producer. If we see a painting titled "Campbell's Chicken Noodle Soup," we're unlikely to believe that Campbell's has branched into the art business. Nor, upon hearing Janis Joplin croon "Oh Lord, won't you buy me a Mercedes-Benz?," would we suspect that she and the carmaker had entered into a joint venture. **A title tells us something about the underlying work but seldom speaks to its origin:**

> Though consumers frequently look to the title of a work to determine what it is about, they do not regard titles of artistic works in the same way as the names of ordinary commercial products. Since consumers expect an ordinary product to be what the name says it is, we apply the Lanham Act with some rigor to prohibit names that misdescribe such goods. But most consumers are well aware that they cannot judge a book solely by its title any more than by its cover.

Having read thousands of opinions while writing this book, I would suggest that most judges should use fewer long quotes and should introduce the ones they do use more thoughtfully and strategically. The Commonwealth tradition in particular appears to favor quoting whole passages *in seriatim* with no analysis whatsoever to guide the reader. Sometimes, though, as in the Australian example below from Justice Kirby, we see a refreshing deviation from the so-and-so-said-such-and-such-in-some-case approach:

Michael Kirby, *Green v. The Queen*, dissenting

The Court was prepared to attribute to the ordinary person the age (in the sense of immaturity) of the actual accused. **But it left no doubt that it was drawing a distinction between the fact and effect of the provocation and the standard of self-control:**

> "[T]he fact that the particular accused lacks the power of self-control of an ordinary person by reason of some attribute or characteristic which must be taken into account in identifying the content or gravity of the particular wrongful act or insult will not affect the reference point of the objective test, namely, the power of self-control of a hypothetical 'ordinary person'."

And here, Canadian Chief Justice Beverly McLachlin uses a thoughtful lead-in to add even more power to the striking rhetoric of the case she quotes:

Beverly McLachlin, *R. v. Keegstra*, dissenting

Continuity has been stressed in cases such as *RWDSU v. Dolphin Delivery Ltd.*, that **recognized both the deep roots** of freedom of expression in Canadian society, and the key role it has played in our democratic development:

> Freedom of expression is not, however, a creature of the *Charter*. It is one of the fundamental concepts that has formed the basis for the historical development of the political, social and educational institutions of western society. Representative democracy, as we know it today, which is in great part the product of free expression and discussion of varying ideas, depends upon its maintenance and protection.

Of course, sometimes a good judge uses a quote not to prop it up but to shoot it down. What's good for similarities is also good for contrasts. In presenting a case's background below, Justice Scalia describes a videotape in evidence, and then uses a block quote to contrast his description with the description of the court below (about to be reversed), suggesting that the lower court has ignored the evidence before its eyes:

Antonin Scalia, *Scott v. Harris*

There is, however, an added wrinkle in this case: existence in the record of a videotape capturing the events in question. There are no allegations or indications that this videotape was doctored or altered in any way, nor any contention that what it depicts differs from what actually happened. The videotape quite clearly contradicts the version of the story told by respondent and adopted by the Court of Appeals. For example, the Court of Appeals adopted respondent's assertions that, during the chase, "there was little, if any, actual threat to pedestrians or other motorists, as the roads were mostly empty and [respondent] remained in control of his vehicle." Indeed, **reading the lower court's opinion, one gets the impression that respondent, rather than fleeing from police, was attempting to pass his driving test:**

> "[T]aking the facts from the non-movant's viewpoint, [respondent] remained in control of his vehicle, slowed for turns and intersections, and typically used his indicators for turns. He did not run any motorists off the road. Nor was he a threat to pedestrians in the shopping center parking lot, which was free from pedestrian and vehicular traffic as the center was closed. Significantly, by the time the parties were back on the highway and Scott rammed [respondent], the motorway had been cleared of motorists and pedestrians allegedly because of police blockades of the nearby intersections."

Not all the justices agreed that it was proper for the Court to make its own assessment of the videotape. In dissent, Justice Stevens suggested that the majority ignored the teaching of *Tennessee v. Garner*, which in his view requires a jury, not a court, to decide whether deadly force was used. Justice Stevens heightens the contrast between the majority's position and *Garner* by quoting from each, and then by introducing the *Garner* quote by telegraphing its essence:

> **John Paul Stevens, *Scott v. Harris*, dissenting**
>
> Although *Garner* may not, as the Court suggests, "establish a magical on/off switch that triggers rigid preconditions" for the use of deadly force, **it did set a threshold under which**

the use of deadly force would be considered constitutionally unreasonable:

> "Where the officer has probable cause to believe
> that the suspect poses a threat of serious physi-
> cal harm, either to the officer or to others, it is not
> constitutionally unreasonable to prevent escape by
> using deadly force. Thus, if the suspect threatens the
> officer with a weapon or there is probable cause to
> believe that he has committed a crime involving the
> infliction or threatened infliction of serious physical
> harm, deadly force may be used if necessary to pre-
> vent escape, and if, where feasible, some warning has
> been given."

Block quotations can be powerful—but they often invite skim-
ming, skipping, or outright irritation. Don't use block quotes just to
stockpile material that "sounds good" or that may "provide helpful
background." Use long quotes sparingly, and only when the gist of
the quote supports a particular point you need to make. Above all,
introduce long quotes by giving the reader the gist, so that the reader
understands why reading copied material is worth the effort.

Speaking of making readers work hard for information, let's
talk next about one of legal writing's most controversial tools: the
footnote.

Troubled Waters: The Footnoters' Dilemma

"Phony excrescences." "An abomination." These and other choice
epithets for footnotes pervade former D.C. Circuit Judge Abner
Mikva's famous article "Goodbye to Footnotes."[1] Mikva didn't like
footnotes because (1) they are hard to read, requiring readers to

search for the note and then try to find their place again, (2) they invite dicta that should have been cut, (3) they can be exploited to sneak doctrinal innovations under colleagues' radar screens, and (4) they can turn into battlegrounds between the majority and the dissenters. Some judges have taken a principled stand against footnotes; Justice Holmes is said to be the only Supreme Court justice on the Hughes court who did not use footnotes in his opinions.[2]

All of Judge Mikva's objections are well taken. And yet as the examples below show, many great judges do use footnotes for the same reasons that many great advocates do: (1) to show that a principle is well established, (2) to distinguish authorities, (3) to counter objections, and (4) to buttress a point.

Here, for example, Justice Scalia uses a footnote to support his contention that ample precedent belies the majority's assessment of a key decision about the scope of "violent crimes" for sentencing purposes:

Antonin Scalia, *Sykes v. United States*, dissenting

The Court's accusation that Sykes "overreads the opinions of this Court," apparently applies to his interpretation of *Begay*'s "purposeful, violent, and aggressive" test, which the Court now suggests applies only "to strict liability, negligence, and recklessness crimes." But that makes no sense. If the test excluded only those unintentional crimes, it would be recast as the "purposeful" test, since the last two adjectives ("violent, and aggressive") would do no work. For that reason, perhaps, all 11 Circuits that have addressed *Begay* "overrea[d]" it just as Sykes does *—and as does the Government.

* See *United States v. Holloway*, 630 F.3d 252, 260 (C.A.1 2011); *United States v. Brown*, 629 F.3d 290, 295–296 (C.A.2 2011) *(per curiam); United States v. Lee*, 612 F.3d 170, 196 (C.A.3 2010); *United States v. Jenkins*, 631 F.3d 680, 683 (C.A.4 2011);

United States v. Harrimon, 568 F.3d 531, 534 (C.A.5 2009);
United States v. Young, 580 F.3d 373, 377 (C.A.6 2009); *United
States v. Sonnenberg,* 628 F.3d 361, 364 (C.A.7 2010); *United
States v. Boyce,* 633 F.3d 708, 711 (C.A.8 2011); *United States
v. Terrell,* 593 F.3d 1084, 1089–1091 (C.A.9 2010); *United
States v. Ford,* 613 F.3d 1263, 1272–1273 (C.A.10 2010); *United
States v. Harrison,* 558 F.3d 1280, 1295–1296 (C.A.11 2009).

Footnotes are also a good place to distinguish authorities that
don't pose enough of a challenge to warrant discussion in the body
of your analysis. Below, for instance, in a dissenting opinion, Judge
Wald uses a footnote to distinguish cases cited not by one of the parties, but by the majority:

Patricia Wald, *Steffan v. Perry,* **dissenting**

The majority declares that Steffan's concession that "the military may discharge those who engage in *homosexual conduct*
whether on or off duty"[7] "frames the dispute." We agree, but
Steffan's concessions should be understood for what they
are—concessions on issues not properly presented by this
case, and that certainly do not warrant the majority's intimation that he was *obliged* to make them.

[7] The majority writes:

Steffan concedes that the military may constitutionally terminate service of all those who engage
in homosexual conduct—wherever it occurs and at
whatever time the conduct takes place. *See Dronenburg
v. Zech,* 741 F.2d 1388, 1398 (D.C. Cir. 1984) . . . ; *Beller
v. Middendorf,* 632 F.2d 788, 812 (9th Cir. 1980). . . .

> Neither case, however, suggests that the military may constitutionally discharge members who engage in *any* "homosexual conduct" at *any* time, as the regulations under review in this case purport to do. The issue in *Dronenburg* was . . . .

Just as footnotes can help distinguish cases that aren't serious enough to warrant treatment in the text, so can they address statutory or policy arguments that undermine the losing party's position but that are peripheral to your main arguments. Here, for example, trial judge Michael Ponsor uses a footnote to undercut the government's argument that Congress always assumes that statutes will not apply retroactively unless it explicitly indicates otherwise. While Ponsor's main argument will attack the government's interpretation of the Saving Statute, his footnote raises doubt about the government's understanding of Congress's intentions:

Michael Ponsor, *United States v. Watts*

Following on this, the government argues, because the court must "assume that Congress is aware of existing law when it passes legislation," the court must also assume that Congress intended the Saving Statute to bar retroactive application to the [Fair Sentencing Act]. The culmination of this process of logic is that the court has no alternative but to sentence Mr. Watts to five years in prison, despite Congress's determination that the statute was mistaken, unjust, and racially tainted.[16] An examination of the muddied jurisprudential history of the General Saving Statute reveals the impertinence of the government's position.

[16] If Congress had explicitly stated that the [Fair Sentencing Act] would not be retroactive, the situation would of course be entirely different. Significantly, on the same day that it passed

the Fair Sentencing Act, the House considered but did not pass the Drug Sentencing Reform and Cocaine Kingpin Trafficking Act of 2009. Notably, this Act contained a specific provision that "There shall be no retroactive application of any portion of this Act." Congress apparently felt the need to include this provision, which under the government's view here would have been superfluous given the General Saving Statute.

Footnotes can also be used to preempt potential objections. In the next example, Judge Schiltz uses a footnote to concede that although his interpretation of a key case conflicts with some other courts' interpretations, he is sticking to his guns all the same:

Patrick Schiltz, *Newton v. Walker*

The Court therefore does not read *Cook* to hold that injuries from a taser are de minimis as a matter of law, particularly because such a reading would be inconsistent with the results in *Brown* and *Shekleton*.[3] Walker's motion for summary judgment is therefore denied as to Newton's excessive-force claim.

[3] **The Court notes that judges in this District have taken differing views of** *Cook*. *Compare Orsak v. Metro. Airports Comm'n Airport Police Dep't*, ("*Cook* did not hold that the injury associated with a taser is *de minimis*. Rather, the court balanced the *Graham* factors with the extent of the force used and held that the officer had a 'legitimate reason' to deploy the taser.") *with McClennon v. Kipke* (citing *Cook* for the proposition that "the Eighth Circuit has held that in the absence of evidence of long-term effects, the use of a Taser does 'not inflict any serious injury.'" (quoting *Cook*)). **The Court agrees with** *Orsak***'s reading of** *Cook***, and respectfully disagrees with** *McClennon***'s.**

Finally, great judges use footnotes to buttress their arguments on the merits. In our final example, Justice Ginsburg uses a footnote to undermine the claim that admitting women to the Virginia Military Institute will destroy the school and its adversative system:

Ruth Bader Ginsburg, *United States v. Virginia*

The notion that admission of women would downgrade VMI's stature, destroy the adversative system and, with it, even the school, is a judgment hardly proved,[12] a prediction hardly different from other "self-fulfilling prophec[ies]", *see Mississippi Univ. for Women*, once routinely used to deny rights or opportunities.

[12] *See* 766 F.Supp., at 1413 (describing testimony of expert witness David Riesman: "[I]f VMI were to admit women, it would eventually find it necessary to drop the adversative system altogether, and adopt a system that provides more nurturing and support for the students."). Such judgments have attended, and impeded, women's progress toward full citizenship stature throughout our Nation's history. Speaking in 1879 in support of higher education for females, for example, Virginia State Senator C.T. Smith of Nelson recounted that legislation proposed to protect the property rights of women had encountered resistance. A Senator opposing the measures objected that "there [was] no formal call for the [legislation]," and "depicted in burning eloquence the terrible consequences such laws would produce." The legislation passed, and a year or so later, its sponsor, C.T. Smith, reported that "not one of [the forecast "terrible consequences"] has or ever will happen, even unto the sounding of Gabriel's trumpet."

Footnotes can address—at length—arguments that do not deserve the full-text treatment but that still provide valuable context for some readers. The key words here are "valuable context" and "some readers." If you need to respond to an argument but don't want to give it more credence than it deserves, a footnote can be the answer.

The Meat of an opinion must withstand scrutiny from the parties, the public, legislatures, appellate courts, and legal scholars. Make your analysis more compelling by anticipating reader questions and then answering them in an order that makes sense, by explaining how the authorities connect to your conclusions, and by explaining why you have rejected viable counterarguments. The analysis can then take shape with a beginning, middle, and end. Headings, subheadings, and a traditional or modified outline structure can help the reader navigate from one point to the next. Within a section, umbrella paragraphs and bridge transitions make it easy for the reader to follow the discussion as well.

Practice Pointers for the Analysis

- Remember these six questions to organize your legal analysis:
  1) What logical questions might occur to a reader who is skeptical of your reasoning, and in what order? Answer those questions one at a time with just a sentence or two apiece.
  2) Why should your answers be trusted? Under each answer, list the applicable authorities, facts, and reasons, and then explain the connection between authority and answer in your own words. Quote and copy sparingly at this juncture.
  3) Is your answer to any question likely to be controversial? If so, acknowledge all viable counterarguments ("To be sure," "Although it is true that," and so forth) and explain why they should not prevail.

4) What natural or logical divisions would make the analysis easier to navigate? Consider breaking down the overall structure by topic, by party, by motion, by claim, by chronology, or by any other principle that bestows a beginning, middle, and end onto the analysis.

5) Use traditional outline structure (I, II, III; A, B, C), a modified structure, bullet points, headings, or other visual cues to organize your analysis. If you or your court disfavor these devices and prefer either the uninterrupted-essay approach or the continually numbered-paragraphs approach, break up long paragraphs so that the analysis isn't overwhelming.

6) Finally, add cues to help the reader navigate at the micro level within the sections. Start with a short "umbrella" paragraph previewing the analysis; add a short "umbrella" paragraph at the start of each section; always present old information before new; add transitions within and between paragraphs to show how your points connect to one another; and end each section with a short conclusion.

Try these techniques on your analyses as well:

- When analogizing, home in on key facts that link the cases while avoiding extraneous facts.
- When distinguishing, avoid getting bogged down; focus on the key points of difference, and omit extraneous facts.
- Whether you are analogizing or distinguishing, favor merged snippets and single-sentence quotations in parentheticals over block quotes regurgitated from the case you're analyzing.
- Use parentheticals for apt single-sentence quotations. Otherwise, use them to explain why a case is on point—or not. Begin with a participial phrase describing exactly what

the court did and why. Because parentheticals can be hard to read, make sure that yours follow parallel structure.

- If you must use a block quote, don't just dump the quote and run; use the lead-in sentence to tell the reader what the quote has to say about the point you're making, and why the reader should care. Think of it as introducing a stranger to a friend.
- Don't be afraid of the occasional footnote to discuss arguments and authorities that do not warrant treatment in the text but that might still interest the reader. For example, a footnote can be a great place to acknowledge the history of a law, to distinguish a line of cases, or to incorporate a policy argument.

Part 4

The Words

Style Must-Haves

Sentence-Level Strategies 163

  A. What a Breeze: Direct, Natural, "Impure" Diction 163

      Elena Kagan, *Arizona Free Enterprise Club v. Bennett*, dissenting 165

      Elena Kagan, *Arizona Free Enterprise Club v. Bennett*, dissenting 165

      Elena Kagan, *Kloeckner v. Solis* 166

      Elena Kagan, *Scialabba v. Cuellar de Osorio* 166

      Lord Denning, *Thornton v. Shoe Lane Parking* 167

      Richard Posner, *United States v. Gutman* 167

      Frank Easterbrook, *In Re Sinclair* 168

      John Roberts, *Rumsfeld v. Forum for Academic & Inst. Rights* 168

      John Roberts, *FCC v. AT&T* 169

      John Roberts, *Rancho Viejo v Norton*, dissenting from a denial of *en banc* rehearing 170

      Benjamin Goldgar, *In Re Brent* 171

      O. Rogeriee Thompson, *United States v. Seng Tan* 172

  B. The Starting Gate: Short Sentence Openers 174

      Edward Carnes, *Hamilton v. Southland Christian School* 174

      Oliver Wendell Holmes Jr., *Abrams v. United States*, dissenting 174

      Beverly McLachlin, *Seaboyer v. H.M. The Queen* 176

      John Roberts, *Already LLC v. Nike, Inc.* 176

      O. Rogeriee Thompson, *United States v. Seng Tan* 177

      Benjamin Goldgar, *In re Earley* 177

D.P. Marshall, *Little Rock School Dist. v. North Little Rock School Dist.* 177

Lord Sumption, *Prest v. Petrodel* 178

Patrick Schiltz, *Newton v. Walker* 178

Lord Hoffmann, *A(FC) and others (FC) v. Secretary of State for the Home Department,* dissenting 178

Elena Kagan, *Florida v. Harris* 179

C. Size Matters: The Pithy Sentence 179

Frank Easterbrook, *United States v. Dumont* 181

Edward Carnes, *Southland Christian School v. Hamilton* 181

Lord Denning, *Thornton v. Shoe Lane Parking* 182

Lady Hale, *Dunhill v. Burgin* 182

Lord Sumption, *Prest v. Petrodel* 183

D.P. Marshall, *Little Rock School Dist. v. North Little Rock School Dist.* 183

Elena Kagan, *Florida v. Harris* 184

John Roberts, *Attorney General's Office v. Osborne* 184

D.P. Marshall, *Tucker v. Southwestern Energy Co.* 185

D. Talk to Me: Variety in Sentence Form 185

D.P. Marshall, *Tucker v. Southwestern Energy Co.* 186

Lord Hoffmann, *A(FC) and others (FC) v. Secretary of State for the Home Department,* dissenting 186

Beverly McLachlin, *Seaboyer v. H.M. The Queen* 186

Richard Posner, *Cecaj v. Gonzalez* 187

Antonin Scalia, *Scott v. Harris* 187

Alex Kozinski, *Mattel v. MCA Records* 187

John Roberts, *Attorney General's Office v. Osborne* 188

E. Parallel Lives: Parallel Constructions 188

Patrick Schiltz, *Newton v. Walker* 190

Oliver Wendell Holmes Jr., *Abrams v. United States* 190

Lord Hoffmann, *A(FC) and others (FC) v. Secretary of State for the Home Department,* dissenting 190

Frank Easterbrook, *In re Sinclair* 191

Oliver Wendell Homes Jr., *United States v. Schwimmer* 191

Louis Brandeis, *Whitney v. California,* concurring 192

Robert Jackson, *Zorach v. Clauson,* dissenting 192

Frank Easterbrook, *In re Sinclair* 193

Lady Hale, *Dunhill v. Burgin* 193

Learned Hand, *NLRB v. Federbush Co.* 193

Lord Sumption, *Petroleo Brasileiro S.A. v. E.N.E. Kos 1 Ltd.* 194

Benjamin Goldgar, *In re Brent* 194

Antonin Scalia, *Scott v. Harris* 195

Michael Musmanno, *Schwartz v. Warwick-Phila Corp.* 196

Word-Level Strategies 196

  A. Lean and Mean: Words and Phrases to Avoid 197

    Interlude: 16 Key Edits 197

Edward Carnes, *Ash v. Tyson* 197

Lord Denning, *Cummings v. Granger* 198

Michael Kirby, *Wurridjal v. Commonwealth of Australia* 198

Benjamin Goldgar, *In re Earley* 198

Michael Kirby, *Wurridjal v. Commonwealth of Australia* 198

Ruth Bader Ginsburg, *Astrue v. Capato* 199

Frank Easterbrook, *In re Sinclair* 199

John Roberts, *Snyder v. Phelps* 199

Patrick Schiltz, *Newton v. Walker* 200

Benjamin Goldgar, *In re Earley* 200

Beverly McLachlin, *Seaboyer v. H.M. the Queen* 200

Lord Hoffmann, *A(FC) and others (FC) v. Secretary of State for the Home Department*, dissenting 200

Edward Carnes, *Hamilton v. Southland Christian School* 201

Shira Scheindlin, *New York Magazine v. Metropolitan Transit Authority* 201

Benjamin Goldgar, *In re Brent* 201

Lord Denning, *Cummings v. Granger* 202

Benjamin Goldgar, *In re Brent* 202

Lord Denning, *Lloyds Bank Ltd. v. Bundy* 202

Lady Hale, *Dunhill v. Burgin* 202

  B. Zingers: Evocative Verbs 203

John Roberts, *Attorney General's Office v. Osborne* 203

Oliver Wendell Holmes Jr., *McFarland v. American Sugar Refining Co.* 204

Robert Jackson, *Zorach v. Clauson*, dissenting 204

Lord Denning, *Lazarus Estates Ltd. v. Beasley* 204

Diane Wood, *JCW Investments, Inc. v. Novelty, Inc.* 205

Alex Kozinski, *United States v. Alvarez*, concurring 205

Antonin Scalia, *Scott v. Harris* 206

John Roberts, *Nike v. Already LLC* 206

Robert Jackson, *Zorach v. Clauson*, dissenting 207

John Paul Stevens, *Attorney General's Office v. Osborne*, dissenting 207

O. Rogeriee Thompson, *United States v. Seng Tan* 207

Frank Easterbrook, *In re Sinclair* 208

John Roberts, *League of United Latin Am. Citizens v. Perry*, dissenting 208

Beverly McLachlin, *Seaboyer v. The Queen* 208

Interlude: 55 Zinger Verbs 209

C. A Dash of Style: The Dash 210

John Paul Stevens, *Attorney General's Office v. Osborne*, dissenting 210

Patrick Schiltz, *Newton v. Walker* 210

Frank Easterbrook, *In re Sinclair* 211

Beverly McLachlin, *Seaboyer v. H.M. The Queen* 211

Benjamin Goldgar, *In re Earley* 211

Alex Kozinski, *United States v. Alvarez*, concurring 212

Antonin Scalia, *Romer v. Evans*, dissenting 212

Frank Easterbrook, *United States v. Bradley* 212

Louis Brandeis, *Olmstead v. United States*, dissenting 212

Lord Denning, *Thornton v. Shoe Lane Parking* 213

Interlude: the Hyphen 213

O. Rogeriee Thompson, *United States v. Seng Tan* 213

Patrick Schiltz, *Newton v. Walker* 213

Lord Sumption, *Prest v. Petrodel* 214

D.P. Marshall, *Cunningham v. Loma Systems* 214

Antonin Scalia, *Scott v. Harris* 214

Antonin Scalia, *Stenberg v. Carhart*, dissenting 215

D. Good Bedfellows: The Semicolon 215

 Frank Easterbrook, *FTC v. QT, Inc.* 215

 John Paul Stevens, *Attorney General's Office v. Osborne*,
   dissenting 216

 Patrick Schiltz, *Newton v. Walker* 216

 Learned Hand, *Cheney Bros. v. Doris Silk Corp.* 216

 Michael Kirby, *Green v. The Queen,* dissenting 217

E. Drum Roll: The Colon 218

 Beverley McLachlin, *Schmeiser v. Monsanto* 218

 Lord Denning, *Thornton v. Shoe Lane Parking* 218

 Alex Kozinski, *Mattel v. MCA Records* 218

 Antonin Scalia, *Romer v. Evans*, dissenting 219

 Jan Paulsson, *Pantechniki v. Albania* 219

F. Take Me by the Hand: Seamless Transitions 219

 Richard Posner, *Cecaj v. Gonzalez* 221

 Patricia Wald, *Hubbard v. EPA* 221

 Lady Hale, *Dunhill v. Burgin* 222

 Patrick Schiltz, *Shiraz Hookah LLC v. City of Minneapolis* 223

 Benjamin Goldgar, *In re Brent* 224

 Interlude: 135 Transition Words and Phrases 225

G. Bridge the Gap: Linked Paragraphs 228

 Beverly McLachlin, *Seaboyer v. H.M. the Queen* 228

 John Paul Stevens, *Attorney General's Office v. Osborne*,
   dissenting 229

 D.P. Marshall, *Tucker v. Southwestern Energy Co.* 229

 John Roberts, *Attorney General's Office v. Osborne* 230

 Benjamin Goldgar, *In re Brent* 230

 O. Rogeriee Thompson, *United States v. Seng Tan* 231

 Lord Sumption, *Petroleo Brasileiro S.A. v. E.N.E. Kos 1
   Ltd.* 232

Practice Pointers for Style Must-Haves 233

 Sentence Strategies 233

 Word Strategies 233

We are tempted to divorce style from substance, wanting to believe that an opinion rises or falls based on pure legal acumen. But as Justice Benjamin Cardozo once put it, "The opinion will need persuasive force, or the impressive virtue of sincerity and fire, or the mnemonic power of alliteration and antithesis, or the terseness and tang of the proverb, and the maxim. Neglect the help of these allies, and it may never win the day."[1]

I don't think Cardozo was suggesting that an order granting a motion *in limine* needs abundant alliteration or rhetorical figures worthy of Cicero. So there's no need for a daily dose of language like Cardozo's "The criminal is to go free because the constable has blundered." That said, opinion writers do need an eye and ear for style. You don't want to institutionalize or sterilize your voice. As Lord Denning has suggested, let your writing live and breathe instead through a sympathetic style and a strong dramatic arc:

> I try to make my judgment live...I start my judgment, as it were, with a prologue—as the chorus does in one of Shakespeare's plays—to introduce the story. Then I go from act to act as Shakespeare does—each with its scenes—drawn from real life...I draw the characters as they truly are—using their real names...I avoid long sentences like the plague: because they lead to obscurity. It is no good if the hearer cannot follow them...I refer sometimes to previous authorities—I have to do so—because I know that people are prone not to accept my views unless they have support in the books. But never at much length. Only a sentence or two. I avoid all reference to pleadings and orders—They are mere lawyer's stuff. They are unintelligible to everyone else. I finish with a conclusion—an epilogue—again as the chorus does in Shakespeare. In it I gather the threads together and give the result.[2]

You can sense the joy in Lord Denning's vision, and I hope it's contagious. The techniques in the next two chapters should be fun for judge and reader alike.

I'll focus in this chapter with what I consider "must haves" in great judicial style. First we'll consider sentence-level techniques for diction, length, weight, structure, and variety. Then we'll dive deep into easy word-level edits, power verbs, punctuation devices, and transitions.

The next chapter will turn to some nonessential "nice to haves" that make an opinion not just easy and even enjoyable to read, but provocative and even enduring: metaphors, similes, examples, analogies, allusions, and rhetorical devices.

Sentence-Level Strategies

Let's start with general prose-style techniques. This section will share strategies for modulating your level of diction along with the weight, length, structure, and form of your sentences.

A. What a Breeze: Direct, Natural, "Impure" Diction

A key challenge for ambitious judges is to settle on a style that's inviting and engaging but not crass or self-consciously cute. That said, if you survey the world's consumers of judicial opinions—law students, lawyers, and judges alike—you'll rarely hear that the problem with opinions is that they're just too darn catchy and casual. Instead, readers moan that opinions are too stuffy and formal.

In that spirit, I share below examples of down-home, "impure" diction that might very well push you past your comfort zone—and I do so by design. Were I to have written this book a half-century ago, I would not necessarily endorse a conversational style. Even Judge Posner, who favors direct and "impure" writing himself, points out that justices as great as Brandeis and Cardozo had a loftier, "purer," and more formal voice that worked very well for their purposes—and perhaps for their eras.

But is such a style the way to go today? I'd say no, and for two reasons.

First of all, the contemporary era resists formality. And second, writing in a profound, imperious style requires a rare innate talent. U.S. Supreme Court Justice Anthony Kennedy, for example, often adopts the mien of a philosopher king when he writes. But as one tough critic put it, "His prose alternates between bureaucratic and grandiose, resulting in sentences that manage to be pompous and clueless at the same time, like this gem from *Bush* v. *Gore*: 'None are more conscious of the vital limits on judicial authority than are the members of this Court, and none stand more in admiration of the Constitution's design to leave the selection of the President to the people, through their legislatures, and to the political sphere.'"[3] One of my own favorites is this Kennedy quote from the gay-rights case *Lawrence v. Texas*: "The instant case involves liberty of the person both in its spatial and more transcendent dimensions." Even in more-routine cases, Justice Kennedy often pens sentences such as this one: "This brief, separate concurrence is written to underscore that covenants like the one Nike filed here ought not to be taken as an automatic means for the party who first charged a competitor with trademark infringement suddenly to abandon the suit without incurring the risk of an ensuing adverse adjudication."*

So unless you're a born poet, don't try to wax eloquent. Relax the diction instead. Although all judges are capable of drafting overwrought, overwritten, and convoluted sentences, few have the

---

* Incidentally, you don't need a comma after "brief." You include commas between adjectives only when the adjectives modify the noun separately. Hint: if you can't put the word "and" before the last adjective, then no comma. It's not a "brief and separate concurrence." It's a "brief separate concurrence."

clarity of mind and the editing chops to express their thoughts naturally and directly.

For inspiration on this front, let me share some excerpts from one of the greatest living examples of a judge with an "impure" style: U.S. Supreme Court Justice Elena Kagan. Although her woman-on-the-street vernacular can sometimes distract, Kagan's style is a refreshing antidote to the stilted and haughty tone that keeps so many other judges from connecting with their audience.

Part of her talent stems from simple diction choices. Like her Right-leaning colleague Justice Scalia, she inhabits the direct and witty side of the judicial style spectrum. One of her strategies, especially when she is eager to persuade, is to mime the sort of language that her readers might use:

Elena Kagan, *Arizona Free Enterprise*
*Club v. Bennett***, dissenting**

Except in **a world gone topsy-turvy,** additional campaign speech and electoral competition is not a First Amendment injury.

Or the sort of language that might provoke a chuckle, if not some friendly eye-rolling:

Elena Kagan, *Arizona Free Enterprise*
*Club v. Bennett***, dissenting**

So [Petitioners] are making a novel argument: that Arizona violated *their* First Amendment rights by disbursing funds to *other* speakers even though they could have received (but chose to spurn) the same financial assistance. **Some people might call that** *chutzpah*.

Oh sure, you say—how hard is it to write an engaging dissent about election law? Point taken. So let's put Kagan to the test by seeing how clearly she writes when the issues are dull and dry. In the majority opinion below, Kagan had to wend her way through a labyrinth of conflicting statutory language on the not-so-scintillating subject of federal employees' procedural rights upon termination of employment. Displaying empathy and even frustration as she speaks to her constituency candidly, Kagan eventually throws up her hands on the reader's behalf:

Elena Kagan, *Kloeckner v. Solis*

If you need to **take a deep breath** after all that, you're not alone. It would be hard to dream up a more round-about way of bifurcating judicial review of the [agency's] rulings in mixed cases.

Suddenly, we realize that the problem isn't us, it's the statutes—and that's Kagan's very point.

Addressing the reader directly, professor style, is indeed one of Kagan's opinion-writing hallmarks:

Elena Kagan, *Scialabba v. Cuellar de Osorio*

A word to the wise: Dog-ear this page for easy reference, because these categories crop up regularly throughout this opinion.

The devices Kagan uses—shunning jargon, talking to the reader in the imperative or with the second person "you," projecting her own reactions, mimicking natural oral language—bring her closer to her intended audience in a way that few other judges could even dream of. Not to mention making the substance easier to read and understand.

Most of the world's best-known judges have broken the mold in a similar way. Take this priceless explanation of an adhesion contract, courtesy of Lord Denning:

> ### Lord Denning, *Thornton v. Shoe Lane Parking*
>
> These cases were based on the theory that the customer, on being handed the ticket, could refuse it and decline to enter into a contract on those terms. He could ask for his money back. **That theory was, of course, a fiction. No customer in a thousand ever read the conditions. If he had stopped to do so, he would have missed the train or the boat.**

Judge Posner, Lord Denning's American heir apparent, is yet another judge who favors unusually direct, candid, and "impure" prose, as I mentioned above. Unlike Kagan, though, who has an unabashedly populist yet upbeat style, Posner has a bit of an edge:

> ### Richard Posner, *United States v. Gutman*
>
> When a codefendant drops out in the course of trial, **a juror would have to be pretty stupid not to surmise that he had pleaded guilty**; and if this knowledge were grounds for mistrial it would be impossible for a defendant in a multiple defendant case to plead guilty after trial began.

Posner's Seventh Circuit colleague Judge Easterbrook sometimes pushes the envelope even further, even adopting in the example below metaphors from astronomy to discuss the problem of divining legislative intent, of all things:

Frank Easterbrook, *In Re Sinclair*

Some cases **boldly stake out a middle ground**, saying, for example, "only the most extraordinary showing of contrary intentions from [the legislative history] would justify a limitation on the 'plain meaning' of the statutory language." This implies that **once in a blue moon** the legislative history trumps the statute (as opposed to affording a basis for its interpretation) but **does not help locate such strange astronomical phenomena**. These lines of cases have coexisted for a century, and many cases contain statements associated with two or even three of them, not recognizing the tension.
  What's a court to do?

To be fair, some might find this imagery off-putting. But keep in mind that Judge Easterbrook is targeting case law, not the parties themselves, and so we should cut him a little slack.

That said, a lighter touch can be even more effective. Chief Justice Roberts has a knack for deploying wry humor to his advantage. Take this example from a case about whether Congress violated the Constitution by withholding federal funding from law schools that excluded the military from on-campus recruiting:

John Roberts, *Rumsfeld v. Forum for Academic & Inst. Rights*

We have held that high school students can appreciate the difference between speech a school sponsors and speech the

---

> school permits because legally required to do so .... **Surely students have not lost that ability by the time they get to law school.***

Let's consider another John Roberts classic in this soft-sarcasm vein. This one comes from his opinion in an otherwise dry dispute about whether a corporation, in this case AT&T, had a right to "personal" privacy under the Freedom of Information Act. The corporation argued that it did, because it was a "person," the root word of "personal." Roberts snips away at those threads through a playful tour of the dictionary, ending with a dig that I imagine might have made even a few AT&T executives chuckle:

> **John Roberts, *FCC v. AT&T***
>
> We reject the argument that because "person" is defined for purposes of FOIA to include a corporation, the phrase "personal privacy" in exemption 7(c) reaches corporations as well. The protection in FOIA against disclosure of law enforcement information on the ground that it would constitute an unwarranted invasion of personal privacy does not extend to corporations. **We trust that AT&T won't take it personally**.

There's a fine line between gentle humor and outright mockery, of course. When Chief Justice Roberts was first nominated to the U.S. Supreme Court, his opponents made hay over a single line in a dissent from a denial of rehearing that he had written on the D.C. Circuit. The case was about whether the arroyo toad could be

---

* Insert an "it is" before "legally required."

protected under the Endangered Species Act, with the subtext that perhaps the Act was unconstitutional altogether. Here is Roberts's infamous line, which proved to be one of the few stumbling blocks in his meteoric rise:

John Roberts, *Rancho Viejo v Norton*, dissenting from a denial of *en banc* rehearing

The panel's approach in this case leads to the result that regulating the taking of **a hapless toad that, for reasons of his own, lives his entire life in California** constitutes regulating "Commerce . . . among the several states."

Part of what fueled the objection to this line was substantive, of course. For his critics, Roberts's approach to the commerce clause here was radical. But part of the objection was decidedly stylistic, so much so that a pro-environment Web site took on the name "The Hapless Toad." On the one hand, few judges have Roberts's gift for rhythm and cadence that inspired him to pen a phrase like "a hapless toad that, for reasons of his own, lives his entire life in California." But on the other hand, Roberts's wry language here could strike some as disdainful, if not callous. Perhaps that's exactly why so few judges even attempt to write with flair. In the end, of course, these judgment calls often depend on how receptive you expect your readers to be—and perhaps on the extent to which you're seeking to make the record books or the legal news.

Just in case the hapless-toad example is intimidating, controversial, or both, I want to end with a couple of more straightforward, and perhaps more realistic, examples of the "impure" style. The first comes from Bankruptcy Judge Goldgar. Notice the pattern in what

I've highlighted below: each bolded phrase is close to what Goldgar would likely have used were he recounting the case out loud:

Benjamin Goldgar, *In Re Brent*

Liou's misrepresentations to the court were quite serious, far worse than simply **checking the wrong box on a bunch of forms**.

Liou unquestionably **should have known better**. He has represented debtors in chapter 13 bankruptcies for almost fifteen years and is a regular practitioner in this court. His practice of modifying the [Model Retention Agreement] with an addendum was not only inconsistent with the basic principle underlying the court's flat fee arrangement but plainly so. If, as he now says, he did not actually intend to conceal anything or mislead anyone, he should certainly have realized that was the effect. **The call is not even a close one.** All told, Liou's **moral compass badly needs repair**.

Although reliance on counsel is not usually relevant to the question of whether there has been a Rule 9011 violation, it can be relevant to the sanction itself. The problem for Liou is that the record shows he consulted Sukowicz about fee agreements other than the MRA. He never sought Sukowicz's advice about using the MRA with the addendum and then representing on his fee applications that he had entered into the MRA, the specific violation here. Liou **gets no points** for consulting counsel over a different ethical problem.

Finally, Liou asks to be recognized for "taking corrective action." After the December 2010 show cause order suggested his conduct was sanctionable, Liou says he amended the MRAs and withdrew and then refiled any pending fee applications. But Liou's "corrective action" was **half-hearted at best**. He filed amended MRAs in only thirty-three cases and withdrew fee applications in only eighteen. In several instances, moreover, Liou **added insult to injury** by committing yet another set of Rule 9011 violations. Ten of the thirty-three amended MRAs were not true amendments at all but, as described earlier, simply had the word "amended" added to the title and the phrase "see attached addendum" **scratched out**. The debtors in these cases evidently never saw, let alone signed, the amended agreements. **There is no such thing in Illinois law** as a unilateral contract amendment, as Liou surely knew.

In Goldgar's style, you can almost feel the air lifting you up: lots of short and crisp words, idiomatic turns of phrase, and visual imagery.

Our final example really pushes the limits, and it may push your buttons as well. It's from a relatively new judge, First Circuit Judge O Thompson. She favors an unusually conversational tone and even indulges in slang (her use of "legit" and "gobs" are head-turners), all to breathe life into an otherwise dry tale of financial shenanigans:

O. Rogeriee Thompson, *United States v. Seng Tan*

A federal jury convicted James Bunchan and Seng Tan, a husband and wife team, of numerous mail-fraud, money-laundering, and conspiracy crimes committed in furtherance of a classic pyramid scheme that swindled some 500 people out of roughly $20,000,000 in the early to mid-2000s. Fellow scammer Christian Rochon pled guilty to similar charges. . . .

Here is how it all worked. Bunchan tasked Tan with drumming up new members, something she was born to do, apparently. . . . . As "CEO Executive National Marketing Director,"

Tan ran informational seminars for potential investors, meeting them at hotels, their homes, and elsewhere. She usually made quite an entrance, showing up in a chauffeur-driven Mercedes. . . .

When prospective investors asked her point-blank whether they had to sell company merchandise to get money, Tan answered no. She and Bunchan reduced their promises to writing, with Tan even signing letters guaranteeing monthly returns basically forever. One member who got cold feet and asked for her investment back received a letter from Tan saying that she (Tan) would return her money if [the marketing scheme] went belly up. . . .

The scheme started out swimmingly. [The marketing schemes] used newly-invested money to trick old investors into thinking that the good times were here to stay. Not knowing any better, members were ecstatic. Bunchan and Tan were too, obviously. And with cash pouring in, the pair used the companies' coffers as their own personal piggy bank.*

If I can use a breezy expression myself to characterize the examples in this section, it would be "Lighten Up." Direct and brisk wording choices do more than just boost the chances that you'll find your name in a casebook one day or even in the pantheon of "Great Judicial Writers." They make your substantive points more memorable as well. And they also bring you closer to your readers, infusing your analysis with a populist and democratic flavor.

---

* As much as I like the style here generally, I cringe at the teenager-like phrase "basically forever." That one goes too far in my view, and in exchange for a more-staid expression there, I'd change "numerous" to "many" toward the start.

B. The Starting Gate: Short Sentence Openers

Few people have accused the English language of being beautiful and lyrical. So if you're not vigilant about sentence structure, starting too many sentences with long, heavy words will deaden your prose and lull the reader to sleep. In fact, one reason that most legal writing is so tedious is that so many lawyers and judges are unconsciously addicted to starting sentences with the longest transitional devices imaginable, such as *Moreover, Additionally, However,* and *Consequently.*

Below, for example, Judge Carnes might have opened his sentence like this: "Consequently, her testimony contradicted..." But here's what he wrote instead:

Edward Carnes, *Hamilton v. Southland Christian School*

So[] her testimony contradicted John Ennis' testimony that he had never heard her say she was sorry and that he would not have fired her if she had.

Carnes's knack for short, crisp words pushes through to the end of his sentence as well.

For a lighter effect, then, favor starting your sentences with one-syllable words like *this* and *that* or *if, and, but, yet,* and *nor*. Take this well-known passage by Justice Holmes:

Oliver Wendell Holmes Jr., *Abrams v. United States*, dissenting

If you have no doubt of your premises or your power and want a certain result with all your heart, you naturally express your wishes in law and sweep away all opposition. **To** allow opposition by speech seems to indicate that you think the speech impotent, as when a man says he has squared the circle, or that you do not care whole-heartedly for a result, or that you doubt either your power or your premises. **But** when men have realized that time has upset many fighting faiths, they may come to believe even more than they believe the very foundations of their own conduct that the ultimate good is better reached by free trade in ideas, that the best test of truth is the power of thought to get itself accepted in the competition of the market, and that truth is the only ground upon which their wishes safely can be carried out. **That** at any rate is the theory of our Constitution. **It** is an experiment, as all life is an experiment. **Every** year, if not every day, we have to wager our salvation upon some prophecy based upon imperfect knowledge. **While** that experiment is part of our system, I think that we should be eternally vigilant against attempts to check the expression of opinions that we loathe and believe to be fraught with death, unless they so imminently threaten immediate interference with the lawful and pressing purposes of the law that an immediate check is required to save the country.

Holmes's sentences start out sprightly and conversationally, each with a one-syllable word, gradually building on a dose of assonance and alliteration—"imminent immediate interference," "pressing purposes"—toward a climactic final sentence. The tone is calm, reflective, and thoughtful, a far cry from the fearmongering that Holmes cautions against.

Short demonstrative adjectives and pronouns ("this," "that," "these," or "those") can serve as good sentence-starters as well:

Beverly McLachlin, *Seaboyer v. H.M. The Queen*

These principles and procedures are familiar to all who practice in our criminal courts. **They** are common sense rules based on basic notions of fairness, and as such properly lie at the heart of our trial process. **In short**, they form part of the principles of fundamental justice enshrined in s. 7 of the Charter. **They** may be circumscribed in some cases by other rules of evidence, but as will be discussed in more detail below, the circumstances where truly relevant and reliable evidence is excluded are few, particularly where the evidence goes to the defence.*

And never forget the coordinating conjunctions (remember "fanboys": for, and, nor, but, or, yet, so). Chief Justice John Roberts loves to use them to start his sentences even—or especially—in something as dry as a procedural recap:

John Roberts, *Already LLC v. Nike, Inc.*

[Already LLC] never stated that these shoes would arguably infringe Nike's trademark yet fall outside the scope of the covenant. **Nor** did it do so on appeal to the Second Circuit. **And** again, it failed to do so here, even when counsel for Already was asked at oral argument whether his client had any intention to design or market a shoe that would even arguably fall outside the covenant.

---

* I'd change "circumstances where" to "circumstances in which" and would probably change "particularly where" to "particularly when."

Coordinating conjunctions work just as well when you're relaying facts:

O. Rogeriee Thompson, *United States v. Seng Tan*

But Tan's promises were too good to be true. She started having trouble signing up new investors. **So** WMDS and 1UOL stopped mailing out the monthly checks.

Members revolted, naturally .... **And** she herself decided which lucky member would get a check from the new money—an ill-conceived stopgap measure, it turns out.

Benjamin Goldgar, *In re Earley*

By filing its proof of claim, then, Triad established that it had a valid claim for $11,680.10. **But** the proof of claim did not establish that the claim was secured. Despite the claim's allowance, Earley remained entitled to contest Triad's secured status. **And** he has contested it, proposing a plan that treats Triad's claim as unsecured.

And when you're setting forth the issues before the court:

D.P. Marshall, *Little Rock School Dist. v. North Little Rock School Dist.*

The motions are rooted in good-faith arguments from the Settlement Agreement, the two stipulations, and various approving Orders. **And** this dispute is about the kinds of schools (and their students) in Pulaski County, the hub of the case.

Or the law itself:

Lord Sumption, *Prest v. Petrodel*

For years after it was decided, *Cape Industries* was regarded as having settled the general law on the subject. **But** for much of this period, the Family Division pursued an independent line, essentially for reasons of policy arising from its concern to make effective its statutory jurisdiction to distribute the property of the marriage upon a divorce.

Patrick Schiltz, *Newton v. Walker*

In *Chambers*, the Eighth Circuit clarified that a plaintiff need not show more than de minimis injury in order to prevail on a claim of excessive force. **But** because the Eighth Circuit's previous case law had not been clear on this point, the police officers who had been sued in *Chambers* were entitled to qualified immunity.

Lord Hoffmann, *A(FC) and others (FC) v. Secretary of State for the Home Department*, dissenting

If the finger of suspicion has pointed and the suspect is detained, his detention must be reviewed by the Special Immigration Appeals Commission. **They** can decide that there were no reasonable grounds for the Home Secretary's suspicion. **But** the suspect is not entitled to be told the grounds upon which he has been suspected. **So** he may not find it easy to explain that the suspicion is groundless. **In** any case, suspicion of being a supporter is one thing and proof of wrongdoing is another.

In fact, if one monosyllabic sentence opener adds punch, why not two?

> ### Elena Kagan, *Florida v. Harris*
>
> The defendant, for example, may contest the adequacy of a certification or training program, perhaps asserting that its standards are too lax or its methods faulty. **So too,** the defendant may examine how the dog (or handler) performed in the assessments made in those settings.

One last gloss: I hope these examples will put to rest any doubts you might have about the propriety of starting sentences with *But* or *And* or *Because*. The alleged prohibition on doing so is one of the greatest grammatical canards of all time: although it's true that English teachers across the globe tell students to avoid starting sentences with conjunctions (alas, I even hear about supposed bans on starting sentences with "prepositions"), the only point of this alleged "rule" is to help students avoid sentence fragments such as "I like school. But not homework."

To sum up, sentences carry weight. So to lighten the reader's load, avoid starting too many sentences with such heavy-handed clunky openers as *Additionally* and *However*. Favor one-syllable openers that propel your readers forward instead.

Sentences also have a length, of course, and that's the challenge we will turn to next.

C. Size Matters: The Pithy Sentence

Read the following passage:

> A contractor's road work site located in Albania was overrun and ransacked by looters in the midst of significant civil

> disturbances in March 1997. It is estimated that of the total adult population of the country, two-thirds of the citizens experienced a significant decrease in savings due to Ponzi schemes which were thought to involve complicity on the part of government officials. After numerous instances of rioting were visited upon the country, hundreds of people were killed and eventually, the government ceased to function.

Decent, but slow going. Now read the version that international-arbitration guru Jan Paulsson actually wrote:

> A contractor's road work site in Albania was overrun and ransacked by looters during significant civil disturbances in March 1997. It is estimated that two-thirds of the country's adult population lost much of its savings to Ponzi schemes in which government officials were thought to be complicit. Waves of rioting battered the country. Hundreds of people were killed. The government fell.

I plucked this passage from a 41-page award of his, a tour de force with not a single comma. That's right: nothing but short, controlled, declarative sentences. Although I'm not sure that even Jan Paulsson would recommend that anyone else write this tautly all day long, striving to do so is a worthy goal indeed. There's nothing wrong with commas, of course, but banning them for a time is an excellent writing workout.

Short sentences add a pulse to your prose while giving the reader much-needed breaks. Below, for example, Judge Easterbrook mixes up sentences of varied lengths to relay key facts:

Frank Easterbrook, *United States v. Dumont*

The Grateful Dead play rock music. Their style, often called "acid rock" because it mimics the effects some persons obtain after using LSD, is attractive to acid-heads. Wherever the Dead appear, there is demand for LSD in the audience. Demand induces supply. Vendors follow the band around the country; law enforcement officials follow the vendors.*

A series of short sentences can really pack a punch, as in this unusual opening from Judge Carnes:

Edward Carnes, *Southland Christian School v. Hamilton*

A woman of childbearing age was hired as a teacher at a small Christian school. **Then she got pregnant, married, and fired. In that order. Then she filed a lawsuit. She lost on summary judgment. This is her appeal.**

In fewer than 40 words, Judge Carnes's short sentences introduce the parties while recapping the key facts and procedural history. He even throws in a sentence fragment—"in that order"—that helps grab the reader's attention.

Of course, some readers and judges worry about a tipping point here. There's a fine line indeed between tight sentences and staccato

---

* Note Judge Easterbrook's fourth sentence, which juxtaposes two related clauses with a semicolon, a technique I'll return to later in this chapter.

breathlessness, if not a distracting affectation. Even Lord Denning has been criticized for taking the whole short-sentence thing too far. I happen to love excerpts such as the one below, but for some readers, these ultra-short sentences might be too much of a good thing:

> **Lord Denning, *Thornton v. Shoe Lane Parking***
>
> The customer pays his money and gets a ticket. He cannot refuse it. He cannot get his money back. He may protest to the machine, even swear at it. But it will remain unmoved. He is committed beyond recall. He was committed at the very moment when he put his money into the machine. The contract was concluded at that time.

One solution is to identify apt moments for a stray short sentence. The end of a paragraph presents one such opportunity. Below, Lady Hale spools out the defendant's argument with longish sentences, but then she dismisses the point with a halting "This cannot be right":

> **Lady Hale, *Dunhill v. Burgin***
>
> [O]n the defendant's argument, the claimant's capacity would depend upon whether she had received good advice, bad advice or no advice at all. If she had received good advice or if she had received no advice at all but brought her claim as a litigant in person, then she would lack the capacity to make the decisions which her claim required of her. But if, as in this case, she received bad advice, she possessed the capacity to make the decisions required of her as a result of that bad advice. **This cannot be right.**

Her colleague Lord Sumption uses a similar technique in critiquing a lower court ruling:

Lord Sumption, *Prest v. Petrodel*

[I]f, as the judge thought, the property of a company is property to which its sole shareholder is "entitled, either in possession or reversion", then that will be so even in a case where the sole shareholder scrupulously respects the separate personality of the company and the requirements of the Companies Acts, and even in a case where none of the exceptional circumstances that may justify piercing the corporate veil applies. This is a proposition which can be justified only by asserting that the corporate veil does not matter where the husband is in sole control of the company. **But that is plainly not the law.**

Not that short final sentences need not undermine what comes before. They can also function as a confident wrap-up:

D.P. Marshall, *Little Rock School Dist. v. North Little Rock School Dist.*

Eleven of the seventeen currently operating charter schools are in Pulaski County. These schools were authorized to enroll 5,518 students in the 2011-2012 school year; and they did enroll 4,498 the fall of 2011. Thus, more than 4,000 students, black and non-black, currently attend open-enrollment charters in Pulaski County. **Expectations settled.**

And here is Justice Kagan, turning a short sentence into her grand finale:

Elena Kagan, *Florida v. Harris*

The question—similar to every inquiry into probable cause—is whether all the facts surrounding a dog's alert, viewed through the lens of common sense, would make a reasonably prudent person think that a search would reveal contraband or evidence of a crime. A sniff is up to snuff when it meets that test. **And here, Aldo's did.***

(Note that the ends of the last two examples aren't even complete sentences. They're just fragments.)

Another hot spot for a short sentence is at the start of a new paragraph:

John Roberts, *Attorney General's Office v. Osborne*

These procedures are similar to those provided for DNA evidence by federal law and the law of other States, and they are not inconsistent with the "traditions and conscience of our people" or with "any recognized principle of fundamental fairness."

And there is more. While the Alaska courts have not had occasion to conclusively decide the question, the Alaska Court of Appeals has suggested that the State Constitution provides an additional right of access to DNA. . . .

---

* In the first sentence, "similar to" should be "as with," because she isn't actually comparing a question to an inquiry. Instead, she's comparing a question raised in this case to the question raised in every inquiry into probable cause. And for some readers, the "sniff is up to snuff" language might seem a little too cute.

> **D.P. Marshall, *Tucker v. Southwestern Energy Co.***
>
> The legal adequacy of the strict-liability claim should be decided on a full record at the summary-judgment stage.
>
> **Now to trespass**. The Tuckers allege that alpha methylstyrene, a component of some fracking fluid, has made their well water undrinkable and unsafe. . . .

The more sentences per page, the better. At least once each page, in fact, write a sentence that begins and ends on the same line. Making your average sentence length sink makes your readability soar, leading to happier readers and a more-confident tone.

D. Talk to Me: Variety in Sentence Form

"O mighty Caesar! Dost thou lie so low? Are all thy conquests, glories, triumphs, spoils, shrunk to this little measure?"

That lovely passage from *Julius Caesar* offers a prime example of the provocative rhetorical question. If great judicial style is defined as engaging an imaginary reader, then isn't the occasional question a useful arrow in your quiver?*

Truth be told, I hesitate to include this module in the "Must-Haves" group. My larger point here is not that you need questions per se, but that you need a variety of sentence types. And it just so happens that the occasional question is your best bet in that department.

In their simplest incarnation, questions need not be "rhetorical" at all. Simply presenting a legal issue as a question and then

---

* Yes, I know that my own rhetorical question doesn't deserve to inhabit the same page as Shakespeare's, but I also hope that it's also a more realistic example for my readers.

answering it, call-and-response style, can already liven up an opinion, as in these examples:

D.P. Marshall, *Tucker v. Southwestern Energy Co.*

Have the companies engaged in an ultra-hazardous activity? If the companies' gas-production activities (1) necessarily present a risk of serious harm which cannot be eliminated by the exercise of utmost care and (2) are not a matter of common usage, the answer is "yes."

Lord Hoffmann, *A(FC) and others (FC) v. Secretary of State for the Home Department*, dissenting

What is meant by "threatening the life of the nation"? The "nation" is a social organism, living in its territory (in this case, the United Kingdom) under its own form of government and subject to a system of laws which expresses its own political and moral values. When one speaks of a threat to the "life" of the nation, the word life is being used in a metaphorical sense.

You can also craft questions that are rhetorical in feel—they are worded to stack the deck—but that you answer all the same:

Beverly McLachlin, *Seaboyer v. H.M. The Queen*

These examples leave little doubt that [Canada's rape-shield law] has the potential to exclude evidence of critical relevance to the defence. **Can it honestly be said, as the Attorney General for Ontario contends, that the value of such evidence will always be trifling when compared with its potential to mislead the jury? I think not.**

> **Richard Posner, *Cecaj v. Gonzalez***
>
> Do Albanian police routinely beat people who fail to carry identification? Maybe so, but taken together with the other evidence in the case the beating was further evidence of persecution.

Justice Scalia's example below suggests that the answer could go either way:

> **Antonin Scalia, *Scott v. Harris***
>
> **So how does a court go about weighing the perhaps lesser probability of injuring or killing numerous bystanders against the perhaps larger probability of injuring or killing a single person?** We think it appropriate in this process to take into account not only the number of lives at risk, but also their relative culpability. It was respondent, after all, who intentionally placed himself and the public in danger by unlawfully engaging in the reckless, high-speed flight that ultimately produced the choice between two evils that Scott confronted.

Finally, the classic rhetorical question, formerly known as *erotema*, works particularly well if you want to weave together provocative examples:

> **Alex Kozinski, *Mattel v. MCA Records***
>
> The problem arises when trademarks transcend their identifying purpose. Some trademarks enter our public discourse and become an integral part of our vocabulary. **How else do**

> you say that something's "the Rolls Royce of its class?"
> What else is a quick fix, but a Band-Aid? Does the average
> consumer know to ask for aspirin as "acetyl salicylic acid"?

Or if you want to weave together provocative threats about consequences. Imagine if Chief Justice Roberts had simply written that "An endless array of issues would likely present themselves" rather than the series of questions he penned below:

John Roberts, *Attorney General's Office v. Osborne*

Establishing a freestanding right to access DNA evidence for testing would force us to act as policymakers, and our substantive-due-process rulemaking authority would not only have to cover the right of access but a myriad of other issues. We would soon have to decide if there is a constitutional obligation to preserve forensic evidence that might later be tested. **If so, for how long? Would it be different for different types of evidence? Would the State also have some obligation to gather such evidence in the first place? How much, and when?**

The occasional question can add variety to your prose, persuade skeptics, preempt likely objections, put opponents on the defensive, and peer into the future. Are you inspired to include one yourself?

E. Parallel Lives: Parallel Constructions

Think of "Give me liberty or give me death" or "We shall not fail or falter; we shall not weaken or tire" or "Ask not what your country can do for you; ask what you can do for your country." Parallel constructions give the reader a mental anchor for a sentence or for an entire passage.

Parallelism glitches, by contrast, often make for a tough reading. Take this sentence from former U.S. Supreme Court Justice David Souter, dissenting in the DNA-testing case called *Attorney General v. Osborne*:

> Changes in societal understanding of the fundamental reasonableness of government actions work out in much the same way that individuals reconsider issues of fundamental belief.

If you imagine stacking the two key phrases vertically, the faulty parallel will jump off the page. The first phrase has "changes" as its subject, while the second has "individuals." It's a jarring switch. To fix the glitch, we need a pair of subjects of the same type followed by two similar verbs. How about "society reconsiders" and "individuals reexamine"?

> Society reconsiders which government actions are fundamentally reasonable just as individuals reexamine their fundamental beliefs.

And because it's often better to present old information before new, let's switch the order as well:

> Just as individuals reexamine their fundamental beliefs, society revisits which government actions are fundamentally reasonable.

The new version is hardly worthy of Cicero or Churchill, but at least it's clearer. Nods to parallelism create better balance and rhythm as well.

Having an eye for balance and symmetry is half the battle. Below, for instance, Judge Schiltz properly repeats a preposition—"on"—before the second object of "rely" and not just the first:

Patrick Schiltz, *Newton v. Walker*

Because all of Newton's claims arise out of his arrest, **Newton must rely on the Fourth Amendment rather than on substantive due process.** The Court therefore grants Walker's motion for summary judgment on Newton's substantive-due-process claim.

Other times, you want to join the repetition of a preposition with a pair of correlative conjunctions such as "not . . . but":

Oliver Wendell Holmes Jr., *Abrams v. United States*

The defendants are to be made to **suffer not for** what the indictment alleges, **but for** the creed that they avow.

Lord Hoffmann, *A(FC) and others (FC) v. Secretary of State for the Home Department*, dissenting

The real threat to the life of the nation, in the sense of a people living in accordance with its traditional laws and political values, **comes not from terrorism but from laws such as these.**

> **Frank Easterbrook, *In re Sinclair***
>
> The "plain meaning" rule of *Caminetti* **rests not on** a silly belief that texts have timeless meanings divorced from their many contexts, **not on** the assumption that what is plain to one reader must be clear to any other (and identical to the plan of the writer), **but on** the constitutional allocation of powers.

After a verb with multiple objects, a binding word such as "that" can work well, too:

> **Oliver Wendell Homes Jr., *United States v. Schwimmer***
>
> And recurring to the opinion that bars this applicant's way, I would suggest **that** the Quakers have done their share to make the country what it is, **that** many citizens agree with the applicant's belief, **and that** I had not supposed hitherto that we regretted our inability to expel them because they believed more than some of us do in the teachings of the Sermon on the Mount.

Repeating "that" above is a conscious choice, and an admirable one.* Justice Brandeis's passage below is even more ambitious than Holmes's: buttressing the binding effect of "that" are both his

---

* Many writers are too quick to cut the word "that" from their sentences, creating miscues like "The Court held Plaintiff failed to prove." See my article available online entitled "Stop Cutting 'That.'"

repetition of the end of one phrase at the beginning of the next and his elision of the final conjunction "and":

Louis Brandeis, *Whitney v. California*, concurring

[Those who won our independence] recognized the risks to which all human institutions are subject. But they knew **that** order cannot be secured merely through fear of punishment for its infraction; **that** it is hazardous to discourage thought, hope and imagination; **that** fear breeds repression; **that** repression breeds hate; **that** hate menaces stable government; **that** the path of safety lies in the opportunity to discuss freely supposed grievances and proposed remedies.

The same, minus the missing "and," holds for the below, where Justice Jackson repeats the "to" each time in a series of infinitives:

Robert Jackson, *Zorach v. Clauson*, dissenting

The very purpose of a Bill of Rights was **to withdraw** certain subjects from the vicissitudes of political controversy, **to place** them beyond the reach of majorities and officials, **and to establish** them as legal principles to be applied by the courts.*

---

* Grammar sticklers will even insist that the repeated "to" isn't even optional here, because without it you'd be splitting an infinitive before both "place" and "establish."

And for the below, where Judge Easterbrook binds a parallel sequence by repeating "what":

Frank Easterbrook, *In re Sinclair*

What came out of conference, what was voted for by House and Senate, **what was** signed by the President, says that pending Chapter 11 cases may not be converted.*

Sustaining and echoing the same structure throughout a sentence can create another type of parallelism, especially when you want to draw a contrast.

Lady Hale does so here:

Lady Hale, *Dunhill v. Burgin*

There are two issues in this case, **both of them simple to state** but **neither of them simple to answer.**

As Learned Hand does here:

Learned Hand, *NLRB v. Federbush Co.*

What to an outsider will be no more than the vigorous presentation of a conviction, **to an employee may be** the manifestation of a determination which it is not safe to thwart.

---

* Note the nice rhetorical touch of eliminating the "and" before the third element in the series.

And Lord Sumption here:

Lord Sumption, *Petroleo Brasileiro S.A. v. E.N.E. Kos 1 Ltd.*

[T]he more foreseeable the owners' loss, **the more likely** it is to be an ordinary incident of the chartered service and therefore outside the scope of the indemnity.

All our examples so far are at the level of a single sentence. Parallelism across sentences easily spills over into rhetorical devices, which we'll discuss in the next chapter on "Nice-to-Haves." But for now we can see parallelism as a path toward clearer sentence structure. Simply repeating a word or phrase in sentence after sentence can give the reader an anchor that aids readability and comprehension. Here, for example, Judge Goldgar uses the phrase "the addendum allowed" as a structural anchor for an entire passage:

Benjamin Goldgar, *In re Brent*

Liou is mistaken. **The addendum allowed** Liou to tack on an 18% annual charge for late payments of attorney's fees—fees generated in the bankruptcy case—increasing those fees in the process. **It allowed** him to charge attorney's fees for "necessary post-termination work," meaning fees resulting from the bankruptcy case (e.g., "drafting itemizations of work performed") following the debtor's termination of Liou's representation. **It allowed** him to charge attorney's fees at a $295 hourly rate for "services not specified in the Model Retention Agreement," services necessarily related to the bankruptcy

---

case since the MRA only concerns the bankruptcy case. **And it allowed** him to charge "two hours of Attorney time" to prepare a motion . . . .*

And here, Justice Scalia intones the royal "we see" four times:

> **Antonin Scalia,** *Scott v. Harris*
>
> The videotape tells quite a different story. There **we see** respondent's vehicle racing down narrow, two-lane roads in the dead of night at speeds that are shockingly fast. **We see** it swerve around more than a dozen other cars, cross the double-yellow line, and force cars traveling in both directions to their respective shoulders to avoid being hit. **We see** it run multiple red lights and travel for considerable periods of time in the occasional center left-turn-only lane, chased by numerous police cars forced to engage in the same hazardous maneuvers just to keep up. Far from being the cautious and controlled driver the lower court depicts, what **we see** on the video more closely resembles a Hollywood-style car chase of the most frightening sort, placing police officers and innocent bystanders alike at great risk of serious injury.

If you remember The Incredible Case of the Spilled Asparagus Sauce from Part 1, it is there that we shall end this section. Below, former Pennsylvania Supreme Court Justice Musmanno serves us a whopping 161-word sentence that exploits anchoring and repetition, along with a delicious blend of *What a Breeze*-type plain talk

---

* Note how Judge Goldgar mercifully spares us the mechanical "Moreover" or "Additionally" that many other judges would have tacked onto the start of each sentence.

and such terms as "concatenation," "terpsichorean," "watsui," and "frug" (dances, those latter two). He does all this to explain why a negligence action against the owner of a banquet hall should not have been dismissed:

Michael Musmanno, *Schwartz v. Warwick-Phila Corp.*

A nonsuit must be based on fact and not on supposition, on testimony and not conjecture, on realities and not guesses. **Since no one questioned** the presence of asparagus and sauce on the dance floor where assuredly it should not have been, **since there is no evidence** it was carried there by guests because the trial judge's hypothesis that it could have gotten there hanging on to the men's coattails or women's dresses must be dismissed as visionary, **since there was direct evidence** that waiters transported asparagus across the floor aloft on trays, and there was evidence that waiters physically jostled dancers **and, since it is not difficult to conclude** that in a clash between a hurrying waiter and a dancer writhing in the throes of a watusi, frug, twist, jerk or buzzard, the resulting jolt would tilt the tray, cascading asparagus and sauce to the floor to throw the terpsichorean gymnasts off balance, it is reasonable, proper, and fair to conclude that **this concatenation of circumstances made out a prima facie case of negligence** against the establishment running the wedding feast.

A feast it is indeed, at least at the sentence level!

Word-Level Strategies

Our second set of style tips will span the gamut from word-level edits to powerful verbs, elegant and varied punctuation, and smooth, seamless transitions.

A. Lean and Mean: Words and Phrases to Avoid

Judge Posner has urged opinion writers to resist being "jargonista[s]" and to avoid, among other things, "legal clichés (such as 'plain meaning,' 'strict scrutiny,' 'instant case,' 'totality of circumstances,' 'abuse of discretion,' 'facial adequacy,' 'facial challenge,' 'chilling effect,' 'canons of construction,' 'gravamen' and 'implicates' . . .)."[4]

No doubt some of these chestnuts, especially "instant case" and "gravamen," are the stuff of legal-writing parodies. But so many of the other cited terms have universally understood legal meaning that I'm not sure that there's always a superior alternative (and Posner doesn't always offer one as part of his critique). Indeed, in my experience, there's too much talk about avoiding what's often called "legalese"—"heretofore" and "therein"—and not nearly enough about making the sorts of edits to "normal" English expressions that professional editors make to professional prose all day long.

In that spirit, I offer below a hit list of common wordy or heavy expressions followed by lighter, tighter choices. And of course, in the spirit of the rest of the book, I show you well-known judges making the exact choices I'm recommending.

Interlude: 16 Key Edits

1. *Avoid* "with respect to," "with regard to," "regarding," "concerning," and, for British English types, "with regards to" and "in regard to."

   Favor **"on" or "about" or "for" or "as for."**

Edward Carnes, *Ash v. Tyson*

The court granted Tyson's motion for summary judgment **as to** all of the other claims.

---

2. *Avoid* "subsequent to."
   Favor **"after."**

Lord Denning, *Cummings v. Granger*

After the accident the plaintiff's handbag and shoe were found in the middle of the yard.

---

3. *Avoid* "moreover" and "furthermore" and "additionally."
   Favor **"also."**

Michael Kirby, *Wurridjal v. Commonwealth of Australia*

[A] growing number of judges in this Court have lately referred to international legal materials. That development is inevitable. It is **also** desirable, natural and legally correct.

---

4. *Avoid* "inter alia."
   Favor **"among other things."**

Benjamin Goldgar, *In re Earley*

Among other things, the automatic stay prevents an Illinois garnishment lien.

---

5. *Avoid* "prior to."
   Favor **"before."**

Michael Kirby, *Wurridjal v. Commonwealth of Australia*

This Court has generally insisted upon first analyzing the impugned legislative language **before** determining a contested issue of constitutional validity.

6. *Avoid* "even assuming" or "even assuming arguendo" or "assuming arguendo" or "arguendo."

   Favor **"even if."**

Ruth Bader Ginsburg, *Astrue v. Capato*

We conclude that the SSA's reading is better attuned to the statute's text and its design to benefit primarily those supported by the deceased wage earner in his or her lifetime. And **even if** the SSA's longstanding interpretation is not the only reasonable one, it is at least a permissible construction that garners the Court's respect under [*Chevron*].

---

7. *Avoid* "assists in."

   Favor **"helps."**

Frank Easterbrook, *In re Sinclair*

Legislative history **helps** us learn what Congress meant by what it said, but it is not a source of legal rules competing with those found in the U.S. Code.

---

8. *Avoid* "in the present case," "in the instant case," "in the case at bar," or even "in this case."

   Favor **"here," and put it inside the sentence.**

John Roberts, *Snyder v. Phelps*

The jury **here** was instructed that it could hold Westboro liable for intentional infliction of emotional distress based on a finding that Westboro's picketing was "outrageous."

---

9. *Avoid* "is not required to."

   Favor **"need not."**

Patrick Schiltz, *Newton v. Walker*

In *Chambers*, the Eighth Circuit clarified that a plaintiff **need not** show more than de minimis injury in order to prevail on a claim of excessive force.

---

10. *Avoid* "in its response to the Motion" and other long procedural descriptors.

    Favor **"responds."**

Benjamin Goldgar, *In re Earley*

Earley **responds** that under [case], pre-petition liens on wages do not survive bankruptcy.

---

11. *Avoid* "demonstrates."

    Favor **"shows"** or **"proves."**

Beverly McLachlin, *Seaboyer v. H.M. the Queen*

The examples **show** that the evidence may well be of great importance to getting at the truth and determining whether the accused is guilty or innocent under the law—the ultimate aim of the trial process.

Lord Hoffmann, *A(FC) and others (FC) v. Secretary of State for the Home Department*, dissenting

The Home Secretary has adduced evidence, both open and secret, **to show** the existence of a threat of serious terrorist outrages.

12. *Avoid* "therefore" or "consequently" or "accordingly."
    Favor **"so"** or **"thus"** or **"then."**

Edward Carnes, *Hamilton v. Southland Christian School*

So[] her testimony contradicted John Ennis' testimony that he had never heard her say she was sorry and that he would not have fired her if she had.

Shira Scheindlin, *New York Magazine v. Metropolitan Transit Authority*

[T]he content of the Ad includes political satire—it pokes fun at the Mayor's alleged penchant for taking credit for all of New York's achievements. The question, **then,** is whether the inclusion of political satire in the motif of the Ad removes it from the category of commercial speech in which it would otherwise clearly fall.

---

13. *Avoid* "in order to."
    Favor **"to."**

Benjamin Goldgar, *In re Brent*

To be sanctionable, a misstatement or omission must be more than an innocent mistake; in making the misstatement or omission, the attorney must have been "culpably careless."

14. *Avoid* "pursuant to."
    Favor **"Under"**

Lord Denning, *Cummings v. Granger*

The only case put before the judge or before us was that the keeper was strictly liable **under** the *Animals Act* 1971.

---

15. *Avoid* "proceeded."
    Favor **"went on."**

Benjamin Goldgar, *In re Brent*

The addendum **went on** to describe six charges for which the debtor would be liable.

---

16. *Avoid* "where" for conditions.
    Favor **"when" or "if."**

Lord Denning, *Lloyds Bank Ltd. v. Bundy*

There are cases in our books in which the courts will set aside a contract, or a transfer of property, **when** the parties have not met on equal terms–**when** the one is so strong in bargaining power and the other so weak—that, as a matter of common fairness, it is not right that the strong should be allowed to push the weak to the wall.

Lady Hale, *Dunhill v. Burgin*

If she had received good advice or **if** she had received no advice at all but brought her claim as a litigant in person, then she would lack the capacity to make the decisions which her claim

> required of her. But **if**, as in this case, she received bad advice, she possessed the capacity to make the decisions required of her as a result of that bad advice.

Speaking of word choice, let's turn next to the persuasive power of the vivid verb.

B. Zingers: Evocative Verbs

"The word was the Verb, and the Verb was God."—Victor Hugo.

Choice verbs enliven your prose, painting pictures in the reader's mind that animate your legal analysis. In the passage below, for example, Chief Justice Roberts might have written that granting criminal defendants a constitutional right to DNA testing would "interfere with" a legislative response to the issue.

But look at the verb he chose instead:

> **John Roberts,** *Attorney General's Office v. Osborne*
>
> The elected governments of the States are actively confronting the challenges DNA technology poses to our criminal justice systems and our traditional notions of finality, as well as the opportunities it affords. To suddenly constitutionalize this area would **short-circuit** what looks to be a prompt and considered legislative response.*

"Short-circuit" conjures up sparks, malfunctions, destruction: the very sorts of images the Chief wants you to see.

---

* Also note the purposeful and proper split infinitive here as well: "to suddenly constitutionalize this area." Had Roberts put "suddenly" anywhere else in the sentence, he would have muddled the meaning.

Roberts is hardly the only great judge to favor zinger verbs for subtle jabs. Take these examples from Justice Holmes, Justice Jackson, Lord Denning, and Judge Wood:

A statute isn't "filled with" severities:

Oliver Wendell Holmes Jr., *McFarland v. American Sugar Refining Co.*

The statute **bristles** with severities that touch the plaintiff alone.

A metaphoric wall isn't "convoluted":

Robert Jackson, *Zorach v. Clauson*, dissenting

The wall which the court was professing to erect between church and state has become even more **warped and twisted** than I expected.

Fraud doesn't "have a deleterious effect"

Lord Denning, *Lazarus Estates Ltd. v. Beasley*

No court in this land will allow a person to keep an advantage which he has obtained by fraud. No judgment of a court, no order of a Minister, can be allowed to stand if it has been obtained by fraud. Fraud **unravels** everything.

And a party doesn't just try to "include" too much:

Diane Wood, *JCW Investments, Inc. v. Novelty, Inc.*

Novelty contends that rather than copy, it merely made a similar doll based on the same comic archetype, that of "a typical man wearing jeans and a T-shirt in a chair doing the 'pull my finger' joke." That, Novelty argues, is the idea, not the expression, and the reason that the two dolls are similar is they are both based on that idea. The district court found that Novelty tried to **shoehorn** too much into the "idea" and that the only idea here is that of a "plush doll that makes a farting sound and articulates jokes when its finger is activated."

Especially good "zingers" often appeal to the senses. Here, in a case about whether the government can criminalize lying about war medals, rather than using an obvious verb like "contradicts," Judge Kozinski makes the reader hear a "thwack" as the dissenters' argument bounces off the Supreme Court's marble façade:

Alex Kozinski, *United States v. Alvarez*, concurring

The dissent dismisses these difficulties by creating a doctrine that is so complex, ad hoc and subjective that no one but the author can say with assurance what side of the line particular speech falls on. This not only **runs smack up against** the Supreme Court's admonition against taking an "'ad hoc,' 'freewheeling,' 'case-by-case' approach" in the First Amendment area, but results in the "courts themselves … becom[ing] inadvertent censors."

Zingers can color the facts, too, and not just the legal findings. You'll recall that in *Scott v. Harris,* the U.S. Supreme Court had to decide if it was constitutional for a policeman to use his cruiser to run a fleeing driver off the road. Contrast Justice Scalia's evocative use of "ramming" with the case syllabus's antiseptic "terminated." (It's no coincidence that "ram" is one of those concrete one-syllable Anglo-Saxon verbs that Orwell touted in "Politics and the English Language": "*break, stop, spoil, mend, kill.*")

Antonin Scalia, *Scott v. Harris*

We consider whether a law enforcement official can, consistent with the Fourth Amendment, attempt to stop a fleeing motorist from continuing his public-endangering flight by **ramming** the motorist's car from behind. Put another way: Can an officer take actions that place a fleeing motorist at risk of serious injury or death in order to stop the motorist's flight from endangering the lives of innocent bystanders?

And in these other examples, judges reach for their Inner Thesaurus to exploit connotations. Some verbs conjure up *threats* more than "invoke" would:

John Roberts, *Nike v. Already LLC*

According to Already, allowing Nike to unilaterally moot the case "subverts" the important role federal courts play in the administration of federal patent and trademark law. It allows companies like Nike to register and **brandish** invalid trademarks to intimidate smaller competitors, avoiding judicial review by issuing covenants in the rare case where the little guy fights back.*

---

* Note that "to unilaterally moot" is another purposeful split infinitive from the chief justice!

Others convey *domination* more than "criticize" would:

Robert Jackson, *Zorach v. Clauson*, dissenting

The same epithetical jurisprudence used by the Court today to **beat down** those who oppose pressuring children into some religion can devise as good epithets tomorrow against those who object to pressuring them into a favored religion.

Still others suggest *sanctimony* more than "endorses" would:

John Paul Stevens, *Attorney General's Office v. Osborne*, dissenting

On two equally problematic grounds, the Court today **blesses** the State's arbitrary denial of the evidence Osborne seeks.

Or *condemnation* more than "tricked," "confused" or "cheated" would:

O. Rogeriee Thompson, *United States v. Seng Tan*

Witness after witness testified that Tan was the one who had met them at their homes and other locales; who had **bedazzled** them into believing that their lump-sum investments would get them and their heirs monthly checks till the end of time, all without their ever having to market or sell a single company product; who had tried to **bluff** them into thinking that everything was and would remain just great, even as she knew that the companies could not write them checks; and who had then **scammed** other innocents out of serious money using the same phony come-on—a desperate bid to pull the companies out of their death spiral.

Or *bemusement* more than "are replete with" would:

Frank Easterbrook, *In re Sinclair*

Yet the advice from the Supreme Court about how to deal with our situation seems scarcely more harmonious than the advice from the legislature. The reports **teem with** statements such as: "When we find the terms of a statute unambiguous, judicial inquiry is complete."

Or *baseness* more than "dividing us up" would:

John Roberts, *League of United Latin Am. Citizens v. Perry*, dissenting

It is a sordid business, this **divvying us up** by race.

Or *good intentions gone awry* more than "misses" would:

Beverly McLachlin, *Seaboyer v. The Queen*

The operation of s. 276 permits the infringement of the rights enshrined in ss. 7 and 11(*d*) of the *Charter*. In achieving its purpose—the abolition of the outmoded, sexist-based use of sexual conduct evidence—it **overshoots** the mark and renders inadmissible evidence which may be essential to the presentation of legitimate defences and hence to a fair trial.

Interlude: 55 Zinger Verbs

Here's a list of vivid verbs to spice up your writing:

Afflict	Leap
Besiege	Mark
Bleed	Marry
Bless	Mask
Blink	Meander
Block	Mimic
Bludgeon	Mince
Brandish	Mint
Burst	Mock
Chisel	Morph
Clamor	Muzzle
Clone	Pluck
Coin	Plunge
Constrict	Pocket
Cut against	Savor
Dodge	Scour
Duck	Shoehorn
Dupe	Skate
Echo	Skirt
Eclipse	Slash
Erode	Smack of/up against
Etch	Strike
Evoke	Stymie
Falter	Sunder
Feign	Teem
Flinch	Thwart
Flout	Wring
Hoodwink	

C. A Dash of Style: The Dash

I suggested above that the occasional question, whether rhetorical or answered, is an effective way to engage with your readers or at least to spice up your prose. Other underused tools for your punctuation arsenal: the dash, the semicolon, and the colon.

The em-dash has long been a favorite of great writers, whether legal, judicial, or otherwise. Properly formatted, it looks like one long line, twice as long as a hyphen (and the same width as a typeface block). Properly used, it emphasizes a word or phrase that might otherwise go unnoticed.

Use dashes midsentence to elaborate on a key point, as Justice Stevens does here, elaborating on a lower court's reasoning:

John Paul Stevens, *Attorney General's Office v. Osborne*, dissenting

The final reason offered by the state court—**that further testing would not be conclusive on the issue of Osborne's guilt or innocence**—is surely a relevant factor in deciding whether to release evidence for DNA testing.

As Judge Schiltz does here, detailing the plaintiff's injuries:

Patrick Schiltz, *Newton v. Walker*

[T]he injuries suffered by Newton—**including extreme pain, bruises, a bleeding cut, and feelings of depression, embarrassment, and humiliation**—are not materially distinguishable from the injuries suffered by the plaintiffs in *Brown* and *Shekleton*.

And as Judge Easterbrook does here, musing on legislative history:

> **Frank Easterbrook, *In re Sinclair***
>
> Legislative history may show the meaning of the texts—**may show, indeed, that a text "plain" at first reading has a strikingly different meaning**—but may not be used to show an "intent" at variance with the meaning of the text.*

Midsentence dashes can also piggyback on an earlier word in the sentence and offer a sort of parenthetical explanation, as Chief Justice McLachlin does here with "effect":

> **Beverly McLachlin, *Seaboyer v. H.M. The Queen***
>
> [Canada's rape-shield statute] goes further than required to protect privacy because it fails to permit an assessment of the effect on the witness of the evidence—**an effect which may be great in some cases and small in others**—in relation to the cogency of the evidence.**

As Judge Goldgar does here, recasting "debtor":

> **Benjamin Goldgar, *In re Earley***
>
> [T]he lien cannot attach to wages the debtor—**now a debtor in the bankruptcy sense**—earns thereafter.

---

* Also note how Judge Easterbrook's example plays on both parallelism and repetition, repeating "may show" as an anchor before offering up a contrast with what legislative history "may not be used to show."

** "Required" doesn't modify anything here. Try "further than it must."

Another way to use midsentence dashes is to highlight a point that you ultimately reject:

Alex Kozinski, *United States v. Alvarez*, concurring

Yet the regime the dissenters agitate for today—**one that criminalizes pure speech simply because it's false**—leaves wide areas of public discourse to the mercies of the truth police.

Antonin Scalia, *Romer v. Evans*, dissenting

Thus, this "singling out" of the sexual practices of a single group for statewide, democratic vote—**so utterly alien to our constitutional system, the Court would have us believe**—has not only happened, but has received the explicit approval of the United States Congress.

And if you have a literary bent, you can also use a single dash to make the reader pause on a phrase at the end of a sentence:

Frank Easterbrook, *United States v. Bradley*

[Jailhouse lawyer] Deutsch is a con man, a fraud, a phony, a humbug, a mountebank—**in short, an imposter.**

Louis Brandeis, *Olmstead v. United States*, dissenting

They conferred, as against the government, the right to be let alone—**the most comprehensive of rights and the right most valued by civilized men.**

> **Lord Denning,** *Thornton v. Shoe Lane Parking*
>
> In order to give sufficient notice, [the condition] would need to be printed in red ink with a red hand pointing to it—**or something equally startling.**

Interlude: the Hyphen

Does the phrase "small business owners" conjure up the height-challenged, or does it refer to a mom-and-pop shop? If you spot an ambiguity there, you'll find yourself in good company with the world's most fastidious writers, who make a point of sprinkling hyphens into their multiword phrases, often called "unit modifiers" or "phrasal adjectives," to clarify what's what:

> **O. Rogeriee Thompson,** *United States v. Seng Tan*
>
> Tan has two more **insufficient-evidence claims**, both of which target her **money-laundering convictions** under 18 U.S.C. § 1957. Neither persuades, however.

> **Patrick Schiltz,** *Newton v. Walker*
>
> Newton also brings **common-law** claims of assault and battery against Walker. As Walker conceded at oral argument, the **official-immunity** analysis under which he seeks summary judgment on the state claims essentially duplicates the **qualified-immunity** analysis under which he seeks summary judgment on the federal **excessive-force** claim.

> **Lord Sumption, *Prest v. Petrodel***
>
> Whether assets legally vested in a company are beneficially owned by its controller is a highly **fact-specific** issue.

> **D.P. Marshall, *Cunningham v. Loma Systems***
>
> In short, Tyson cites no authority—binding, persuasive, or otherwise—for its **contributory-negligence argument**.

The above examples all track the best practices for phrasal hyphenation. That said, I am not as rigid as some in this regard, in part because hyphenation is not always needed for clarity, and in part because many great judges and other great writers frankly flout these "rules" with gusto.

I'd also distinguish the pure grammatical usage of hyphens from a usage popularized by Justice Scalia, a big fan of what you might call the "hyphenated combo phrase." In the examples below and in many others, Scalia uses hyphens to coin a phrasal unit for dramatic effect:

> **Antonin Scalia, *Scott v. Harris***
>
> [W]e are loath to lay down a rule requiring the police to allow fleeing suspects to get away whenever they drive *so recklessly* that they put other people's lives in danger. It is obvious the perverse incentives such a rule would create: Every fleeing motorist would know that escape is within his grasp, if only he accelerates to 90 miles per hour, crosses the double-yellow line a few times, and runs a few red lights. The Constitution assuredly does not impose this invitation to **impunity-earned-by-recklessness**.

> **Antonin Scalia, *Stenberg v. Carhart*, dissenting**
>
> The most that we can honestly say is that we disagree with the majority on their **policy-judgment-couched-as-law.***

D. Good Bedfellows: The Semicolon

When you're comparing or contrasting two thoughts in a single sentence, a semicolon is an elegant and persuasive alternative to writing two choppy sentences (in other words, an alternative to something as clumsy as "To err is human. However, to forgive is divine.")

In the example below, Judge Easterbrook uses a semicolon to juxtapose two effects of fraud:

> **Frank Easterbrook, *FTC v. QT, Inc.***
>
> Deceit such as the tall tales that defendants told about the Q-Ray Ionized Bracelet will lead some consumers to avoid treatments that cost less and do more; the lies will lead others to pay too much for pain relief or otherwise interfere with the matching of remedies to medical conditions.

---

* Justice Scalia, ever the grammarian, somewhat surprisingly uses the plural pronoun "their" to refer to the collective noun "majority." That usage is typical in British English but is unusual in formal American English. Is he personalizing the views of the individual justices in the majority, consciously or not?

A similar device is used here by Justice Stevens, who contrasts what he sees as a hyperbolic prediction with a more modest one:

John Paul Stevens, *Attorney General's Office v. Osborne*, dissenting

In the same way, a decision to recognize a limited right of postconviction access to DNA testing would not prevent the States from creating procedures by which litigants request and obtain such access; it would merely ensure that States do so in a manner that is nonarbitrary.

And here, for a simpler point, Judge Schiltz cleanly contrasts how police officers are trained with how they are not:

Patrick Schiltz, *Newton v. Walker*

Class A does not provide any training to the police officers or policies for the officers to follow; the officers are trained by the [Minneapolis Police Department] and, as noted, follow [their policies].

Also consider this lovely example from Judge Learned Hand, one that toggles between "to exclude" and "to prevent . . . to set up":

Learned Hand, *Cheney Bros. v. Doris Silk Corp.*

To exclude others from the enjoyment of a chattel is one thing; **to prevent any imitation of it, to set up a monopoly** in the plan of its structure, gives the author a power over his fellows vastly greater, a power which the Constitution allows only Congress to create.

Note that in all these examples, the writer spares us a common but superfluous transition after the semicolon like "however," "rather," or "by contrast," transitions that you never need if you're using a semicolon to sharpen a contrast.

Our final semicolon example is a bit different. Here, Justice Kirby is using semicolons in a list, but not to obey a grammatical precept (in other words, not because at least one item in the list already includes a comma):

Michael Kirby, *Green v. The Queen*, dissenting

In my view, the "ordinary person" in Australian society today is not so homophobic as to respond to a non-violent sexual advance by a homosexual person as to form an intent to kill or to inflict grievous bodily harm. He or she might, depending on the circumstances, be embarrassed; treat it at first as a bad joke; be hurt; [be] insulted. He or she might react with the strong language of protest; might use as much physical force as was necessary to effect an escape; and where absolutely necessary assault the persistent perpetrator to secure escape.

Instead, Justice Kirby is slowing down the pace of a list of ways to respond to an unwanted sexual advance—perhaps miming the deliberative process that the judge believes the "ordinary person" should go through as well.

E. Drum Roll: The Colon

The simplest and most familiar use of a colon is to introduce a list, as in this example by Chief Justice McLachlin:

Beverley McLachlin, *Schmeiser v. Monsanto*

The Patent Act permits **two alternative types of remedies: damages and an accounting** of profits.

But a colon can do much more. It can provide a drumroll for key substance on the horizon, as does Lord Denning's colon here:

Lord Denning, *Thornton v. Shoe Lane Parking*

[The contract] **can be translated into offer and acceptance in this way:** the offer is made when the proprietor of the machine holds it out as being ready to receive the money.

In many great judges' hands, a colon also offers an emphatic alternative for a humdrum wordy phrase like "due to the fact that." Judge Kozinski provides an excellent example below:

Alex Kozinski, *Mattel v. MCA Records*

Hoffman **controls:** Barbie Girl is not purely commercial speech, and is therefore fully protected.

As does Justice Scalia here:

Antonin Scalia, *Romer v. Evans*, dissenting

In *Bowers v. Hardwick*, we held that the Constitution does not prohibit what virtually all States had done from the founding of the Republic until very recent years—making homosexual conduct a crime. That holding is unassailable, except by those who think that the Constitution changes to suit current fashions. **But in any event it is a given in the present case: Respondents' briefs did not urge overruling *Bowers*,** and at oral argument respondents' counsel expressly disavowed any intent to seek such overruling.

A colon can also train the reader's eye on an issue or question, as in this example by Jan Paulsson:

Jan Paulsson, *Pantechniki v. Albania*

It comes down to this: does the word "investment" in Article 25(1) carry some inherent meaning which is so clear that it must be deemed to invalidate more extensive definitions of the word "investment" in other treaties?

F. Take Me by the Hand: Seamless Transitions

Smooth and evocative transitions are the final ingredient in our recipe for superb judicial style. If you want the reader to accompany you from one sentence or paragraph to the next, you should snap your points together like the pieces in a jigsaw puzzle. Through the examples below, I'll share ways to deploy a varied set of transitional words and phrases, to engage your readers by addressing them in the second person, and to build bridge transitions between paragraphs.

The more I dissect the prose of the best legal and judicial writers, the more I tip my hat to the underappreciated world of precise and varied transitions. As I mentioned above in our discussion of starting-gate sentences, all lawyers and judges are comfortable with *consequently* and *moreover.* But that's the problem: these heavy-handed transitions become a crutch that communicates little to the reader other than that another point is on the way. Here are some typical examples plucked randomly from some judicial decisions:

> No redemption occurred within the statutory time limit. **Consequently,** a treasurer's deed to the real property was issued in June.
>
> In his response and objections, he argues only that he had notified several officials of his complaints and given them ample time to address them. **Moreover,** he contends he was unaware that he was required to appeal his initial grievance.
>
> **Certainly,** Plaintiff has adduced some evidence of misrepresentation. **However,** such evidence does not by itself demonstrate the requisite knowledge of falsity.
>
> These misrepresentations also support its argument that many (if not all) of Plaintiff's marks have been abandoned, which would also render them invalid. **Additionally,** Defendant has put forth substantial evidence calling into severe question many of the representations made by [the expert] in his declaration submitted to the Court.
>
> Plaintiff has failed to offer any evidence or arguments that establish that this Court failed to make the correct legal finding in the Memorandum Opinion and Order and Final Judgment. **Furthermore,** Plaintiff has failed to meet the requisite legal standard for the Court to grant a motion pursuant to Rule 60(b) of the Federal Rules of Civil Procedure.

In the examples below, by contrast, the judges sprinkle in one logical transitional device per point, all the while shunning the front-loaded cumbersome transitions that we saw above, and that I already suggested avoiding in the *Starting Gate* chapter on sentence weight.

Here's Judge Posner:

Richard Posner, *Cecaj v. Gonzalez*

Thus, the immigration judge's finding that Cecaj was not a victim of persecution on account of his political activity is not supported by substantial evidence. **Even so,** he is not entitled to asylum unless he has a well-founded fear of being persecuted should he be returned to Albania. Political conditions have changed in that country since he left in 2001—the Democratic Party (not the New Democratic Party, however) gained control of the government last year. **Maybe** Cecaj will be safe if he returns and resumes his political career. **But** once past persecution is shown, the burden shifts to the government to establish that the alien lacks a well-founded fear of future persecution.

And here's Judge Wald:

Patricia Wald, *Hubbard v. EPA*

The only "entitlement" that the EPA deprived Hubbard of was the job offer he would have received except for the constitutional deprivation. Instatement is the specific relief for that deprivation; it gives Hubbard "the very thing" he was owed. **On the other hand**, any loss of income attributable to Hubbard's being denied the job, like any emotional distress or harm to reputation that he may have suffered as well, is a consequence of the denial of the offer of employment. **And** the classic remedy for that loss is money damages. **That is why** courts ordinarily award back pay only in the amount necessary to compensate the plaintiff for the loss that resulted from the unlawful deprivation of employment. . . . **Thus,** back pay essentially pays the plaintiff for the economic losses suffered as a result of the employer's wrong; it does not return to the plaintiff anything which was rightfully his in the first place.

And here's Lady Hale:

Lady Hale, *Dunhill v. Burgin*

In truth, such judicial statements, made in the context of a different issue from that with which we are concerned, are of little assistance. **But** they serve to reinforce the point that, on the defendant's argument, the claimant's capacity would depend upon whether she had received good advice, bad advice or no advice at all. **If** she had received good advice or if she had received no advice at all but brought her claim as a litigant in person, then she would lack the capacity to make the decisions which her claim required of her. **But if,** as in this case, she received bad advice, she possessed the capacity to make the decisions required of her as a result of that bad advice. This cannot be right.

And here, on the trial side, we have Judge Schiltz:

Patrick Schiltz, *Shiraz Hookah LLC v. City of Minneapolis*

As noted, although the Ordinance does not single out any particular type of tobacco seller or buyer, Shiraz alleges that the Ordinance effectively creates a classification between, **on the one hand**, hookah shops and hookah smokers, and, **on the other hand**, cigar shops and cigar smokers. Assuming that Shiraz is correct, the Ordinance **nonetheless** survives rational-basis review.

To begin with, regulating smoking in public places for the protection of public health is plainly a legitimate government purpose. Shiraz argues, **though**, that even if the City has a legitimate interest in regulating smoking in public places, the City still has not provided a rational basis for effectively banning tobacco sampling at hookah shops while simultaneously permitting tobacco sampling at cigar shops. Shiraz is confused about who bears the burden of proof. The Supreme Court has made clear that "[t]he burden is on the one attacking the legislative arrangement to negative every conceivable basis which might support it, whether or not the basis has a foundation in the record." **In other words,** it is not the City's burden to prove that the Ordinance has a rational basis; instead, it is Shiraz's burden to prove that the Ordinance does not have a rational basis. **And,** to meet that burden, Shiraz must identify and refute "every conceivable basis" which might support the Ordinance.*

---

* As I mentioned in the semicolon chapter, the "instead" after the semicolon is superfluous.

And Judge Goldgar:

Benjamin Goldgar, *In re Brent*

Liou, **however**, claims otherwise. He contends, **first**, that he did in fact enter into the [Model Retention Agreement] in each case, and the representation in each form fee application was **therefore** "true in its literal sense." Not so. **Certainly**, in each case Jackson and the debtor signed the document, and in no case did Jackson and the debtor alter the document physically by inserting or deleting terms on any of its pages. **But** the addendum Liou admits using in conjunction with the MRA added terms that changed the compensation to which Jackson was entitled in the bankruptcy case. The addition of **those terms** in a separate document modified the MRA, making it a different agreement, **as much as if** they had been written into the MRA's own margins. **Having added those terms**, Liou could not truthfully represent to the court that he had entered into the MRA. **At best,** the representation was a half-truth, and a half-truth "can be just as misleading, sometimes more misleading, than an absolutely false representation."*

If you're duly inspired by these examples, let me share what I believe is the most comprehensive list available of transitions for judges and other legal writers. I've arranged these 135 signposts according to the role of the point in question. Although in the name of fullness I include such overused transitions as "Moreover" and

---

* I much appreciate the quick short sentences like "Not so" and the varied sentence structure. That said, I'm not a big fan of using "certainly" to introduce a concession. For alternatives, consider "To be sure" or even "True enough."

"Consequently," I'd recommending favoring the shorter words (along with the phrases made up of short words):

Interlude: 135 Transition Words and Phrases

To provide another point

Additionally	Further
And	Furthermore
Along with	In addition
Also	Moreover
Another reason	Nor
As well (as)	To X, Y adds Z
Besides	What is more

To conclude

Accordingly	In sum
All in all	In summary
Consequently	In the end
Hence	Then
In brief	Therefore
In conclusion	Thus
In short	To summarize

To extract the essence

At bottom	In essence
At its core	In the end
At its root	The bottom line is that
In effect	

To show cause and effect

And so	In consequence
And therefore	On that basis
And thus	So
As a result	That is why
Because	To that end
For	To this end
For that reason	With that in mind

To draw an analogy or comparison

As in X, Y	In the same way
As with X, Y	Just as X, so Y
By analogy	Like X, Y
By extension	Likewise
Here	Similarly
In each case	So too here
In like manner	So too with

To draw a contrast

At the same time	In contrast
But	In the meantime
By contrast	Nevertheless
Despite	Not
For all that	Rather
Instead	Unlike (in)
However	Yet

To give an example

As an example	For instance
As in	For one thing
By way of example	Imagine (as first word of
First, second, third, etc.	sentence)
For example	Including

In that regard
Like
Say
Such as

Suppose (as first word of
sentence)
Take (as first word of sentence)
To illustrate

To concede a point or to preempt a counterargument

All of that may be true, but
All the same
Although
At least
At the same time
Even assuming
Even if
Even so
Even still
Even though

Even under
For all that
Of course
On the other hand
Otherwise
Still
That said
Though some might argue
To be sure
True enough

To redirect

At any rate
(Even) more to the point

In all events
In any event

To emphasize or expand

Above all
All the more because
All the more reason
All the more X because Y
By extension
Especially
Even more (so)
If anything
In effect

In fact
In other words
In particular
Indeed
Not only X, but (also) Y
Particularly
Put another way
Put differently
Simply put

G. Bridge the Gap: Linked Paragraphs

Readers crave smooth transitions not just between sentences but between paragraphs as well. Otherwise, it's hard to know how the first sentence of a new paragraph connects to what came before.

One solution is to build a bridge between paragraphs by repeating or recasting a key term from the end of the first. In the example below, for instance, Chief Justice McLachlin repeats the phrase "this problem" in the second paragraph, referring to the opening sentence of the first paragraph. Her repetition connects the two points in the reader's mind:

> **Beverly McLachlin, *Seaboyer v. H.M. the Queen***
>
> **The problem which arises is that a trial is a complex affair, raising many different issues.** Relevance must be determined not in a vacuum, but in relation to some issue in the trial. Evidence which may be relevant to one issue may be irrelevant to another issue. What is worse, it may actually mislead the trier of fact on the second issue. Thus the same piece of evidence may have value to the trial process but bring with it the danger that it may prejudice the fact-finding process on another issue.
>
> **The law of evidence deals with this problem** by giving the trial judge the task of balancing the value of the evidence against its potential prejudice. Virtually all common law jurisdictions recognize a power in the trial judge to exclude evidence on the basis that its probative value is outweighed by the prejudice which may flow from it.

And here, Justice Stevens's bridge does not reprise the exact words "liberty interest" from the opening paragraph before. Instead, he recasts that interest as a right in the new paragraph:

> **John Paul Stevens, *Attorney General's Office v. Osborne*, dissenting**
>
> It is therefore far too late in the day to question the basic proposition that convicted persons such as Osborne retain a constitutionally protected measure of interest in liberty, including **the fundamental liberty of freedom from physical restraint.**
>
> **Recognition of this right** draws strength from the fact that 46 States and the Federal Government have passed statutes providing access to evidence for DNA testing, and 3 additional states (including Alaska) provide similar access through court-made rules alone[.]

In the slight twist below, Judge Marshall addresses deficiencies in the plaintiffs' pleading by using a conversational transition—"this is not to say that"—to bridge to the first paragraph:

> **D.P. Marshall, *Tucker v. Southwestern Energy Co.***
>
> As they stand, the complaints (especially the Tuckers') are mostly a matter of "after this, therefore because of this"—bad things happened after the fracking, and therefore because of the fracking. But this fallacy is not sound as a matter of logic or law.
>
> **This is not to say that** the Berrys and the Tuckers must now plead (or eventually prove) their case with the exactitude required in a car-wreck case. As the Arkansas Supreme Court recognized decades ago in a case about damage to a water well from underground blasting, "there is no feasible way to prove *exactly* what happens beneath the surface from such explosion."

And here, in another contrasting bridge, Chief Justice Roberts uses the phrase "Against this prompt and considered response" to invoke the legislative approaches he discusses in the paragraph before:

John Roberts, *Attorney General's Office v. Osborne*

DNA testing has an unparalleled ability both to exonerate the wrongly convicted and to identify the guilty. It has the potential to significantly improve both the criminal justice system and police investigative practices. The Federal Government and the States have recognized this, and have developed special approaches to ensure that this evidentiary tool can be effectively incorporated into established criminal procedure— **usually but not always through legislation.**

Against this prompt and considered response, the respondent, William Osborne, proposes a different approach: the recognition of a freestanding and far-reaching constitutional right of access to this new type of evidence.

These last two examples from Judge Goldgar and Judge Thompson show other ways of using a bridge transition to signal a shifting of gears:

Benjamin Goldgar, *In re Brent*

Flat fees benefit courts because they save judicial time "that a busy bankruptcy court would otherwise be required to spend dealing with detailed fee applications." **Indeed, the large volume of chapter 13 cases makes full judicial review of a detailed fee application in each case not only "administratively burdensome,"** but, as one noted authority has suggested, "almost inconceivable."

Flat fee systems are flexible enough, however, to take into account that unusual animal, the complex or involved chapter 13 case. When fees above the flat fee are warranted, either for services beyond those spelled out in the Rights and Responsibilities agreement or for extraordinary work, attorneys are generally permitted to petition for additional compensation.

O. Rogeriee Thompson, *United States v. Seng Tan*

Tan's no-knowledge argument runs something like this. She neither owned nor ran WMDS or 1UOL. . . . Also, she had married Bunchan because she was lonely, not because she wanted in on his con game. And because of cultural taboos, she never discussed company "issues" with him. Ultimately, she had no reason to suspect that anything was "rotten" at either company, and she was as much a victim as the poor investors her husband had duped. **Or so she argues.**

But Tan's theory does not hold together, given the government-friendly standard of review. Witness after witness testified that Tan was the one who had met them at their homes and other locales; who had bedazzled them into believing that their lump-sum investments would get them and their heirs monthly checks till the end of time, all without their ever having to market or sell a single company product; who had tried to bluff them into thinking that everything was and would remain just great, even as she knew that the companies could not write them checks; and who had then scammed other innocents out of serious money using the same phony come-on—a desperate bid to pull the companies out of their death spiral.

Yet another effective bridging technique is simply to list reasons that the last thing you wrote is true, as we see in this Lord Sumption example:

Lord Sumption, *Petroleo Brasileiro S.A. v. E.N.E. Kos 1 Ltd.*

The scope of the indemnity in clause 13, like that of the corresponding implied term, **is very wide** ("all consequences or liabilities that may arise"). **But it is not "complete", nor is it unlimited.**

In the first place, it has to be read in the context of the owners' obligations under the charterparty as a whole. The owners are not entitled to an indemnity against things for which they are being remunerated by the payment of hire. There is therefore no indemnity in respect of the ordinary risks and costs associated with the performance of the chartered service.

As we ring down the curtain on our "Must-Haves," keep in mind the broad goal here: an opinion that is easy, and perhaps even enjoyable, to read. Both the law itself and the need for precision pose many obstacles indeed, and I'm not suggesting that a judicial opinion needs to read like *The Economist* with a few citations to case law. That said, by relaxing the diction, shortening sentence openers, avoiding legalisms, varying sentence structure and form, striving for parallel constructions, and smoothing out transitions, you can guide your readers on a pleasant journey while still laying all your substantive points bare.

If, however, your goal is even more ambitious: to craft striking language that endures, turn to the next section.

Practice Pointers for Style Must-Haves

Sentence Strategies

- As your default style, strive for natural and direct speech. Avoid the common trap of overwritten, overwrought prose.
- Replace cumbersome sentence openers like *Additionally* and *However* with short conjunctions and short, light phrases.
- Try to write one sentence per page that starts and stops on the same line.
- For variety and reader engagement alike, include the occasional question or rhetorical question.
- Check all series and comparisons for parallel form.

Word Strategies

- Replace the common wordy phrases listed in Part 4 with the suggested lighter or shorter alternatives.
- For key passages, replace abstract or trite verbs with "zinger" verbs. Consult my list of 55.
- Use the occasional pair of dashes to highlight a word or phrase that would otherwise go unnoticed.
- For strong comparisons or contrasts, consider using a semicolon.
- Use the occasional colon as a replacement for causal words and phrases like *because* or *due to the fact that.*
- Broaden the array of transition words and phrases that you use to link your points.
- Consider linking the beginning of a new paragraph with something that the reader remembers from the end of the paragraph before.

Part 5

THE WORDS

"Nice-to-Haves" in Style

It Is What It Is: Metaphors 237

    Oliver Wendell Holmes Jr., *New York Trust Co. v. Eisner* 238

    Oliver Wendell Holmes Jr., *Towne v. Eisner* 238

    Oliver Wendell Holmes Jr., *Rock Island A. & L. R. Co. v. United States* 238

    Oliver Wendell Holmes Jr., *Bain Peanut Co. v. Pinson* 238

    Oliver Wendell Holmes Jr., *United States v. Abrams*, dissenting 239

    Robert Jackson, *West Virginia State Bd. of Education v. Barnette* 239

    Louis Brandeis, *New State Ice Co. v Liebmann*, dissenting 240

    John Roberts, *Virginia Office for Protection & Advocacy v. Stewart,* dissenting 240

    Antonin Scalia, *Webster v. Reproductive Health Services*, concurring 241

    Antonin Scalia, *Lee v. Weisman*, dissenting 241

    Learned Hand, *Harrison v. United States* 242

    Learned Hand, *NLRB v. Federbush Co.* 242

As If: Similes 243

    Richard Posner, *Singletary v. Continental Illinois Nat'l Bank & Trust Co.* 243

    Robert Jackson, *Edwards v. California* 243

    Robert Jackson, *Korematsu v. United States*, dissenting 244

    Antonin Scalia, *Lamb's Chapel v. Center Moriches Union Free School District*, concurring 244

    Brett Kavanaugh, *Belize Social Development Ltd. v. Government of Belize*, dissenting 245

Richard Posner, *Mayo v. Lane* 245

John Roberts, *Brigham City v. Stuart* 246

That Reminds Me: Examples and Analogies 247

Oliver Wendell Holmes Jr., *Schenck v. United States* 247

Frank Easterbrook, *Doe v. Elmbrook School Dist.* 247

Diane Wood, *JCW Investments, Inc. v. Novelty, Inc.* 248

Richard Posner, *Cecaj v. Gonzalez* 248

Alex Kozinski, *Mattel v. MCA Records* 248

Alex Kozinski, *United States v. Alvarez*, concurring 249

Frank Easterbrook, *FTC v. QT, Inc.* 251

Elena Kagan, *Florida v. Jardines*, concurring 252

Elena Kagan, *Arizona Free Enterprise Club v. Bennett,* dissenting 253

Elena Kagan, *Arizona Christian School Tuition Org. v. Winn,* dissenting 254

Treasure Trove: Literary and Cultural References 255

Diane Wood, *Ritter v. Ross* 255

Antonin Scalia, *Smith v. United States* 256

John Roberts, *Already LLC v. Nike* 256

Oliver Wendell Holmes Jr., *Lochner v. New York,* dissenting 257

Lord Denning, *The Siskina* 257

Lord Hoffmann, *A(FC) and others (FC) v. Secretary of State for the Home Department*, dissenting 258

Antonin Scalia, *Coy v. Iowa* 258

Ruth Bader Ginsburg, *Shelby County v. Holder*, dissenting 259

Richard Posner, *Albright v. Oliver* 260

Frank Easterbrook, *Federal Trade Commission v. QT, Inc.* 260

Antonin Scalia, *National Endowment for Arts v. Finley,* concurring 261

Antonin Scalia, *Barnes v. Glen Theatre, Inc.*, concurring 261

John Roberts, *Already LLC v. Nike* 262

Elena Kagan, *Scialabba v. Cuellar de Osorio* 262

John Roberts, *Sprint Comm. Co. L.P. v. APCC Servs. Inc.*, dissenting 262

John Roberts, *Pennsylvania v. Nathan Dunlap*, dissenting
from denial of *certiorari* 263

That's Classic: Rhetorical Devices 264

John Roberts, *Shelby County v. Holder* 264

John Roberts, *Parents Involved in Community Schools
v. Seattle* 265

John Roberts, *Already LLC v. Nike* 265

Benjamin Cardozo, *People v. Defore* 265

John Roberts, *Morse v. Frederick* 266

Robert Jackson, *Brown v. Allen*, concurring 266

Robert Jackson, *American Communications Associate
v. Douds* 266

Robert Jackson, *Zorach v. Clauson*, dissenting 266

Benjamin Cardozo, *Berkovitz v. Arbib & Houlberg* 267

Robert Jackson, *Thomas v. Collins* 267

Practice Pointers for Style Nice-to-Haves 268

Great judicial writing, like all great writing, paints pictures, pro-
vokes thought, and sometimes even stokes emotion. These goals
are all the more daunting, of course, when the subject matter is dry
and abstract. That's why a choice metaphor, simile, example, analogy, allusion, or rhetorical figure can be one of the best ways to tap
into your readers' collective experience. Less is more, and for most
opinions, you'll do well to include just a single burst of creativity
drawn from just one of the techniques in this section.

It Is What It Is: Metaphors

Vivid and concrete metaphors have prompted some of the most
memorable lines in legal history. Imagine if Justice Holmes had

written the following line: "History proves a more reliable guide to this problem than does logic." Instead, he wrote this:

> **Oliver Wendell Holmes Jr., *New York Trust Co. v. Eisner***
>
> Upon this point a **page of history is worth a volume of logic.**

What if he had written that "words are subject to changing meanings" rather than this?

> **Oliver Wendell Holmes Jr., *Towne v. Eisner***
>
> **A word is not a crystal, transparent and unchanged, it is the skin of a living thought** and may vary greatly in color and content according to the circumstances and the time in which it is used.

Or "bureaucracy poses innumerable challenges to citizens who deal with the government" rather than this?

> **Oliver Wendell Holmes Jr., *Rock Island A. & L. R. Co. v. United States***
>
> Men must **turn square corners** when they deal with the Government.

Or "the inner workings of government must be flexible on occasion" rather than this?

> **Oliver Wendell Holmes Jr., *Bain Peanut Co. v. Pinson***
>
> We must remember that the **machinery of government** would not work if it were not allowed **a little play in its joints.**

Or "exemplary and deserving thoughts will prevail if they are meritorious" rather than this?

> **Oliver Wendell Holmes Jr., *United States v. Abrams*, dissenting**
>
> But when men have realized that time has upset many fighting faiths, they may come to believe even more than they believe the very foundations of their own conduct that the ultimate good desired is better reached by **free trade in ideas**—that the best test of truth is the power of the thought to get itself accepted **in the competition of the market**, and that truth is the only ground upon which their wishes safely can be carried out.

Holmes is but one of many distinguished judges who have exploited the power of the judicial metaphor. Justice Jackson, in finding against a public school that had expelled Jehovah's Witness students for refusing to salute the flag, surely didn't write a line like "An immutable characteristic of the Constitution is that the government shall not prescribe societal or religious norms." Instead, he strove for the heavens in one of the most eloquent and quoted passages in American legal history:

> **Robert Jackson, *West Virginia State Bd. of Education v. Barnette***
>
> **If there is any fixed star in our constitutional constellation, it is that no official, high or petty, can prescribe what shall be orthodox** in politics, nationalism, religion, or other matters of opinion or force citizens to confess by word or act their faith therein.

Justice Brandeis, for his part, gifted us the enduring image of the state as a "laboratory" of democracy:

Louis Brandeis, *New State Ice Co. v Liebmann*, dissenting

To stay experimentation in things social and economic is a grave responsibility. Denial of the right to experiment may be fraught with serious consequences to the Nation. **It is one of the happy incidents of the federal system that a single courageous State may, if its citizens choose, serve as a laboratory**; and try novel social and economic experiments without risk to the rest of the country.

Among contemporary judges, Chief Justice Roberts conjures up below a memorable and uncharacteristically graphic metaphor to make a point about why a state would care about the identity of the plaintiff that had sued it:

John Roberts, *Virginia Office for Protection & Advocacy v. Stewart*, dissenting

[T]here is indeed a real difference between a suit against the State brought by a private party and one brought by a state agency. It is **the difference between eating and cannibalism; between murder and patricide.** While the ultimate results may be the same—a full stomach and a dead body—it is the means of getting there that attracts notice. I would think it more an affront to someone's dignity **to be sued by a brother than to be sued by a stranger.** While neither may be welcomed, that does not mean they would be equally received.

Justice Scalia is yet another modern master of the judicial metaphor, particularly of the caustic variety (not for nothing was he recently named "The Most Sarcastic Justice" in an academic study):

Antonin Scalia, *Webster v. Reproductive Health Services*, concurring

It thus appears that the **mansion** of constitutionalized abortion law, constructed overnight in *Roe v. Wade*, must be disassembled **doorjamb by doorjamb**, and never entirely brought down, no matter how wrong it may be.

Antonin Scalia, *Lee v. Weisman*, dissenting

As its instrument of destruction, **the bulldozer of its social engineering**, the Court invents a boundless, and boundlessly manipulable, test of psychological coercion, which promises to do for the Establishment Clause what the *Durham* rule did for the insanity defense. Today's opinion shows more forcefully than volumes of argumentation why our Nation's protection, **that fortress which is our Constitution**, cannot possibly rest upon the changeable philosophical predilections of the Justices of this Court, but must have deep foundations in the historic practices of our people.*

---

* It would be "historical," not "historic." "Historic" refers to epochal events, not events that happen over time.

Judge Learned Hand, for his part, could hold his own in the metaphor-as-wit department:

Learned Hand, *Harrison v. United States*

[C]onspiracy, **that darling of the modern prosecutor's nursery.**

And in the negative-metaphor department as well:

Learned Hand, *NLRB v. Federbush Co.*

Words are not pebbles in alien juxtaposition; they have only a communal existence; and not only does the meaning of each interpenetrate the other, but all in their aggregate take their purport from the setting in which they are used, of which the relation between the speaker and the hearer is perhaps the most important part.

I wish I could share a magic formula for the magic metaphor, but if such a formula existed, then metaphors wouldn't pack much of a punch, would they? That said, one unifying force in these enduring examples is real-world physicality, from skin and pebbles to pages and mansions. Readers remember what they can see in their mind's eye. And don't discount the virtue of creative surprise—of challenging yourself to look at a legal problem from a faraway prism, whether it be sociological, anthropological, corporeal, scientific, economic, astronomical, mechanical, or even architectural.

As If: Similes

If pebble and mansion metaphors haven't sated you, let's turn next to some judicial similes of the giraffe and ghoul variety. Here, too, physicality, visual imagery, and surprise are the keys to rendering the abstract concrete, relatable, and evocative.

Below, for example, Judge Posner shuns humdrum language like "It is necessary for limitations periods and accrual dates to originate from identical statutes." He trots out an unexpected bestial simile instead:

> **Richard Posner, *Singletary v. Continental Illinois Nat'l Bank & Trust Co.***
>
> To take the period of limitations from one statute and the accrual date from another, however, is **like grafting a giraffe's head onto an alligator's body**.

And imagine if Justice Jackson had written that "It is of paramount important that the Constitution measure up to the promise embodied in its words" rather than this heart-felt pecuniary simile in this passionate plea about citizenship:

> **Robert Jackson, *Edwards v. California***
>
> Unless this Court is willing to say that citizenship of the United States means at least this much to the citizen, then our heritage of constitutional privileges and immunities is only **a promise to the ear to be broken to the hope, a teasing illusion like a munificent bequest in a pauper's will**.

And here, in another enduring Jackson example, another simile livens up a point about the seductive dangers of a vague, abstract legal standard like "urgent need":

Robert Jackson, *Korematsu v. United States*, dissenting

A military order, however unconstitutional, is not apt to last longer than the military emergency. Even during that period a succeeding commander may revoke it all. But once a judicial opinion rationalizes such an order to show that it conforms to the Constitution, or rather rationalizes the Constitution to show that the Constitution sanctions such an order, the Court for all time has validated the principle of racial discrimination in criminal procedure and of transplanting American citizens. **The principle then lies about like a loaded weapon ready for the hand of any authority that can bring forward a plausible claim of an urgent need.**

Still other similes, like Justice Scalia's famous jab at the separation-of-church-and-state doctrine, toy with humor and even shock, all the while personifying (or, in this case, spirit-ifying?) the otherwise obtuse:

Antonin Scalia, *Lamb's Chapel v. Center Moriches Union Free School District*, concurring

Like some ghoul in a late-night horror movie that repeatedly sits up in its grave and shuffles abroad, after being repeatedly killed and buried, *Lemon* stalks our Establishment Clause jurisprudence once again, frightening little children and school attorneys of Center Moriches Union Free School District. Its most recent burial, only last Term, was, to be sure, not fully six feet under . . . . Over the years, however, no fewer than five of the currently sitting Justices have, in their own opinions, personally driven pencils through the creature's heart (the author of today's opinion repeatedly), and a sixth has joined an opinion doing so.

If ghastly horror flicks are fair game, why not chainsaws? Mandamus below morphs into something beyond mere "overkill":

Brett Kavanaugh, *Belize Social Development Ltd. v. Government of Belize*, dissenting

Even if we think the District Court erred under the Federal Arbitration Act by entering a temporary stay, its error was hardly "extraordinary." **Mandamus for this case is akin to using a chainsaw to carve your holiday turkey.** Indeed, if you ask me which is the more extraordinary—the District Court's temporary stay or this Court's invocation of mandamus jurisdiction under these circumstances—I would say the latter.

Still other times, as in this Judge Posner example, an extended simile can concretize a point about the merits of a specific case—here, an abstract damages issue:

Richard Posner, *Mayo v. Lane*

In short there is no indication either that Mrs. Mayo has been injured by the order barring her from visiting Illinois prisons (and so might obtain damages) or that she would derive a benefit from rescission of the order (and so might be aided by the injunction she seeks). She is **like a person who is in a room locked from the outside but does not know the room is locked and does not attempt to leave** during the time it is locked. More precisely, she is **like a person standing outside a locked room, neither knowing the room is locked nor desiring to enter it**. Such a person incurs no harm from the fact that the door is locked.

Similes, like metaphors, can be cast in the negative, too, in a "Don't Get Any Ideas" sense. Below, Chief Justice Roberts uses a clever negative sports simile to make his point about police officers' expansive authority:

John Roberts, *Brigham City v. Stuart*

In these circumstances, the officers had an objectively reasonable basis for believing both that the injured adult might need help and that the violence in the kitchen was just beginning. . . . . The role of a peace officer includes preventing violence and restoring order, not simply rendering first aid to casualties; **an officer is not like a boxing (or hockey) referee, poised to stop a bout only if it becomes too one-sided.**

As with metaphors, there's no ready recipe here: part of what makes these similes work is that they're so unexpected. But also as with metaphors, the challenge is to render the eminently abstract as eminently concrete. A simple and memorable image or flight of words—whether that be a *Lemon* ghoul or the lubricated joints of governmental machinery—can help your prose reach your readers directly and, if you're lucky, offer an enduring image that can shape the law itself.

That Reminds Me: Examples and Analogies

Metaphors and similes work best when they conjure up a short, vivid, and enduring image. Examples and analogies, by contrast, draw much of their force from the power of narrative. Take Justice Holmes's famous quip about the limits of free expression. Many judges would have written something like "Free speech has well-defined limits and exceptions" or even "The most stringent protection of free speech would not protect a person who made a false statement that resulted in imminent injury to another."

But here's what Holmes famously penned instead:

> **Oliver Wendell Holmes Jr., *Schenck v. United States***
>
> The most stringent protection of free speech would not protect a man in **falsely shouting fire in a theatre and causing a panic**.

Simple analogies can make the sublime seem ridiculous, as in these three examples from the Seventh Circuit's dynamic trio:

> **Frank Easterbrook, *Doe v. Elmbrook School Dist.***
>
> Holding a high school graduation in a church does not "establish" that church any more than **serving Wheaties in the school cafeteria establishes Wheaties as the official cereal**.

Diane Wood, *JCW Investments, Inc. v. Novelty, Inc.*

It is not the idea of a farting, crude man that is protected [in this copyright and trademark case about a farting doll named "Pull My Finger Fred"], but this particular embodiment of that concept. Novelty could have created another plush doll of a middle-aged farting man that would seem nothing like Fred. **He could, for example, have a blond mullet and wear flannel, have a nose that is drawn on rather than protruding substantially from the rest of the head, be standing rather than ensconced in an armchair, and be wearing shorts rather than blue pants.**

Richard Posner, *Cecaj v. Gonzalez*

The immigration judge's analysis of the evidence was radically deficient. He failed to consider the evidence as a whole, as he was required to do by the elementary principles of administrative law. Instead he broke it into fragments. **Suppose you saw someone holding a jar, and you said, "That's a nice jar," and he smashed it to smithereens and said, "No, it's not a jar."** That is what the immigration judge did.

And in this trademark-dilution example from their West Coast counterpart Judge Kozinski:

Alex Kozinski, *Mattel v. MCA Records*

"Dilution" refers to the "whittling away of the value of a trademark" when it's used to identify different products. For example, **Tylenol snowboards, Netscape sex shops and**

Harry Potter dry cleaners would all weaken the "commercial magnetism" of these marks and diminish their ability to evoke their original associations. These uses dilute the selling power of these trademarks by blurring their "uniqueness and singularity," and/or by tarnishing them with negative associations.*

Speaking of Judge Kozinski, I want to end this segment with a tour de force of his from a case called *United States v. Alvarez*. The dispute hinged on whether Congress could criminalize misstatements about whether someone had received military honors. In his concurrence voting to strike down the law, known as The Stolen Valor Act, Kozinski asserted that "living means lying"—a point that many of us might hesitate to concede, at least in public. But let's face it: it's tough to resist the seductive force of Kozinski's memorable parade of dozens of light, funny, familiar examples of quotidian lies:

Alex Kozinski, *United States v. Alvarez*, concurring

Saints may always tell the truth, but for mortals **living means lying**. We lie to protect our privacy ("No, I don't live around here"); to avoid hurt feelings ("Friday is my study night"); to make others feel better ("Gee you've gotten skinny"); to avoid recriminations ("I only lost $10 at poker"); to prevent grief ("The doc says you're getting better"); to maintain domestic tranquility ("She's just a friend"); to avoid social stigma ("I just haven't met the right woman"); for career advancement ("I'm sooo lucky to have a smart boss like you"); to avoid being lonely ("I love opera"); to eliminate a rival ("He has a

---

* Change the "and/or" to just "or."

boyfriend"); to achieve an objective ("But I love you *so* much"); to defeat an objective ("I'm allergic to latex"); to make an exit ("It's not you, it's me"); to delay the inevitable ("The check is in the mail"); to communicate displeasure ("There's nothing wrong"); to get someone off your back ("I'll call you about lunch"); to escape a nudnik ("My mother's on the other line"); to namedrop ("We go way back"); to set up a surprise party ("I need help moving the piano"); to buy time ("I'm on my way"); to keep up appearances ("We're not talking divorce"); to avoid taking out the trash ("My back hurts"); to duck an obligation ("I've got a headache"); to maintain a public image ("I go to church every Sunday"); to make a point ("Ich bin ein Berliner"); to save face ("I had too much to drink"); to humor ("Correct as usual, King Friday"); to avoid embarrassment ("That wasn't me"); to curry favor ("I've read all your books"); to get a clerkship ("You're the greatest living jurist"); to save a dollar ("I gave at the office"); or to maintain innocence ("There are eight tiny reindeer on the rooftop").

And we don't just talk the talk, we walk the walk, as reflected by the popularity of plastic surgery, elevator shoes, wood veneer paneling, cubic zirconia, toupees, artificial turf and cross-dressing. Last year, Americans spent $40 billion on cosmetics—an industry devoted almost entirely to helping people deceive each other about their appearance.

You might call this technique "whole-is-greater-than-sum," because the reader is almost overwhelmed with the force of the list, so much so that the individual items—in part or in sum—escape scrutiny. And yet does cubic zirconium really cause as much harm to real diamond wearers as a fake war hero does to a man who lost his legs while dragging his wounded comrades out of the line of fire? Is sex really an "obligation"? And are cosmetics really meant to deceive us into thinking that the wearer has naturally blue eyelids and red fingernails? Perhaps not, but Kozinski builds up enough momentum to sway even the most skeptical of readers.

So far we've seen relatively compact examples of examples—in isolation or in a series—that help bring an abstract point to life. But some of the bench's very best writers go a step further, conjuring up law-professor-like elaborate hypotheticals that run on for a paragraph if not a page. Of course, a passage that long had better be a home run.

This striking example from Judge Easterbrook invites the reader to "think about" a hypothetical scenario (one in which science-based claims don't require testing), and then to apply his trumped-up fact pattern to the claims at hand:

Frank Easterbrook, *Federal Trade Commission v. QT, Inc.*

Think about the seller of an adhesive bandage treated with a disinfectant such as iodine. The seller does not need to conduct tests before asserting that this product reduces the risk of infection from cuts. The bandage keeps foreign materials out of the cuts and kills some bacteria. It may be debatable *how much* the risk of infection falls, but the direction of the effect would be known, and the claim could not be condemned as false. Placebo-controlled, double-blind testing is not a legal requirement for consumer products.

But how could this conclusion assist defendants? In our example the therapeutic claim is based on scientific principles. For the Q-Ray Ionized Bracelet, by contrast, all statements about how the product works—Q-Rays, ionization, enhancing the flow of bio-energy, and the like—are blather. Defendants might as well have said: **"Beneficent creatures**

> from the 17th Dimension use this bracelet as a beacon to locate people who need pain relief, and whisk them off to their homeworld every night to provide help in ways unknown to our science."

Justice Kagan is similarly imaginative below in a concurrence in a case about a police dog that sniffed for drugs on a defendant's front porch. Like Judge Easterbrook, Kagan adopts a relaxed, confident tone, almost like that of a late-night raconteur:

Elena Kagan, *Florida v. Jardines*, concurring

For me, a simple analogy clinches this case—and does so on privacy as well as property grounds. A stranger comes to the front door of your home carrying super-high-powered binoculars. He doesn't knock or say hello. Instead, he stands on the porch and uses the binoculars to peer through your windows, into your home's furthest corners. It doesn't take long (the binoculars are really very fine): In just a couple of minutes, his uncommon behavior allows him to learn details of your life you disclose to no one. Has your "visitor" trespassed on your property, exceeding the license you have granted to members of the public to, say, drop off the mail or distribute campaign flyers? Yes, he has. And has he also invaded your "reasonable expectation of privacy," by nosing into intimacies you sensibly thought protected from disclosure? **Yes, of course, he has done that too.**

When President Obama put Elena Kagan on the Supreme Court in 2010, she had never been a judge. But as the above excerpt suggests, she soon became one of the High Court's most confident voices, leading the Left flank with her quick wit. Nowhere is this more apparent than in the extended hypotheticals she loves to insert in her dissents. Consider these two virtuoso examples, one from a case about campaign finance, and the other from a case about taxpayer standing to sue the government:

Elena Kagan, *Arizona Free Enterprise Club v. Bennett*, dissenting

Imagine two States, each plagued by a corrupt political system. In both States, candidates for public office accept large campaign contributions in exchange for the promise that, after assuming office, they will rank the donors' interests ahead of all others. . . .

Recognizing the cancerous effect of this corruption, voters of the first State, acting through referendum, enact several campaign finance measures previously approved by this Court. . . . [But] candidates choose not to participate in the public financing system because the sums provided do not make them competitive with their privately financed opponents. . . .

Voters of the second State . . . . realize, based on the first State's experience, that such a program will not work unless candidates agree to participate in it. And candidates will participate only if they know that they will receive sufficient funding to run competitive races. So the voters enact a program that carefully adjusts the money given to would-be officeholders, through the use of a matching funds mechanism, in order to provide this assurance. . . . And just as the voters had hoped, the program accomplishes its mission of restoring integrity to the political system. The second State rids itself of corruption.

Elena Kagan, *Arizona Christian School Tuition Org. v. Winn*, dissenting

Our taxpayer standing cases have declined to distinguish between appropriations and tax expenditures for a simple reason: Here, as in many contexts, the distinction is one in search of a difference. To begin to see why, **consider an example far afield from *Flast* and, indeed, from religion. Imagine that the Federal Government decides it should pay hundreds of billions of dollars to insolvent banks in the midst of a financial crisis. Suppose, too, that many millions of taxpayers oppose this bailout on the ground (whether right or wrong is immaterial) that it uses their hard-earned money to reward irresponsible business behavior.**

In the face of this hostility, some Members of Congress make the following proposal: Rather than give the money to banks via appropriations, the Government will allow banks to subtract the exact same amount from the tax bill they would otherwise have to pay to the U.S. Treasury. Would this proposal calm the furor? Or would most taxpayers respond by saying that a subsidy is a subsidy (or a bailout is a bailout), whether accomplished by the one means or by the other? Surely the latter; indeed, we would think the less of our countrymen if they failed to see through this cynical proposal. . . .

Suppose a State desires to reward Jews—by, say, $500 per year—for their religious devotion. Should the nature of taxpayers' concern vary if the State allows Jews to claim the aid on their tax returns, in lieu of receiving an annual stipend?

The power of these passages stems from the hypotheticals themselves: they seek to back the majority into a corner. But Justice Kagan's prose style is remarkable as well. Her imperative commands ("imagine," "consider," "suppose") speak directly to the reader in the second person, and her rhetorical questions in the second example invite, and even demand, reader engagement.

Treasure Trove: Literary and Cultural References

The three techniques above—metaphors, similes, and examples—require reader empathy and creative juices alike. First you need the good sense to realize that a legal abstraction, whether it be a restraint on freedom of expression or the types of products that are prone to trademark dilution, must be rooted in reality before it can come to life. And then you need to search long and hard until you settle on an apt image or narrative, often an original one, like Holmes's man falsely shouting fire in a crowded theater and causing panic.

But now let's turn to devices requiring a different type of creative output. In the examples below, the source material—idioms, allusions, and folkloric references—is very familiar, not original, and that's the whole point. Your challenge is to find creative ways to link the law with this trove of shared general culture.

In the example below, for instance, Judge Wood cleverly opens an opinion with a proverb that makes a broader point about how a picayune mistake can prompt outsized consequences:

Diane Wood, *Ritter v. Ross*

"For want of a nail the shoe is lost, for want of a shoe the horse is lost, for want of a horse the rider is lost." And for want of $84, a homesite was lost. Specifically, for allegedly failing to pay $84.43 in back taxes, Elmer and Helen Ritter may have permanently lost thirty-eight acres in Rock County, Wisconsin.

Idioms can work well too, but to avoid regurgitating clichés, try to morph them a bit as Justice Scalia does below:

Antonin Scalia, *Smith v. United States*

Having joined forces to achieve collectively more evil than he could accomplish alone, Smith tied his fate to that of the group. His individual change of heart (assuming it occurred) could not put the **conspiracy genie back in the bottle**.

And as Chief Justice Roberts does here, with the added twist of boomeranging a party's own idiomatic exploits against it:

John Roberts, *Already LLC v. Nike*

As counsel told us at oral argument: "once bitten, twice shy." But we have never held that a plaintiff has standing to pursue declaratory relief merely on the basis of being "once bitten." Quite the opposite. Given our conclusion that Nike has met its burden of demonstrating there is no reasonable risk that Already will be sued again, there is no reason for Already to be so shy.

If you want to reach for the next rung of the allusion ladder, consider literary and philosophical references as well. The early years of U.S. Supreme Court opinions favored Locke and Montesquieu. Economists like John Stuart Mill have provided fodder, too. True literary references, by contrast, are rare, and mostly populate dissents.[1] Favored authors include Orwell to Kafka, though references to Orwell's *1984* and Kafkaesque bureaucracies are probably overdone by now, as are quips citing Shakespeare's "let's kill all the lawyers" line, *Alice in Wonderland*'s "The question is whether you can make words mean so many different things," and the ceaseless trial in Dickens's *Bleak House*.

Sometimes these references impart substantive meaning. In his epochal *Lochner* dissent, for example, Holmes didn't write that "The Fourteenth Amendment does not enact laissez-faire economics." Instead, he cited a contemporary classic of libertarian thought:

Oliver Wendell Holmes Jr., *Lochner v. New York*, dissenting

The Fourteenth Amendment does not enact **Mr. Herbert Spencer's Social Statics.**

Even pure literary allusions can be substantive and persuasive. In the example below, Lord Denning invokes the nature poetry of William Cowper, first by quoting it and then by translating it into its legal context:

Lord Denning, *The Siskina*

To wait for the Rule Committee would be to shut the stable door after the steed had been stolen. And who knows that there will ever again be another horse in the stable? Or another ship sunk and insurance moneys here? I ask: why should the judges wait for the Rule Committee? The judges have an inherent jurisdiction to lay down the practice and procedure of the courts; and we can invoke it now to restrain the removal of these insurance moneys. **To the timorous souls I would say in the words of William Cowper**
   'Ye fearful saints fresh courage take
   The clouds ye so much dread
   Are big with mercy, and shall break
   In blessings on your head.'
   Instead of 'saints,' read 'judges'. Instead of 'mercy', read 'justice.' And you will find a good way to law reform!

And in this stirring passage below about whether the United Kingdom can indefinitely detain suspected terrorists, Lord Hoffman invokes Milton the polemicist:

Lord Hoffmann, A(FC) and others (FC) v. Secretary of State for the Home Department, dissenting

Of course the government has a duty to protect the lives and property of its citizens. But that is a duty which it owes all the time and which it must discharge without destroying our constitutional freedoms. There may be some nations too fragile or fissiparous to withstand a serious act of violence. But that is not the case in the United Kingdom. When Milton urged the government of his day not to censor the press even in time of civil war, he said:

"Lords and Commons of England, consider what nation it is whereof ye are, and whereof ye are the governours"

(Milton's *Areopagitica*, one of the greatest defenses of free expression, has peppered several U.S. Supreme Court decisions as well.)

And here, in an opinion about the confrontation clause, Justice Scalia quotes both Shakespeare and the New Testament for the insights they bring to bear on the meaning of "confrontation":

Antonin Scalia, *Coy v. Iowa*

"Then call them to our presence--face to face, and frowning brow to brow, ourselves will hear the accuser and the accused freely speak. . . ." **Richard II, act 1, sc. 1. . . .**

The Roman Governor Festus, discussing the proper treatment of his prisoner, Paul, stated: "It is not the manner of the Romans to deliver any man up to die before the accused has met his accusers face to face, and has been given a chance to defend himself against the charges." **Acts 25:16.**

Justice Scalia's fellow-opera-loving colleague Ruth Bader Ginsburg wasn't yet on the Supreme Court when he displayed his erudition above. She made up for it decades later, however, with her own dual quotations in a recent dissent in *Shelby County v. Holder*, a highly contested case about the Voting Rights Act. As a rejoinder to the majority's claim that Congress failed to recognize that "history did not end in 1965," when the Voting Rights Act was first passed, Ginsburg manages to cite both Shakespeare and Santayana:

Ruth Bader Ginsburg, *Shelby County v. Holder*, dissenting

There is no question, moreover, that the covered jurisdictions have a unique history of problems with racial discrimination in voting. Consideration of this long history, still in living memory, was altogether appropriate. The Court criticizes Congress for failing to recognize that "history did not end in 1965." **But the Court ignores that "what's past is prologue." W. Shakespeare, The Tempest, act 2, sc. 1. And "[t]hose who cannot remember the past are condemned to repeat it."** 1 G. Santayana, The Life of Reason 284 (1905).

Other allusions frankly just add color and interest. Faced with the claim that restrictions on travel are tantamount to prison, Judge Posner reaches for his copy of *Hamlet*:

Richard Posner, *Albright v. Oliver*

[False-imprisonment Plaintiff] was, it is true, "confined" to Illinois; and if **Denmark was a dungeon to Hamlet** (as the latter claimed), we suppose Illinois could be a prison to [Plaintiff] . . . but constitutional torts do not follow the exact contours of their common law counterparts.

Hamlet needs no introduction, of course. But if your allusion might seem obscure, as with the operatic reference below, follow Judge Easterbrook's lead in providing enough background so that your readers can appreciate the gesture without feeling stupid:

Frank Easterbrook, *Federal Trade Commission v. QT, Inc.*

[T]he placebo effect cannot justify fraud in promoting a product. **Doctor Dulcamara was a charlatan who harmed most of his customers even though Nemorino gets the girl at the end of Donizetti's *L'elisir d'amore*.**

Some judges even deploy literary references as part of a populist jab. Take Justice Scalia, an opera buff who also styles himself a judge-of-the-people. In the two culture-war examples below—one about government funding of the arts, and the other about ordinances restricting public nudity—Scalia cleverly mocks the American cultural elites, especially, in a two-for-one, with his citing of a French phrase used by the French decadent poets:

> **Antonin Scalia, *National Endowment for Arts v. Finley*, concurring**
>
> Those who wish to create indecent and disrespectful art are as unconstrained now as they were before the enactment of this statute. **Avant-garde artistes** such as respondents remain entirely free to *épater les bourgeois*; they are merely deprived of the additional satisfaction of having the bourgeoisie taxed to pay for it.

> **Antonin Scalia, *Barnes v. Glen Theatre, Inc.*, concurring**
>
> Perhaps the dissenters believe that "offense to others" ought to be the only reason for restricting nudity in public places generally, but there is no basis for thinking that our society has ever shared that **Thoreauvian "you-may-do-what-you-like-so-long-as-it-does-not-injure-someone-else" beau ideal**—much less for thinking that it was written into the Constitution. The purpose of Indiana's nudity law would be violated, I think, if 60,000 fully consenting adults crowded into the Hoosierdome to display their genitals to one another, even if there were not an offended innocent in the crowd.

The examples above are all canonical. But apt allusions need not invoke Romantic poetry or libertarian philosophy. Films and pop culture can add color as well. Chief Justice Roberts tries to

straddle the fence below, as he places the plaintiff's claims somewhere between the cinematic and the mythological:

John Roberts, *Already LLC v. Nike*

If such a shoe exists, the parties have not pointed to it, there
is no evidence that Already has dreamt of it, and we cannot
conceive of it. It sits, as far as we can tell, on a shelf between
Dorothy's ruby slippers and Perseus's winged sandals.

Just as Justice Kagan squeezes a Peter Pan reference into her
discussion about a statutory scheme hinging on age:

Elena Kagan, *Scialabba v. Cuellar de Osorio*

If an alien was young when a U. S. citizen sponsored his entry,
then **Peter Pan-like**, he remains young throughout the immigration process.

How about rock? Chief Justice Roberts, of all people, in an opinion on Article III standing, of all things, channeled none other than
Bob Dylan:

John Roberts, *Sprint Comm. Co. L.P. v.*
***APCC Servs. Inc.*, dissenting**

"When you got nothing, you got nothing to lose."*

---

* In a move that lit up the blogosphere at the time, the chief justice altered the
original language a bit. Dylan's actual words were "When you ain't got nothing, you got nothing to lose." Maybe Roberts just couldn't bring himself to write
"ain't"?

And on another occasion, in a genre allusion that's more of a pastiche, Roberts even mimed the style of a detective potboiler:

> **John Roberts, *Pennsylvania v. Nathan Dunlap*, dissenting from denial of *certiorari***
>
> North Philly, May 4, 2001. Officer Sean Devlin, Narcotics Strike Force, was working the morning shift. Undercover surveillance. The neighborhood? Tough as a three-dollar steak. Devlin knew. Five years on the beat, nine months with the Strike Force. He'd made fifteen, twenty drug busts in the neighborhood.
>
> Devlin spotted him: a lone man on the corner. Another approached. Quick exchange of words. Cash handed over; small objects handed back. Each man then quickly on his own way. Devlin knew the guy wasn't buying bus tokens. He radioed a description and Officer Stein picked up the buyer. Sure enough: three bags of crack in the guy's pocket. Head downtown and book him. Just another day at the office. . . .
>
> A drug purchase was not the only possible explanation for the defendant's conduct, but it was certainly likely enough to give rise to probable cause.

(When I once shared this passage as a guest-blogger on The Volokh Conspiracy, commenters expressed sheer horror at Roberts's flight-of-fancy here. My advice would be to lighten up. Procedurally, Roberts's denial didn't matter a whit, and although I agree that humor can backfire, a little bit of levity hardly threatens the integrity of the judiciary.)

In the end, allusions and references are by no means necessary. And yet it's probably no coincidence that nearly all of the world's best-known judges include the occasional nod to literature or philosophy. On the writing front, these devices reflect a desire to engage the reader's imagination, to invoke shared culture, and to make the judge appear more "real." They also make "judicial opinion writing" seem more like "writing." And on the jurisprudential front, they signal that the life of the law has been experience indeed. But proceed with caution: the more obscure the reference—say, an operatic reference or a rattled-off phrase in the original French—the more likely you will alienate the very readers you're trying to reach. A Donizetti opera is a far cry from shouting fire in a crowded theater.

That's Classic: Rhetorical Devices

As I suggested in Part 4, parallel structure makes for clearer prose, not to mention grammatical purity. But some judges aim even higher, toying with classical rhetoric devices that help cement points in the reader's mind, all the while dreaming of writing a line or two that might endure for generations.

Some devices are deceptively simple in their focus on repetition. Chief Justice Roberts is a fan of *conduplicato* (simple repetition), *symploce* (repetition at the beginning and end) and *polyptoton* (repetition of a root word but with a twist in the word ending).[2]

In the example below, which is pure *conduplicato*, Roberts's insistence on the word "extraordinary" helps build a case that certain sections of the Voting Rights Act have an intent that's too remote to allow the statute to continue in its current form:

> **John Roberts, *Shelby County v. Holder***
>
> The Voting Rights Act of 1965 employed **extraordinary** measures to address an **extraordinary** problem.

My next Roberts example adds a bit of *polyptoton*, repeating a root word with a different ending, to craft a seemingly self-executing statement that's sure to energize opponents of racial preferences in school admissions while infuriating their supporters:

> **John Roberts, *Parents Involved in Community Schools v. Seattle***
>
> The way to **stop discrimination** on the basis of race is to **stop discriminating** on the basis of race.

Another device, *epistrophe*, plays off a series in which the ends of the items stay consistent:

> **John Roberts, *Already LLC v. Nike***
>
> If such a shoe exists, the parties have not **pointed to it**, there is no evidence that Already has **dreamt of it**, and we cannot **conceive of it**.

Most rhetorical devices are fair game. Consider this famous Cardozo line as an example of *isocolon*, here a pair of short phrases built on a contrast (and on alliteration) between "the criminal" and "the constable":

> **Benjamin Cardozo, *People v. Defore***
>
> The criminal is to go free because the constable has blundered.

Once your goal climbs from clarity to elegance, you can even play with the device known as *chiasmus*, or word scramble, or inversion, as in these examples. Below, the chief justice quotes a phrase from one of his own opinions when he was a judge

266 | POINT TAKEN

on the D.C. Circuit, a traditional breeding ground for the U.S. Supreme Court:

John Roberts, *Morse v. Frederick*

[T]he cardinal principle of judicial restraint—**if it is not necessary to decide more, it is necessary not to decide more**—counsels us to go no further.

And in these examples, Justice Jackson uses parallel construction and inversion within a sentence to craft some of the most enduring lines in U.S. Supreme Court history:

Robert Jackson, *Brown v. Allen*, concurring

We are not final because we are infallible, but we are infallible only because we are final.

Robert Jackson, *American Communications Associate v. Douds*

It is not the function of our Government to keep the citizen from falling into error; it is the function of the citizen to keep the Government from falling into error.

Robert Jackson, *Zorach v. Clauson*, dissenting

The day that this country **ceases to be free for irreligion it will cease to be free for religion**—except for the sect that can win political power.

Justice Cardozo does something similar below, but in two separate sentences:

> **Benjamin Cardozo, *Berkovitz v. Arbib & Houlberg***
>
> Jurisdiction exists that rights may be maintained. Rights are not maintained that jurisdiction may exist.

Justice Jackson was also a master of pure *antithesis*, or sharp contrasts with no "word scramble" needed:

> **Robert Jackson, *Thomas v. Collins***
>
> Very many are the interests which the state may protect against the practice of an occupation; very few are those it may assume to protect against the practice of propagandizing by speech or press.

If there's one thing that characterizes all the style techniques in Parts 4 and 5, it's empathy for the reader's experience. I often get the sense when reading opinions that clerks and judges don't imagine a living, breathing reader on the other side. And yet with just a few tweaks you can bridge this gap, making your opinions both enjoyable and clear. On the "enjoyable" front, perhaps the most important strategy is to lighten your general level of diction. The rhythms, cadences, and word choices of speech should be your starting point, not your enemy. Shorter sentence openers and tighter language push the reader along as well. On the "clear" front, exploit parallel constructions and add variety in sentence structure and form. But most important of all, smooth out the links between paragraphs and points.

The Part 5 "Nice to Have" techniques can be richly rewarding, but they are also daunting and risky. Metaphors, similes, extended examples, allusions, and rhetorical devices are all strong spices meant to season the main ingredients of your opinion, not to be doused indiscriminately. If they seem forced or artificial, or if you sound like you're grandstanding rather than edifying, they will backfire. At the same time, though, a judge has every right, and perhaps even a responsibility, to exploit these classic tools of great writing and rhetoric when the moment's just right.

Practice Pointers for Style Nice-to-Haves

- Although you can be a great opinion writer without ever including a single metaphor, simile, example, analogy, allusion, or rhetorical device, remember that such devices help tap into your readers' collective experience, help make otherwise abstract points stick, and help make judicial writing more like "writing."

- Metaphors and similes work best when they are unexpected and are infused with physicality. Choose your prism from outside the law.

- Examples and analogies should be styled as narratives or hypotheticals. For the former, consider opening with "Imagine," "Take," or "Suppose." For the latter, consider completing an "It's as if . . ." prompt for a particularly potent point.

- Literary and pop-culture references can add flavor as well, but avoid the overused ones, such as an invocation of Orwell's *1984* or a reference to Dickens's *Bleak House*.

- If you're aiming for the record books, play with the tools of classical rhetoric, especially pure repetition, repetition with a twist in word form, and inversion or *chiasmus*.

Part 6

DISSENTS

The Road Not Traveled

A Sordid Tale: Wrong on the Facts 272

    Robert Jackson, *Chicago v. Terminiello*, dissenting 273

    Richard Posner, *Johnson v. Phelan*, dissenting 274

    Antonin Scalia, *Romer v. Evans*, dissenting 275

    Ruth Bader Ginsburg, *National Federation of Independent Business v. Sebelius,* dissenting 276

Piercing the Veil: Wrong on the Law 277

    John Paul Stevens, *Citizens United v. Federal Elections Commission*, dissenting 278

    Antonin Scalia, *Morrison v. Olson*, dissenting 279

    Diane Wood, *A Woman's Choice-East Side Women's Clinic v. Newman*, dissenting 279

    Brett Kavanaugh, *In re Sealed Case*, dissenting 280

    Elena Kagan, *Arizona Free Enterprise Club's Freedom Club PAC v. Bennett*, dissenting 282

    Ruth Bader Ginsburg, *Bush v. Gore*, dissenting 283

    John Roberts, *Miller v. Alabama*, dissenting 284

    Robert Jackson, *Korematsu v. United States*, dissenting 286

    John Paul Stevens, *Citizens United v. Federal Election Campaign*, dissenting 287

    Elena Kagan, *Arizona Christian School Tuition Org. v. Winn*, dissenting 288

Get Real: Wrong on the Policy 290

    A. Anti-Elitist 290

        John Stevens, *Citizens United v. Federal Election Commission*, dissenting 291

Alex Kozinski, *United States v. Pineda-Moreno*, dissenting from a denial of rehearing 292

Robert Jackson, *Terminiello v. City of Chicago*, dissenting 294

Oliver Wendell Holmes Jr., *Lochner v. New York*, dissenting 295

Antonin Scalia, *Lawrence v. Texas*, dissenting 297

B. Anti-Populist 298

Lord Hoffmann, *A(FC) and others (FC) v. Secretary of State for the Home Department*, dissenting 299

Lord Sumption, *Societe Generale v. Geys*, dissenting 300

Michael Kirby, *Wurridjal v. Commonwealth of Australia*, dissenting 301

Michael Kirby, *Kartinyeri v. Commonwealth*, dissenting 302

Robert Jackson, *Terminiello v. City of Chicago*, dissenting 303

John Paul Stevens, *Attorney General's Office v. Osborne*, dissenting 304

Ruth Bader Ginsburg, *Shelby County v. Holder*, dissenting 305

Practice Pointers for Dissents 305

Dissents are different. A product of the English common-law tradition, they are rare, and sometimes even prohibited, in civil-law systems. In a legal culture that prizes strong majority opinions, the mere existence of a dissent can threaten a court's legitimacy. Indeed, when the U.S. Supreme Court dives into controversy, chief justices from Left to Right—from Earl Warren to John Roberts—have turned somersaults to persuade the court to speak with a single voice. If the role of a judge is to be just an "umpire calling balls and strikes," at Chief Justice Roberts once put it, then dissents surely knock that notion off its perch, hinting as they do that the law is a set of personal policy preferences cloaked in black robes.

All the same, dissents are sometimes too tempting to resist. Their initial audience: the court's other judges. As Justice Ruth Bader Ginsburg has put it, "there is nothing better than an impressive dissent to lead the author of the majority opinion to refine and clarify her initial circulation."[1] The occasional dissent will seduce so many judges, she notes, that it can sometimes morph into the majority opinion itself.

And yet even if convincing the majority proves futile, dissents can shape legal history over the long term. In the United States, for example, dissents in *Dred Scott*, the *Civil Rights Cases*, and *Korematsu* all set the groundwork for the Court's reversals decades later. "When history demonstrates that one of the Court's decisions has been a truly horrendous mistake," writes Justice Scalia, "it is comforting . . . to look back and realize that at least some of the justices saw the danger clearly and gave voice, often eloquent voice, to their concern."[2] In a 2008 interview with the *Wall Street Journal* Law Blog, Scalia admitted that his own dissents are not "going to persuade my colleagues and I'm not going to persuade most of the federal bench." Instead, he said, "I'm advocating for the future. Who do you think I'm writing my dissents for? I'm writing for the next generation and for law students."

In the meantime, dissents can do damage control. A powerful dissent can sway both other judges and the bar into interpreting the majority opinion narrowly. And a powerful dissent can also reassure the losing party that its position has been granted due consideration, encouraging would-be advocates to bring future cases to test the limits of the majority's ruling.

Most dramatically, a dissent can issue a clarion call to other branches of government. A recent example in the United States was Justice Ginsburg's dissent in *Ledbetter v. Goodyear Tire & Rubber Co.*, a high-profile case about the limitations period for bringing equal-pay claims. Ginsburg read her dissent from the bench, elevating its status and tossing the equal-pay issue into the legislature's court, so to speak. Her words spurred the U.S. Congress to introduce legislation that eventually became the Lilly Ledbetter Fair Pay Act, the first act of Congress that President Barack Obama signed into law.[3]

So much for the "why." How about the "how"?

The best dissents aren't written like majority opinions that just so happen to reach a different conclusion. They use the majority opinion as a springboard instead, poking holes in the majority's reasoning and highlighting points of disagreement, all the while tipping a hat to the court's authority and dignity.

Duly inspired? Then let's talk about craft. Like great advocates and, for that matter, great majority-opinion writers, the best dissenters work their magic in familiar ways. Some suggest that the majority is wrong about the facts, others that the majority is wrong about the law, and still others that the majority is wrong about the underlying policy. I'll share techniques for each of these three tacks below.

A Sordid Tale: Wrong on the Facts

In Part 2, I pitted together two sections from an Australian majority opinion and an Australian dissent in the same case, all to show how different judges can emphasize or downplay different facts. But turnabout is fair play: spin the facts too far, and dissenters will be lying in wait to call you out for misreading the facts, for mischaracterizing them, or for missing the forest for the trees. (And vice versa, of course, for those majority-opinion writers who deign to acknowledge the dissenters.)

Great dissenters often delight in highlighting facts that the majority prefers to brush aside or to reduce to bloodless euphemism. Justice Jackson reveled in such a technique in the example below. In this freedom-of-expression case, a priest was convicted of breaching the peace while giving a speech in an auditorium surrounded by demonstrators. The majority held that the conviction violated the First Amendment, describing in abstract terms how the speaker "condemned the conduct of the crowd outside and vigorously, if not viciously, criticized various political and racial groups whose activities he denounced as inimical to the nation's welfare."

Seizing on the banality of "vigorously, if not viciously," Justice Jackson offered a far more squeamish take on the speech in question:

Robert Jackson, *Chicago v. Terminiello*, dissenting

Evidence showed that [the speech] stirred the audience not only to cheer and applaud but to expressions of immediate anger, unrest and alarm. **One called the speaker a "God damned liar" and was taken out by the police. Another said that "Jews, niggers and Catholics would have to be gotten rid of." One response was, "Yes, the Jews are all killers, murderers. If we don't kill them first, they will kill us." The anti-Jewish stories elicited exclamations of "Oh!" and "Isn't that terrible!" and shouts of "Yes, send the Jews back to Russia," "Kill the Jews," "Dirty kikes," and much more of ugly tenor. This is the specific and concrete kind of anger, unrest and alarm, coupled with that of the mob outside, that the trial court charged the jury might find to be a breach of peace induced by Terminiello.** It is difficult to believe that this Court is speaking of the same occasion, but it is the only one involved in this litigation.

One man's free speech is another man's fighting words, of course, but the devil is in the details, and Justice Jackson's choice quotes from the trial testimony belie the majority's antiseptic summary. When the majority surveys the record from the heavens, a pointed dissent can guide the reader back to earth. The juxtaposed facts should speak for themselves, but as with Jackson's "It is difficult to believe this Court is speaking of the same occasion," you can end by indulging in a gentle rhetorical jab or two.

In the next example, the dissenting judge targets the majority not for writing about facts euphemistically, but for reaching a conclusion based on few facts at all. The issue was whether a prison violated

274 | POINT TAKEN

an inmate's constitutional rights when a female prison guard was assigned to monitor a male pretrial detainee in the shower. The majority deferred to the prison administrators' judgment and thus found no constitutional violation. In dissent, Judge Posner endorses deference on principle, but he still wonders how the majority could have deferred to a judgment that was never really made. "There is no record," as Posner puts it:

Richard Posner, *Johnson v. Phelan*, dissenting

My colleagues say that we must respect "the hard choices made by prison administrators." I agree. There is no basis in the record, however, for supposing that such a choice was made here, or for believing that an effort to limit cross-sex surveillance would involve an inefficient use of staff— "featherbedding," as my colleagues put it. **There is no record.** The case was dismissed on the complaint. We do not know whether the Cook County Jail cannot afford a thicker sheet or, more to the point, cannot feasibly confine the surveillance of naked male prisoners to male guards and naked female prisoners to female guards. We do not even know what crime Johnson is charged with. My colleagues urge deference to prison administrators, but at the same time speak confidently about the costs of redeploying staff to protect Johnson's rights. It would be nice to know a little more about the facts before making a judgment that condones barbarism.

What if the facts aren't missing or ignored, but, like Rodney Dangerfield, just get no respect, or at least not the respect they deserve? A skilled dissenter can upend the majority's take on the facts that it does report, as Justice Scalia does below in his dissent in *Romer v. Evans*, an early gay-rights case about an anti-gay amendment to the Colorado constitution. The majority attributed the amendment's populist passage to animus toward gays and lesbians, in effect characterizing Colorado voters as bigoted. Scalia slammed his fist in response, penning a well-known line that accuses the majority of being so out of touch that it is aloof to a bona fide culture war:

Antonin Scalia, *Romer v. Evans*, dissenting

The Court has mistaken a Kulturkampf for a fit of spite. The constitutional amendment before us here is not the manifestation of a "'bare desire to harm'" homosexuals, but is rather a modest attempt by seemingly tolerant Coloradans to preserve traditional sexual mores against the efforts of a politically powerful minority to revise those mores through use of the laws.

. . .

The Court's portrayal of Coloradans as a society fallen victim to pointless, hate-filled "gay-bashing" is so false as to be comical. Colorado not only is one of the 25 States that have repealed their antisodomy laws, but was among the first to do so.

(I love the opening line as a writing matter, but I've never quite understood the contrast. *Kulturkampf* refers to Otto von Bismarck's efforts in late-nineteenth-century Germany to suppress the Catholic Church—more of a "fit of spite," in the end, than a bona fide culture war.)

In theory, both Scalia and the majority are grappling with the very same "fact" of a popularly passed referendum. But what the majority sees as a story of animus-fueled bigotry, Scalia sees as a "modest" attempt to bridge a cultural divide and to stall the agenda of a "politically powerful minority." And by contrasting more facts—including the repeal of an anti-sodomy law—with the loaded term of "gay-bashing," Scalia suggests that the majority simply got the whole story wrong.

In some cases, the majority's mistake is not about facts in the record but about facts in the world at large. Below, for example, in the high-stakes case about the constitutionality of the Affordable Care Act, also known as "Obamacare," the majority likened buying health insurance to buying cars or even broccoli. Not so, proclaims Justice Ruth Bader Ginsburg:

Ruth Bader Ginsburg, *National Federation of Independent Business v. Sebelius*, dissenting

Maintaining that the uninsured are not active in the health-care market, the Chief Justice draws an analogy to the car market. An individual "is not 'active in the car market,'" the Chief Justice observes, simply because he or she may someday buy a car. **The analogy is inapt.** The inevitable yet unpredictable need for medical care and the guarantee that emergency care will be provided when required are conditions nonexistent in other markets. That is so of the market for cars, and of the market for broccoli as well. Although an individual *might* buy a car or a crown of broccoli one day, there is no certainty she will ever do so. And if she eventually wants a car or has a craving for broccoli, she will be obliged to pay at the counter before receiving the vehicle or nourishment. She will get no free ride or food, at the expense of another consumer forced to pay an inflated price. Upholding the minimum coverage provision on the ground that all are participants or will be participants in the health-care market would therefore carry no implication that Congress may justify under the Commerce Clause a mandate to buy other products and services.

Justice Ginsburg hijacks the majority's analogy to show why the health-insurance market plays by different rules, all the while poking holes in the premise that people are "active" in the market only on the day they visit their doctor. A message like hers can capture the reader's imagination by explaining why the majority's seductive analogies ultimately fall flat, by one-upping the majority's analogy altogether, or by otherwise appealing to the reader's understanding of the world.

To sum up, a majority opinion will invariably pick and choose which facts it emphasizes, which it downplays, and which it ignores. Because even benign facts are open to interpretation, the majority will have offered its own gloss on any facts that it does highlight. And in some cases, the majority will offer a seductive but ultimately flawed analogy between something intrinsic to the record and something extrinsic in the world. All these choices can fuel a skilled dissenter who believes that the majority decision rises or falls based on its fundamental take on the facts.

Piercing the Veil: Wrong on the Law

Just as umpires disagree about the borders of the strike zone, judges disagree about the borders of the law. A majority will usually root its position in an impressive-looking line of authorities, but on closer inspection, those authorities may be scant, inapt, or twisted beyond recognition. A dissent can thus offer the chance to peek behind the majority's curtain of citations.

In doing so, a strong dissenter can unveil any number of analytical flaws: ignoring key precedent, citing authorities that are distinguishable, failing to grapple with counter-authorities, or cherry-picking cases or quotes. Let's consider these techniques in turn.

Even as they issue paeans to stare decisis, majorities sometimes venture into uncharted waters without admitting as much. Other times, the majority will concede the departure but will still downplay a long line of precedent as dated or as just plain wrong. Either way, an adept dissenter will shine a light on the deviation, accusing the majority of precedential dalliances or worse.

Dissenting in a high-profile campaign-contribution case, Justice John Paul Stevens pulls no punches as he accuses the majority of "a dramatic break from our past" and of "reject[ing] a century of history." The fiery language of "blazes through our precedents" makes his distaste abundantly clear:

John Paul Stevens, *Citizens United v. Federal Elections Commission*, dissenting

The majority's approach to corporate electioneering marks **a dramatic break from our past**. Congress has placed special limitations on campaign spending by corporations ever since the passage of the Tillman Act in 1907. We have unanimously concluded that this "reflects a permissible assessment of the dangers posed by those entities to the electoral process," and have accepted the "legislative judgment that the special characteristics of the corporate structure require particularly careful regulation[.]" The Court today rejects a century of history when it treats the distinction between corporate and individual campaign spending as an invidious novelty born of *Austin* v. *Michigan Chamber of Commerce*. Relying largely on individual dissenting opinions, **the majority blazes through our precedents**, overruling or disavowing a body of case law including *FEC* v. *Wisconsin Right to Life, Inc.*, *McConnell* v. *FEC*, *FEC* v. *Beaumont*, *FEC* v. *Massachusetts Citizens for Life, Inc.*, *NRWC*, and *California Medical Assn.* v. *FEC*.

In Justice Stevens's rendition, the Supreme Court's five key precedents created a steady state that the majority has ignited like Godzilla bruising through Tokyo. As he famously put it elsewhere in his dissent, "The only relevant thing that has changed since *Austin* and *McConnell* is the composition of this Court."

In the examples below, Justice Scalia and Seventh Circuit Judge Wood attack their respective majorities not for diluting a long line of precedent but for turning their backs on a single pivotal case.

Justice Scalia's dissent in an important separation-of-powers dispute gains force because the pivotal case in question dates back to 1935—that is, he says, until it was "swept into the dustbin of repudiated principles":

Antonin Scalia, *Morrison v. Olson*, dissenting

Since our 1935 decision in *Humphrey's Executor v. United States* ... it has been established that the line of permissible restriction upon removal of principal officers lies at the point at which the powers exercised by the officers are no longer purely executive. ... Today, however, *Humphrey's Executor* **is swept into the dustbin of repudiated principles**. ... What *Humphrey's Executor* (and presumably *Myers*) really means, we are now told, is not that there are any "rigid categories of those officials who may or may not be removed at will by the President," but simply that Congress cannot "interfere with the President's exercise of the 'executive power' and his constitutionally appointed duty to 'take care that the laws be faithfully executed.'"

As a variation on that theme, Judge Wood accuses the majority in an abortion-rights case not of ignoring a key case per se but of calling it an "opaque mess" when in fact its holding is "crystal clear":

Diane Wood, *A Woman's Choice-East Side Women's Clinic v. Newman*, dissenting

The careful reader of the majority's opinion will see that the majority regrets the fact that the Supreme Court held in *Stenberg v. Carhart*, that pre-enforcement challenges of abortion statutes, like the one presently before us, are permissible. Nevertheless, *Stenberg* is the law of the land and we must follow its direction, including its endorsement of the constitutional standards governing abortion legislation first articulated by the *Casey* plurality. **That direction is by no means the opaque mess the majority accuses the Supreme Court of creating.** In my view, the Court has not left us with "irreconcilable directives[,]" nor has it put courts of appeals "in a pickle." At the most, if we were reviewing legislation in some field unrelated to abortion (or speech), we might be faced with the problems the majority describes. As for abortion regulation, **the Court's guidance is crystal clear.** In the end, the majority concedes that *Stenberg* governs, which ought to be enough for present purposes to lead to an affirmance of the district court's grant of the injunction.

The tone of all three examples above—from Stevens, Scalia, and Wood alike—betrays more than a whiff of irritation. Our final example below, from D.C. Circuit Judge Kavanaugh, adopts a more circumspect approach. For this dissenting judge, his majority colleagues are a bit too grandiose about the scope of their own appellate review. Unlike many dissenters, though, he admits that the question is not an easy one:

Brett Kavanaugh, *In re Sealed Case*, dissenting

In my judgment, the majority opinion illustrates the magnetic pull that the [federal Sentencing] Guidelines still occasionally exert over appellate courts in cases involving sentences outside the Guidelines range. To be sure, the Supreme Court's remedial opinion in *Booker* was open to multiple readings and could have been interpreted to preserve this kind of Guidelines-centric appellate review.

But the Court's recent decisions in *Rita, Kimbrough*, and *Gall*, as I read them, do not permit such an approach; appellate review is for abuse of discretion and is limited to assessing only whether certain procedural requirements were met and whether the sentence is substantively "reasonable." **Recognizing that the governing Supreme Court decisions are not entirely unambiguous, and despite my serious concerns about the sentencing disparities that could well ensue as a result of the current case law, I think our appellate role in the *Booker-Rita-Kimbrough-Gall* sentencing world is more limited than the majority opinion suggests.*** *See Gall* (reversing Eighth Circuit decision: "On abuse-of-discretion review, the Court of Appeals should have given due deference to the District Court's reasoned and reasonable decision that the § 3553(a) factors, on the whole, justified the sentence."); *Kimbrough* (reversing Fourth Circuit decision: "Giving due respect to the District Court's reasoned appraisal, a reviewing court could not rationally conclude that the 4.5-year sentence reduction Kimbrough received qualified as an abuse of discretion.").

What if the majority has, in your estimation, invoked an authority that has only superficial similarities to the case before the court? That authority is too good to be true, you should then proclaim. As does Justice Kagan in the excerpt below. Bit by bit, she demolishes

---

* When a sentence starts with two complex wind-up phrases before you even get to the subject, streamline them and make them parallel. "Recognizing that. . . . and despite my serious concerns . . . , I. . . ." might have been clearer as "Although I recognize that X and have serious concerns about Y, I think. . . ."

the majority's invocation of a case called *Davis*. The similarity "matters far less than the differences," she contends:

Elena Kagan, *Arizona Free Enterprise Club's Freedom Club PAC v. Bennett*, dissenting

The majority thinks it has one case on its side—*Davis v. Federal Election Comm'n*—and it pegs everything on that decision. But *Davis* relies on principles that fit securely within our First Amendment law and tradition—most unlike today's opinion.

. . . .

Under the First Amendment, **the similarity between *Davis* and this case matters far less than the differences. Here is the similarity: In both cases, one candidate's campaign expenditure triggered ... something. Now here are the differences: In *Davis*, the candidate's expenditure triggered a discriminatory speech restriction, which Congress could not otherwise have imposed consistent with the First Amendment; by contrast, in this case, the candidate's expenditure triggers a non-discriminatory speech subsidy, which all parties agree Arizona could have provided in the first instance. In First Amendment law, that difference makes a difference—indeed, it makes *all* the difference.** As I have indicated before, two great fault lines run through our First Amendment doctrine: one, between speech restrictions and speech subsidies, and the other, between discriminatory and neutral government action. The Millionaire's Amendment fell on the disfavored side of both divides: To reiterate, it imposed a discriminatory speech restriction. The Arizona Clean Elections Act lands on the opposite side of both: It grants a non-discriminatory speech subsidy. **So to**

> say that *Davis* "largely controls" this case is to decline to take our First Amendment doctrine seriously.*

Yet another approach is to suggest that the majority is exaggerating the importance—or the consistency—of cases that you deem outliers at best. In the notorious case *Bush v. Gore*, for example, an obviously miffed Justice Ruth Bader Ginsburg accuses the majority of that very sort of cherry-picking when it rejected the Florida Supreme Court's interpretation of Florida election law:

Ruth Bader Ginsburg, *Bush v. Gore*, dissenting

Rarely has this Court rejected outright an interpretation of state law by a state high court. *Fairfax's Devisee* v. *Hunter's Lessee, NAACP* v. *Alabama ex rel. Patterson*, and *Bouie* v. *City of Columbia*, cited by the Chief Justice, are three such rare instances. But those cases are embedded in historical contexts hardly comparable to the situation here.

. . . *[Ginsburg discusses the three cases, explaining that each involved a state court's explicit defiance of the Supreme Court's mandate]*

The Chief Justice's casual citation of these cases might lead one to believe they are part of a larger collection of cases in which we said that the Constitution impelled us to train a skeptical eye on a state court's portrayal of state law. But one would be hard pressed, I think, to find additional cases that fit the mold. As Justice Breyer convincingly explains, **this case involves nothing close to the kind of recalcitrance by**

---

* Note Justice Kagan's use of parallel construction, varied sentence structure, and varied punctuation.

> a state high court that warrants extraordinary action by
> this Court. The Florida Supreme Court concluded that count-
> ing every legal vote was the overriding concern of the Florida
> Legislature when it enacted the State's Election Code. The
> court surely should not be bracketed with state high courts
> of the Jim Crow South.

They key here is to use language suggesting that the current case "involves nothing close to" whatever you think describes the cited one. But note that Ginsburg goes further, baiting the majority with the suggestion that it is equating the Florida Supreme Court with the recalcitrant courts of the Jim Crow South.

Chief Justice Roberts offers a less-loaded example in a rare dissent below. In *Miller v. Alabama*, the majority held that mandatory life-without-parole sentences for juvenile murderers were unconstitutional. For Roberts, the two cases that the majority cites stand for an anodyne principle: that teenagers are less responsible than adults. But those cases do not, he insists, bar noncapital punishments for juveniles who commit violent murder:

> **John Roberts, *Miller v. Alabama*, dissenting**
>
> [T]he Court's holding does not follow from *Roper* and *Graham*.
> Those cases undoubtedly stand for the proposition that
> teenagers are less mature, less responsible, and less fixed
> in their ways than adults—not that a Supreme Court case
> was needed to establish that. What they do not stand for,
> and do not even suggest, is that legislators—who also
> know that teenagers are different from adults—may not
> require life without parole for juveniles who commit the
> worst types of murder.

That *Graham* does not imply today's result could not be clearer. In barring life without parole for juvenile nonhomicide offenders, *Graham* stated that "[t]here is a line 'between homicide and other serious violent offenses against the individual.'" The whole point of drawing a line between one issue and another is to say that they are different and should be treated differently. In other words, the two are in different categories. . . . A case that expressly puts an issue in a different category from its own subject, draws a line between the two, and states that the two should not be compared, cannot fairly be said to control that issue.

Roper provides even less support for the Court's holding. . . . *Roper* reasoned that the death penalty was not needed to deter juvenile murderers in part because "life imprisonment without the possibility of parole" was available. In a classic bait and switch, the Court now tells state legislatures that—*Roper*'s promise notwithstanding—they do not have power to guarantee that once someone commits a heinous murder, he will never do so again. It would be enough if today's decision proved Justice Scalia's prescience in writing that *Roper*'s "reassurance . . . gives little comfort." To claim that *Roper* actually "leads to" revoking its own reassurance surely goes too far.

   . . . .

Roper and *Graham* attempted to limit their reasoning to the circumstances they addressed—*Roper* to the death penalty, and *Graham* to nonhomicide crimes. Having cast aside those limits, the Court cannot now offer a credible substitute, and does not even try.*

---

* Note the many hallmark Chief Justice Roberts style traits here: the wry comment about teenagers, the "bait and switch" culture reference, the variety in sentence structure and length, and the choice snippets from key cases. Make sure, of course, that your "choice snippets" are used fairly and are not plucked out of their context.

A dissenter can make a similar apples-and-oranges argument about just a single case. In his famous *Korematsu* dissent, for instance, Justice Jackson chided the majority for invoking a case that allowed a curfew restriction on a citizen of Japanese ancestry. But indefinite internment is a far cry from a limited curfew, Jackson noted. Even if "these citizens could be made to stay in their homes during the hours of dark," they should still not be removed from their homes, deported, or otherwise detained:

Robert Jackson, *Korematsu v. United States*, dissenting

[The majority] argues that we are bound to uphold the conviction of Korematsu because we upheld one in *Kiyshi Hirabayashi v. United States*, when we sustained these orders in so far as they applied a curfew requirement to a citizen of Japanese ancestry. **I think we should learn something from that experience.** In that case we were urged to consider only the curfew feature, that being all that technically was involved, because it was the only count necessary to sustain Hirabayashi's conviction and sentence. We yielded, and the Chief Justice guarded the opinion as carefully as language will do.

. . . .

However, in spite of our limiting words we did validate a discrimination on the basis of ancestry for mild and temporary deprivation of liberty. **Now the principle of racial discrimination is pushed from support of mild measures to very harsh ones, and from temporary deprivations to indeterminate ones.** And the precedent which it is said requires us to do so is *Hirabayashi*. The Court is now saying that in *Hirabayashi* we did decide the very things we there said we were not deciding. Because we said that these citizens could be made to stay in their homes during the hours of dark, it is said we must require them to leave home entirely; and if that, we are told they may also be taken into custody for deportation; and if that, it is argued they may also be held for some undetermined time in detention camps. How far the principle of this case would be extended before plausible reasons would play out, I do not know.

Rarely has a judicial omen about the slippery slope been so beautifully written.

Just as some majorities cite cases selectively, others quote from the right cases parsimoniously. In those respects, judges are no different from advocates. When a majority opinion recites a quote that stings, sting back.

Such a technique can be particularly effective when the majority intones a grandiloquent line that seems apt at first blush but that is platitudinous or worse at its core. Justice Stevens expresses his dismay in that regard below, accusing the *Citizens United* majority of overplaying its hand when it quotes from two older election-law cases, *Buckley* and *Bellotti*:

John Paul Stevens, *Citizens United v. Federal Election Campaign*, dissenting

Against this extensive background of congressional regulation of corporate campaign spending, and our repeated affirmation of this regulation as constitutionally sound, the majority dismisses *Austin* as "a significant departure from ancient First Amendment principles." How does the majority attempt to justify this claim? Selected passages from two cases, *Buckley* and *Bellotti*, do all of the work. In the Court's view, *Buckley* and *Bellotti* decisively rejected the possibility of distinguishing corporations from natural persons in the

288 | POINT TAKEN

> 1970's; it just so happens that in every single case in which
> the Court has reviewed campaign finance legislation in the
> decades since, the majority failed to grasp this truth. The
> Federal Congress and dozens of state legislatures, we now
> know, have been similarly deluded.
>
> The majority emphasizes *Buckley*'s statement that "'[t]he
> concept that government may restrict the speech of some ele-
> ments of our society in order to enhance the relative voice of
> others is wholly foreign to the First Amendment.'" But this
> elegant phrase cannot bear the weight that our colleagues
> have placed on it.
>
> . . . .
>
> **The majority grasps a quotational straw** from *Bellotti*,
> that speech does not fall entirely outside the protection of
> the First Amendment merely because it comes from a corpo-
> ration. Of course not, but no one suggests the contrary and
> neither *Austin* nor *McConnell* held otherwise.

You can hear a touch of scorn when Stevens utters the term
"elegant phrase." Maybe he thinks better of his own "grasps a quotational straw" gambit.

Speaking of grasping quotational straws, Justice Kagan, in the
dissent below, attacks a different U.S. Supreme Court majority for
plucking the word "extract" from an earlier opinion to create a test
that she says the very signatories of the opinion would have rejected:

> **Elena Kagan,** *Arizona Christian School Tuition Org.*
> *v. Winn,* **dissenting**
>
> The majority purports to rely on *Flast* to support this new
> "extraction" requirement. It plucks the three words "extrac[t]
> and spen[d]" from the midst of the *Flast* opinion, and suggests

that they severely constrict the decision's scope. And it notes that *Flast* partly relied on James Madison's famed argument in the Memorial and Remonstrance Against Religious Assessments: " '[T]he same authority which can force a citizen to contribute three pence only of his property for the support of any one establishment, may force him to conform to any other establishment in all cases whatsoever.'" And that is all the majority can come up with.

But as indicated earlier, everything of import in *Flast* cuts against the majority's position. Here is how *Flast* stated its holding: "[W]e hold that a taxpayer will have standing consistent with Article III to invoke federal judicial power when he alleges that congressional action under the taxing and spending clause is in derogation of" the Establishment Clause. Nothing in that straightforward sentence supports the idea that a taxpayer can challenge only legislative action that disburses his particular contribution to the state treasury. . . . **So the majority is left with nothing, save for three words *Flast* used to describe the particular facts in that case: In not a single non-trivial respect could the *Flast* Court recognize its handiwork in the majority's depiction.***

Kagan makes those scant "three words" from *Flast* sound a bit like George Carlin's *Seven Dirty Words*.

---

* As I discussed in Part 4, Justice Kagan also has a real knack for vivid verbs: "constrict," "cut against," and "come up with" accompany her beloved "pluck."

Get Real: Wrong on the Policy

Still other great dissents have frankly political undertones. These dissenters are not necessarily flummoxed by the majority's treatment of the record, case law, or statutes. Instead, they recoil against what they see as the majority's attempts to shroud itself in dry doctrine, often in the name of "judicial minimalism" or stare decisis, but at the expense of noxious real-world consequences.

I would further divide this dissents-spilling-into-politics group into two subcategories:

- Anti-elitist: "The majority is elitist and out of touch, with no sense of how its ruling will affect 'real people.'"
- Anti-populist: "The majority is nakedly populist, even cowardly, appealing to the masses without considering the rights of minorities or other disfavored groups."

A. Anti-Elitist

Populist charges of elitism themselves come in two varieties: a Right-leaning critique that the majority either identifies with the interests of the intelligentsia or clings to such abstract values as "diversity" or "justice" with no concern for their limits, and a Left-leaning critique that the majority identifies with the interests of the moneyed or ruling class.

Over on the Left, in his blistering dissent in *Citizens United*, Justice John Paul Stevens rails against the majority on populist grounds. In expressing his disdain for the majority's rejection of limits on corporate-campaign contributions, Stevens depicts a world in which the average citizen will feel disempowered and the average candidate will pander to Big Business. Goodbye democracy,

Stevens suggests, and hello to a world filled with "cynicism and disenchantment":

John Stevens, *Citizens United v. Federal Election Commission*, dissenting

Corporate "domination" of electioneering[] can generate the impression that corporations dominate our democracy. When citizens turn on their televisions and radios before an election and hear only corporate electioneering, they may lose faith in their capacity, as citizens, to influence public policy. A Government captured by corporate interests, they may come to believe, will be neither responsive to their needs nor willing to give their views a fair hearing. The predictable result is cynicism and disenchantment: an increased perception that large spenders "'call the tune'" and a reduced "'willingness of voters to take part in democratic governance.'" To the extent that corporations are allowed to exert undue influence in electoral races, the speech of the eventual winners of those races may also be chilled. Politicians who fear that a certain corporation can make or break their reelection chances may be cowed into silence about that corporation. On a variety of levels, unregulated corporate electioneering might diminish the ability of citizens to "hold officials accountable to the people," and disserve the goal of a public debate that is "uninhibited, robust, and wide-open[.]"

Note that in populist dissents like Stevens's, the judge doesn't apologize for an unabashedly political tone and doesn't appear to fear charges of judicial activism, either. Particularly in the United States, populist dissenters thus hold themselves out as gatekeepers of governmental integrity, stressing the judiciary's checks-and-balances role rather than its umpires-calling-balls-and-strikes role.

This populist strain can appeal to judges with a broad swath of ideological persuasions. In the case below, the police encroached upon a defendant's driveway in order to place a GPS under his car, a search that the Ninth Circuit majority found to be constitutional. But dissenting Judge Kozinski attacked the majority for invoking a seemingly neutral principle that in effect privileges the wealthy. His discussion reminds me of Anatole France's quip that "the law, in its majestic equality, forbids rich and poor alike to sleep under bridges, to beg in the streets, and to steal their bread":

Alex Kozinski, *United States v. Pineda-Moreno*, dissenting from a denial of rehearing

The panel's rationale for concluding that Pineda-Moreno had no reasonable expectation of privacy is even more worrisome than its disregard of Supreme Court precedent: According to the panel, Pineda-Moreno's driveway was open to the public in that strangers wishing to reach the door of his trailer "to deliver the newspaper or to visit someone would have to go through the driveway to get to the house." But there are many parts of a person's property that are accessible to strangers for limited purposes: the mailman is entitled to open the gate and deposit mail in the front door slot; the gas man may come into the yard, go into the basement or look under the house to read the meter; the gardener goes all over the property, climbs trees, opens sheds, turns on the sprinkler and taps into the electrical outlets; the pool man, the cable guy, the telephone repair man, the garbage collector, the newspaper delivery boy (we should be so lucky) come onto the property to deliver their wares, perform maintenance or make repairs. This doesn't mean that we invite neighbors to use the pool, strangers to camp out on the lawn or police to snoop in the garage.*

The panel authorizes police to do not only what invited strangers could, but also uninvited children—in this case crawl under the car to retrieve a ball and tinker with the undercarriage. But there's no limit to what neighborhood kids will do, given half a chance: They'll jump the fence, crawl under the porch, pick fruit from the trees, set fire to the cat and micturate on the azaleas. To say that the police may do on your property what urchins might do spells the end of Fourth Amendment protections for most people's curtilage. **The very rich will still be able to protect their privacy with the aid of electric gates, tall fences, security booths, remote cameras, motion sensors and roving patrols, but the vast majority of the 60 million people living in the Ninth Circuit will see their privacy materially diminished by the panel's ruling.** Open driveways, unenclosed porches, basement doors left unlocked, back doors left ajar, yard gates left unlatched, garage doors that don't quite close, ladders propped up under an open window will all be considered invitations for police to sneak in on the theory that a neighborhood child might, in which case, the homeowner "would have no grounds to complain."

As he put it elsewhere in the dissent, the majority's position was "creepy and un-American." (Kozinski's view was eventually vindicated by the U.S. Supreme Court.)

Other times, populist dissenters accuse the majority of being overly pure or naïve in its approach to such fundamental values as

---

* Note the effective use of this parade of examples—the pool man, the cable guy, the telephone repair man, the garbage collector, the newspaper delivery boy—that recalls the "Everyone Lies" Kozinksi passage that I shared in Part 5.

"justice" or "freedom of expression." The patron saint of the populists is the passage in Justice Jackson's *Terminiello* dissent arguing that the Bill of Rights is not a "suicide pact," a turn of phrase also attributed to Abraham Lincoln.

Jackson suggested there that in overturning a conviction for what today would be called "hate speech," the majority took an absolutist approach to free speech that ignored the dangers of the "herd opinion," as he put it. Through choice language like "herd," "mob," and "endanger," Justice Jackson juxtaposes the majority's lofty fantasy land in which the citizens freely exchange ideas with the hard-scrabble real world in which feckless opportunists spout attack lines and whip crowds into frenzies:

Robert Jackson, *Terminiello v. City of Chicago*, dissenting

As a people grow in capacity for civilization and liberty their tolerance will grow, and they will endure, if not welcome, discussion even on topics as to which they are committed. They regard convictions as tentative and know that time and events will make their own terms with theories, by whomever and by whatever majorities they are held, and many will be proved wrong. But on our way to this idealistic state of tolerance the police have to deal with men as they are. The crowd mind is never tolerant of any idea which does not conform to its herd opinion. It does not want a tolerant effort at meeting of minds. It does not know the futility of trying to mob an idea. Released from the sense of personal responsibility that would restrain even the worst individuals in it if alone and brave with the courage of numbers, both radical and reactionary mobs endanger liberty as well as order. The authorities must control them and they are entitled to place some checks upon those whose behavior or speech calls such mobs into being. **When the right of society to freedom from** probable violence should prevail over the right of an individual to defy opposing opinion, presents a problem that always tests wisdom and often calls for immediate and vigorous action to preserve public order and safety.

Another kind of elitism, some dissenters suggest, percolates when the majority is too quick to embrace a general principle that is not legal, such as the rights of criminal defendants, but economic, political, or ideological. Such is the thrust of Justice Holmes's famous dissent in *Lochner*. Holmes blasts the majority for favoring an unproven "economic theory"—laissez-faire economics—over "the right of a majority to embody their opinions in law":

Oliver Wendell Holmes Jr., *Lochner v. New York*, **dissenting**

This case is decided upon an economic theory which a large part of the country does not entertain . . . . The liberty of the citizen to do as he likes so long as he does not interfere with the liberty of others to do the same, which has been a shibboleth for some well-known writers, is interfered with by school laws, by the Postoffice, by every state or municipal institution which takes his money for purposes thought desirable, whether he likes it or not. **The 14th Amendment does not enact Mr. Herbert Spencer's Social Statics.** The other day we sustained the Massachusetts vaccination law. United States and state statutes and decisions cutting down the liberty to contract by way of combination are familiar to this court. Two years ago we upheld the prohibition of sales of stock on margins, or for future delivery, in the Constitution of California. The decision sustaining an eight-hour law for miners is still recent. Some of these laws embody convictions or prejudices which judges are likely to share. Some may not. **But a Constitution is not intended to embody a particular economic theory, whether of paternalism and the organic relation of the citizen to the state or of laissez faire. It is made for people of fundamentally differing views, and the accident of our finding certain opinions natural and familiar, or novel, and even shocking, ought not to conclude our judgment upon the question whether statutes embodying them conflict with the Constitution of the United States.**

General propositions do not decide concrete cases. The decision will depend on a judgment or intuition more subtle than any articulate major premise. But I think that the proposition just stated, if it is accepted, will carry us far toward the end. Every opinion tends to become a law. **I think that the word 'liberty,' in the 14th Amendment, is perverted when it is held to prevent the natural outcome of a dominant opinion, unless it can be said that a rational and fair man necessarily would admit that the statute proposed would infringe fundamental principles as they have been understood by the traditions of our people and our law.**

The main tools of The Great Dissenter are on full display here: the long list of examples of laws that the Court has upheld (only some of which I've included in this excerpt), the memorable pithy quote ("General propositions do not decide concrete cases"), and the laser-like focus on the unforeseen consequences if the majority's view takes hold.

Our final anti-elitist example comes from the Right. In a powerful dissent in a gay-rights case called *Lawrence v. Texas*, Justice Scalia rails against the majority for "tak[ing] sides in a culture war," and for preferring the "law-profession culture" of the intellegentsia to the culture of everyday Americans:

Antonin Scalia, *Lawrence v. Texas*, dissenting

Today's opinion is the product of a Court, which is the product of a law-profession culture, that has largely signed on to the so-called homosexual agenda, by which I mean the agenda promoted by some homosexual activists directed at eliminating the moral opprobrium that has traditionally attached to homosexual conduct. I noted in an earlier opinion the fact that the American Association of Law Schools (to which any reputable law school must seek to belong) excludes from membership any school that refuses to ban from its job-interview facilities a law firm (no matter how small) that does not wish to hire as a prospective partner a person who openly engages in homosexual conduct. One of the most revealing statements in today's opinion is the Court's grim warning that the criminalization of homosexual conduct is "an invitation to subject homosexual persons to discrimination both in the public and in the private spheres." **It is clear from this that the Court has taken sides in the culture war, departing from its role of assuring, as neutral observer, that the democratic rules of engagement are observed. Many Americans do not want persons who openly engage in homosexual conduct as partners in their business, as scoutmasters for their children, as teachers in their children's schools, or as boarders in their home.** They view this as protecting themselves and their families from a lifestyle that they believe to be immoral and destructive. The Court views it as "discrimination" which it is the function of our judgments to deter. So imbued is the Court with the law profession's anti-anti-homosexual culture, that it is seemingly

> unaware that the attitudes of that culture are not obviously
> "mainstream"; that in most States what the Court calls "dis-
> crimination" against those who engage in homosexual acts is
> perfectly legal; that proposals to ban such "discrimination"
> under Title VII have repeatedly been rejected by Congress;
> that in some cases such "discrimination" is mandated by fed-
> eral statute; . . . and that in some cases such "discrimination"
> is a constitutional right.

Like Justice Holmes, Justice Scalia pointedly uses examples with abandon, both in his list of what "many Americans" want, or don't, and in his list of cultural and legal verities that he claims the majority choose to ignore.

B. Anti-Populist

If the dissenters above accuse their majorities of being out of touch or otherwise elitist, the dissenters below are frustrated over the opposite problem: majority opinions that appear risk-averse, if not cowardly, in pandering to popular will at the expense of an underrepresented or unpopular minority. Our populist dissenters above thus portray themselves as down-to-earth and decidedly democratic. And our anti-populist dissenters below adopt the voice of the prescient maverick who will hold the court to its function as a check against majoritarian views. These divisions do not necessarily split on partisan or ideological lines, either.

A common theme in these dissents is the danger of overreacting to a genuine threat: "We have nothing to fear but fear itself," if you will. Below, for instance, Lord Hoffmann dissents from a ruling that deferred to the Home Secretary's determination that because terrorism "threaten[ed] the life of the nation," the government could detain suspects indefinitely without criminal charges or trial:

Lord Hoffmann, *A(FC) and others (FC) v. Secretary of State for the Home Department*, dissenting

This is a nation which has been tested in adversity, which has survived physical destruction and catastrophic loss of life. I do not underestimate the ability of fanatical groups of terrorists to kill and destroy, but they do not threaten the life of the nation. Whether we would survive Hitler hung in the balance, but there is no doubt that we shall survive Al-Qaeda. The Spanish people have not said that what happened in Madrid, hideous crime as it was, threatened the life of their nation. Their legendary pride would not allow it. Terrorist violence, serious as it is, does not threaten our institutions of government or our existence as a civil community.

For these reasons I think that the Special Immigration Appeals Commission made an error of law and that the appeal ought to be allowed. Others of your Lordships who are also in favour of allowing the appeal would do so, not because there is no emergency threatening the life of the nation, but on the ground that the power of detention confined to foreigners is irrational and discriminatory. I would prefer not to express a view on this point. I said that the power of detention is at present confined to foreigners and I would not like to give the impression that all that was necessary was to extend the power to United Kingdom citizens as well. In my opinion, such a power in any form is not compatible with our constitution. **The real threat to the life of the nation, in the sense of a people living in accordance with its traditional laws and political values, comes not from terrorism but from laws**

> such as these. That is the true measure of what terrorism
> may achieve. It is for Parliament to decide whether to give
> the terrorists such a victory.

The lofty tone of this dissent is of course the very sort of thing
that prompted the dissents in the section above: one man's higher
principle is another man's naïveté.

Anti-populist dissents need not always give voice to "the little
guy." They need only seek to curb majoritarian impulses. Below, for
example, a lone dissenting Lord Sumption takes the side of a bank in
an employment dispute that went all the way to the Supreme Court
of the United Kingdom. He accuses the majority's pro-employee position position of "allow[ing] the law to part company with reality" and
of creating a superficially appealing rule that will be unworkable and
even harmful to the functioning of businesses large and small:

> **Lord Sumption, *Societe Generale v. Geys*, dissenting**
>
> [T]here is no basis for Mr Cavender's assertion that the deci-
> sion in *Gunton* has given rise to no difficulty or injustice.*
> Its application would give rise to significant injustice in this
> case.... It cannot, with respect, be an answer to say, as the
> majority do, that their approach is required in order to pre-
> vent [the bank] from profiting from its own wrong and to
> "negative" the impact of the wrong on Mr Geys. These are
> proper functions of an award of damages. Mr Geys' problem
> is that the particular feature of [the bank's] conduct which
> was wrongful, i.e. the temporal separation of the dismissal

* This construction is a good example of a double negative that's better rendered
in the positive.

and the payment in lieu of notice, has not caused him any significant loss. **It is not part of the purpose of the law to reflect moral indignation about [the bank's] conduct, even assuming that [the bank's] mistake calls for moral indignation**, which I doubt.... [M]ore generally, it is always dangerous to allow the law to part company with reality in this way. It leads to highly technical results, which businessmen and employees are unlikely to anticipate unless they are particularly well advised. In this case, even a mighty corporation like [the bank] misunderstood the position. How are more modest enterprises to do so?

Other times, a dissenter's point is that the majority ignores the lessons of history. Take Justice Kirby's dissent in *Wurridjal v. Commonwealth of Australia* below. To a majority upholding legislation that he believes discriminates against aboriginal Australians, Kirby responds with a complimentary history lesson:

Michael Kirby, *Wurridjal v. Commonwealth of Australia*, dissenting

The claimants in these proceedings are, and represent, Aboriginal Australians. They live substantially according to their ancient traditions. This is not now a reason to diminish their legal rights. Given the history of the deprivation of such rights in Australia, their identity is now recognised as a ground for heightened vigilance and strict scrutiny of any alleged diminution.

. . .

History, and not only ancient history, teaches that there are many dangers in enacting special laws that target people of a particular race and disadvantage their rights

to liberty, property and other entitlements by reference to that criterion. The history of Australian law, including earlier decisions of this Court, stands as a warning about how such matters should be decided. Even great judges of the past were not immune from error in such cases.

. . .

If any other Australians, selected by reference to their race, suffered the imposition on their pre-existing property interests of non-consensual five-year statutory leases, designed to authorise intensive intrusions in to their lives and legal interests, it is difficult to believe that a challenge to such a law would fail as legally unarguable on the ground that no "property" had been "acquired". Or that "just terms" had been afforded, although those affected were not consulted about the same process and although rights cherished by them might be adversely affected. The Aboriginal parties are entitled to have their trial and day in court.

In another case involving aboriginal rights, Kirby sets his sights far beyond Australia, jabbing the majority with references to other countries' penchants for passing racially discriminatory laws:

Michael Kirby, *Kartinyeri v. Commonwealth*, dissenting

Yet, in Australia, if s 51(xxvi) of the Constitution permits all discriminatory legislation on the grounds of race excepting that which amounts to a "manifest abuse", many of the provisions which would be universally condemned as intolerably racist in character would be perfectly valid under the Commonwealth's propositions. The criterion of "manifest abuse" is inherently unstable. **The experience of racist laws** in Germany under the Third Reich and South Africa under apartheid was that of gradually escalating discrimination. Such has also been the experience of other places where adverse racial discrimination has been achieved with the help of the law. By the time a stage of "manifest abuse" and "outrage" is reached, courts have generally lost the capacity to influence or check such laws.

. . .

Both in Germany and in South Africa the special laws enacted would probably have been regarded as unthinkable but a decade before they were made. They stand as a warning to us in the elaboration of our Constitution.

Justice Jackson used a similar approach in his *Terminiello* dissent discussed earlier. Driving home his point that the demonstrations and meeting at issue posed serious threats and should not be mistaken for innocent rallies, Jackson, like Kirby, conjures up images of Nazi Germany:

Robert Jackson, *Terminiello v. City of Chicago*, dissenting

Hitler summed up the strategy of the mass demonstration as used by both fascism and communism: "We should not work in secret conventicles but in mighty mass demonstrations, and it is not by dagger and poison or pistol that the road can be cleared for the movement but by the conquest of the streets. We must teach the Marxists that the future master of the streets is National Socialism, just as it will some day be the master of the state." **First laughed at as an extravagant figure of speech, the battle for the streets became a tragic reality when an organized**

> Sturmabteilung began to give practical effect to its slogan that "possession of the streets is the key to power in the state."

Yet another way to suggest that the majority has tunnel vision is to emphasize dark chapters in legal history, as opposed to world history. After the U.S. Supreme Court ruled that prisoners had no constitutional right to DNA testing post-conviction, for instance, Justice John Paul Stevens bludgeoned the majority opinion with a discredited line of "states' rights" authorities:

> ### John Paul Stevens, *Attorney General's Office v. Osborne*, dissenting
>
> The majority's arguments in this respect bear close resemblance to the manner in which the Court once approached the now-venerable right to counsel for indigent defendants.* Before our decision in *Powell v. Alabama*, state law alone governed the manner in which counsel was appointed for indigent defendants. "Efforts to impose a minimum federal standard for the right to counsel in state courts routinely met the same refrain: 'in the face of these widely varying state procedures,' this Court refused to impose the dictates of 'due process' onto the states and 'hold invalid all procedure not reaching that standard."

Anti-populist policy-based dissents are not just for constitutional cases, of course. Below, in her dissent from a U.S. Supreme Court opinion striking down part of the Voting Rights Act, Justice Ginsburg links her distaste for the majority's move to what she sees

---

* Grammatically, the comparison doesn't quite work: "Arguments" can't bear close resemblance to a "manner." Perhaps "The arguments the majority uses here are much like the ones that were used against the now-venerable right to counsel."

as a pinched understanding of the deliberative process undergirding Congress's reauthorization of the statute in question:

Ruth Bader Ginsburg, *Shelby County v. Holder*, dissenting

When confronting the most constitutionally invidious form of discrimination, and the most fundamental right in our democratic system, Congress' power to act is at its height. . . . Congress approached the 2006 reauthorization of the [Voting Rights Act] with great care and seriousness. The same cannot be said of the Court's opinion today. **The Court makes no genuine attempt to engage with the massive legislative record that Congress assembled.** Instead, it relies on increases in voter registration and turnout as if that were the whole story. Without even identifying a standard of review, the Court dismissively brushes off arguments based on "data from the record," and declines to enter the "debat[e about] what [the] record shows". . . **One would expect more from an opinion striking at the heart of the Nation's signal piece of civil-rights legislation.**

A skillful dissent is not a chance to vent but an opportunity to entice the reader to explore a road not taken. Whether the majority elides key facts, skews the governing law, adopts the views of a favored elite, or downplays the perspective of unpopular factions, a strong dissenter can put the brakes on a decision run amok.

Practice Pointers for Dissents

When your objection is mainly factual:

- Does the majority gloss over unhelpful facts? Highlight those facts in detail and explain why they unmoor the majority's legal conclusions.

- Does the majority misconstrue the facts that it does emphasize? Draw sharp contrasts between competing characterizations of the same record.
- Does the majority trot out a real-world analogy that has seductive appeal but that otherwise misses the mark? Dismantle the analogy or offer one that's more apt.

When your objection is mainly legal:

- Call out the majority for ignoring or glossing over a key case or line of cases without justifying the departure from stare decisis.
- Show how the majority is exaggerating the importance of authorities or is glossing over key points of difference.
- Place isolated quotations in their broader context.

When your objection is that the majority is elitist or identifies with entrenched institutions:

- Characterize the majority as being out of touch with the views of the citizenry or of failing to defer to democratically elected institutions.
  o Show how the majority favors the agenda of the intelligentsia, and note how these views contrast with those of ordinary people as expressed through democratic institutions and representatives.
  o Show how the majority favors the interests of the wealthy and powerful, and address how the rights of ordinary people would fare under the majority's decision.
  o Show how the majority appears to take sides in a legitimate cultural dispute that should await democratic resolution.

When your objection is that the majority is nakedly populist and favors the will of the majority above all else:

- Show how the majority is pandering to the masses and is thus endorsing unworkable legal or policy principles.
  - o Show how popular sentiment has changed over time, and emphasize the court's obligation to provide stable, predictable rules.
  - o Give examples of when the dominant group has sought to suppress the rights of minority groups, and emphasize the court's obligation to protect the less powerful.

It's perhaps fitting that the book ends with these heartfelt passages from personalities as diverse as Justices Kirby, Jackson, Stevens, and Ginsburg. At its best, great judicial writing is part of the larger tradition of great rhetoric—but rhetoric that just so happens to have the full power of the State behind it. It's a daunting responsibility indeed. The challenge is to show your humanity when you write—through candid concessions, empathy for the reader, and an honest, personal style—without going so far that you make your opinions more about you than about the parties and the law.

After more than a year enmeshed in a broad swath of judicial opinions, I've come to appreciate the genre's risks and rewards alike. And I have an ever-greater understanding of the competing pressures on judges and clerks. Still, as I've tried to show throughout, at all levels of the judiciary, some judges truly shine. From opening lines through the facts, from headings to case analysis, from sentence variation to enduring imagery, you have countless opportunities to soar above the norm.

"There is no great writing, only great rewriting," Justice Brandeis famously said. True enough. But here's hoping that the examples in this book inspire you to join the ranks of the exemplary figures who penned them.

Part 7

Appendices

Biographies 310

    Berzon, Marsha 310

    Brandeis, Louis 310

    Cardozo, Benjamin 311

    Carnes, Edward 311

    Denning, Alfred, Baron Denning 311

    Easterbrook, Frank 312

    Ginsburg, Ruth Bader 312

    Goldgar, Benjamin 312

    Hale, Brenda, Baroness Hale of Richmond 313

    Hand, Learned 313

    Hoffman, Leonard, Baron Hoffman 314

    Holmes, Oliver Wendell, Jr. 314

    Jackson, Robert 314

    Kagan, Elena 315

    Kavanaugh, Brett 315

    Kirby, Michael 316

    Kozinski, Alex 316

    McLachlin, Beverley 316

    Marshall, D.P., Jr. 317

    Musmanno, Michael 317

    Paulsson, Jan 318

    Ponsor, Michael 318

    Posner, Richard J. 318

    Rakoff, Jed 319

    Roberts, John 319

    Scalia, Antonin 320

    Scheindlin, Shira 320

Schiltz, Patrick 320

Stevens, John Paul 321

Sumption, Jonathan, Lord Sumption 321

Thompson, O. Rogeriee 321

Traynor, Roger 322

Wald, Patricia 322

Wood, Diane 323

Practice Pointers 323

Biographies

Berzon, Marsha

Marsha Berzon has been a judge on the U.S. Court of Appeals for the Ninth Circuit since 2000. Before that, she was in private practice in Washington, DC and in San Francisco. She has also been affiliated with the Boalt Hall School of Law and the Cornell Law School.

Berzon graduated from the Boalt Hall School of Law in 1973. She clerked for Ninth Circuit Judge James R. Browning and for U.S. Supreme Court Justice William Brennan.

Brandeis, Louis

Louis D. Brandeis was an Associate Justice of the U.S. Supreme Court between 1916 and 1941. Before that, he founded one Boston firm and cofounded another. He taught briefly at Harvard Law School and cofounded the Harvard Law School Association in 1886. As a private attorney, he pioneered the "Brandeis Brief," which incorporated statistical data and expert opinion.

Brandeis graduated from Harvard Law School in 1877. He clerked for Massachusetts Supreme Court Justice Horace Gray.

Cardozo, Benjamin

Benjamin N. Cardozo was an Associate Justice of the U.S. Supreme Court between 1932 and 1938. Before that, he served on the New York State Court of Appeals from 1917 to 1932, including five years as the chief judge. He also served on the Supreme Court of the State of New York and was in private practice in New York from 1891 to 1914. He was a founder of the American Law Institute.

Cardozo attended Columbia Law School, but he joined the bar without receiving his degree.

Carnes, Edward

Edward Earl Carnes has been a judge on the U.S. Court of Appeals for the Eleventh Circuit since 1992 and has served as chief judge since 2013. Before that, he was Assistant Attorney General for the State of Alabama from 1975 to 1992.

Carnes graduated from Harvard Law School in 1975.

Denning, Alfred, Baron Denning

Alfred Thompson Denning, Baron Denning, OM, PC, DL, QC was Master of the Rolls from 1962 to 1982, presiding over the Civil Division of the U.K. Court of Appeal. He was appointed as a Lord of Appeal in Ordinary in 1957, at which time he became Baron Denning. In 1948, he was elevated to the Court of Appeal. In 1945, he became a judge of King's Bench. He had practiced law from 1923 to 1943. Denning was elected President of the English Association in 1964 for his contributions to English prose. He became President of Birkbeck College, University of London in 1953. His report on the Profumo scandal, which absolved the Secretary of State for War of any security breach, became a bestseller.

Lord Denning received two degrees from Oxford University, and was called from Lincoln's Inn to the Bar in 1923.

Easterbrook, Frank

Frank H. Easterbrook has been a judge on the U.S. Court of Appeals for the Seventh Circuit since 1985 and served as chief judge from 2006 to 2013. Before his nomination, he was the University of Chicago Law School's Lee and Brena Freeman Professor of Law. In 1974, he joined the Solicitor General's Office, and he served as Deputy Solicitor General from 1978 to 1979. Easterbrook was elected to the American Law Institute in 1983 and to the American Academy of Arts and Sciences in 1992. In 2004, Easterbrook was named one of the Top 20 Legal Thinkers in America in a *Legal Affairs* poll.

Easterbrook graduated Order of the Coif from the University of Chicago Law School, where he served on the Law Review. He clerked for First Circuit Judge Levin Campbell.

Ginsburg, Ruth Bader

Ruth Bader Ginsburg has been an Associate Justice of the U.S. Supreme Court since 1993. Before that, she was a judge on the U.S. Court of Appeals for the District of Columbia Circuit for 13 years. Ginsburg served on the American Law Institute from 1978 to 1993. Her extensive ACLU work included a directorship along with seven years as general counsel. She was a professor at Rutgers University School of Law from 1963 to 1972 and at Columbia Law School from 1972 to 1980. In 2009, *Forbes* named Ginsburg 48th of the world's 100 Most Powerful Women.

Ginsburg graduated from Columbia Law School in 1959 after transferring from Harvard; she served on both schools' law reviews. She clerked for Judge Edmund Palmieri of the Southern District of New York.

Goldgar, Benjamin

A. Benjamin Goldgar has been a judge on the U.S. Bankruptcy Court for the Northern District of Illinois since 2003. Goldgar previously worked for the Illinois Attorney General's Office and practiced law with Keck, Mahin & Cate from 1982 to 1995.

Goldgar graduated from Northwestern University School of Law in 1982.

Hale, Brenda, Baroness Hale of Richmond

Lady Hale is Deputy President of the U.K. Supreme Court. She was appointed to the Court, then known as the Law Lords, in 2004, and was the youngest person ever given that honor. With that appointment, she also became Baroness Hale of Richmond, a life peer of the House of Lords. Lady Hale was a Lord of Appeal in Ordinary from 1999 to 2003, the first woman to be so named. She was a judge of the high court's family division from 1994 to 1999. Before that, she taught law at Manchester University. For 10 years beginning in 1984, she served on the U.K.'s Law Commission. Lady Hale is the author of *Women and the Law*. In 1994, she was made a Dame Commander of the Order of the British Empire.

Lady Hale graduated from Cambridge University in 1966 and was called to the Bar from Gray's Inn.

Hand, Learned

Learned Hand was a judge on the U.S. Court of Appeals for the Second Circuit from 1924 until 1961, having been promoted from the U.S. District Court for the Southern District of New York, where he served beginning in 1909. At age 37, he was one of the youngest people ever appointed to the federal bench; he served for almost 50 years and wrote about four thousand opinions. Along with Benjamin Cardozo, he was an early leader of the American Law Institute.

Hand graduated with honors from Harvard Law School in 1896, where he served on the Law Review.

Hoffman, Leonard, Baron Hoffman

Lord Hoffman is a retired senior judge in the United Kingdom. He was a Lord of Appeal in Ordinary from 1995 to 2009 and, upon his appointment, was created a life peer by the title of Baron Hoffmann. He is also a Non-Permanent Judge of the Court of Final Appeal of Hong Kong and has served as director of the Amnesty International Charity Ltd. since 1990.

Lord Hoffman was described by *Legal Business* magazine as "the most dominant personality in the Lords by a mile."

He attended Oxford as a Rhodes Scholar and was Stowell Civil Law Fellow at University College, Oxford. He was called to the Bar from Gray's Inn in 1964.

Holmes, Oliver Wendell, Jr.

Oliver Wendell Holmes Jr. was an Associate Justice of the U.S. Supreme Court from 1902 until his retirement in 1932. He was known as "The Great Dissenter." He was appointed to the Massachusetts Supreme Judicial Court in 1882 after working in private practice and teaching law at Harvard. In 1870, Holmes became editor of the American Law Review. During the Civil War, he served in the 20th Massachusetts Volunteers, known as the Harvard Regiment, and was wounded three times. His book *The Common Law* was published in 1881 and remains a classic of American legal scholarship.

Holmes graduated from Harvard Law School in 1866.

Jackson, Robert

Robert H. Jackson was an Associate Justice of the U.S. Supreme Court from 1941 until his death in 1954. While on the Court, he also served as prosecutor for the International Military Tribunal in Nuremberg. Jackson served as Attorney General from 1940 to 1941, as Solicitor General from 1938 to 1939, and as Assistant Attorney General for the Tax Division from 1936 to 1938. During the early New Deal, he was special counsel to the Treasury Department and to the Securities & Exchange Commission, and he was also general counsel to the Bureau of Internal Revenue. He was in private practice in New York from 1913 to 1934.

Jackson attended Albany Law School, but he never graduated, passing the bar exam without a degree.

Kagan, Elena

Elena Kagan has been an Associate Justice of the U.S. Supreme Court since 2010. Before working in the Clinton administration, she taught law at Harvard and the University of Chicago. She was Solicitor General from 2009 to 2010. From 2003 to 2009, she was the Dean of Harvard Law School.

Kagan graduated magna cum laude from Harvard Law School in 1986. She clerked for D.C. Circuit Judge Abner Mikva and for Supreme Court Justice Thurgood Marshall.

Kavanaugh, Brett

Brett Kavanaugh has been a judge on the U.S. Court of Appeals for the D.C. Circuit since 2006. In 1992, Kavanaugh earned a one-year fellowship to the Office of the Solicitor General. Kavanaugh served as an Associate Counsel in the Office of Independent Counsel in 1994-1997 and then again in 1998, when he played a key role in the Whitewater investigation. He was in private practice in 1997 and in 1999 to 2001. Kavanaugh served as Associate Counsel and then Senior Associate Counsel for President George W. Bush between 2001 and 2003. He later served as Assistant to President Bush.

Kavanaugh graduated from Yale Law School in 1990. He clerked for Third Circuit Judge Walter K. Stapleton, for Ninth Circuit Judge Alex Kozinski, and for Supreme Court Justice Anthony Kennedy.

Kirby, Michael

Michael Kirby, AC, CMG, served as a Justice of the High Court of Australia from 1996 to 2013. He has also been a judge on the Federal Court of Australia, President of the New South Wales Court of Appeal, and President of the Court of Appeal of the Solomon Islands. From 1975 to 1984, he chaired the Australian Law Reform Commission. He has been an Honorary Visiting Professor at 12 universities. From 2013 to 2014, he headed a United Nations commission of inquiry into human-rights abuses in North Korea. He now edits *The Laws of Australia* and serves as an arbitrator for the International Center for the Settlement of Investment Disputes.

Kirby earned a Master of Laws degree with First Class honors from Sydney University in 1967.

Kozinski, Alex

Alex Kozinski is the Chief Judge of the U.S. Court of Appeals for the Ninth Circuit. A native of Romania, he was only 35 years old when President Reagan appointed him to the court in 1985. Before that, he was Chief Judge of the U.S. Court of Federal Claims from 1982 to 1985 and worked in private practice from 1977 to 1981.

Kozinski graduated from UCLA Law School in 1975. He clerked for then-Ninth Circuit Judge Anthony Kennedy and for Chief Justice Warren Burger.

McLachlin, Beverley

Beverley McLachlin became Chief Justice of the Supreme Court of Canada in 2000. She was elevated to the Supreme Court of Canada in 1989 after a brief stint as Chief Justice of the Supreme Court of British Columbia and after four years on the British Columbia Court of Appeal. From 1974 to 1981, McLachlin was an Associate Professor of the Faculty of Law at the University of British Columbia. She practiced law in Alberta and in British Columbia from 1969 to 1974.

McLachlin received her Bachelor of Laws degree with high honors from the University of Alberta in 1968.

Marshall, D.P., Jr.

Denzil Price Marshall Jr. has been a judge on the U.S. District Court for the Eastern District of Arkansas since 2010. Before that, Marshall served on the Arkansas Court of Appeals from 2006 to 2009. From 1991 to 2006, he was a principal at the law firm of Barrett & Deacon.

Marshall graduated from Harvard Law School in 1989. He clerked for Eighth Circuit Judge Richard Arnold.

Musmanno, Michael

Michael A. Musmanno was a Justice on the Pennsylvania Supreme Court from 1951 until his death in 1968. Musmanno was one of the most influential state-court judges in American history. A decorated veteran of both world wars, he later served in Congress, where he was known as a strong advocate for unions and for the disadvantaged. He also wrote many articles and books, including a novel.

Musmanno was a military judge and also presided at the Nuremberg trials. He was a defense lawyer in the Sacco & Vanzetti trial and is well known for his writings about the case.

Musmanno graduated from Georgetown Law School in 1918.

Paulsson, Jan

Jan Paulsson is an arbitrator at the International Center for Investment Disputes, the President of the International Council for Commercial Arbitration, and the head of the International Arbitration Institute. He holds the Michael Klein Distinguished Scholar Chair at the University of Miami School of Law. Paulsson has participated as counsel or arbitrator before many international tribunals, including the International Court of Justice in The Hague.

Paulsson graduated from Yale Law School in 1975, where he edited the *Yale Law Journal*.

Ponsor, Michael

Michael Ponsor has been a judge on the U.S. District Court for the District of Massachusetts since 1994. Before that, he was a U.S. magistrate. Ponsor has taught at Western New England College of Law since 1988, and was also an adjunct professor at Yale Law School from 1989 to 1991. His novel, *The Hanging Judge,* was published in 2013. He is the 2015 recipient of the Legal Writing Institute's Golden Pen Award.

Ponsor graduated from Yale Law School in 1975. He clerked for District Court of Massachusetts Judge Joseph Tauro.

Posner, Richard J.

Richard J. Posner is a judge on the U.S. Court of Appeals for the Seventh Circuit, and served as Chief Judge from 1993 to 2000. He has taught at the University of Chicago Law School since 1969, and has also worked for the Solicitor General. He has published more than 30 books. In 2004, Posner was named one of the Top 20 Legal Thinkers in America in a *Legal Affairs* poll. Posner has been named an Honorary Bencher of the Inner Temple and a corresponding fellow of the British Academy.

Posner graduated from Harvard Law School in 1962, and has since received honorary degrees from a dozen other universities, including Georgetown and Yale. Posner clerked for U.S. Supreme Court Justice William Brennan.

Rakoff, Jed

Jed S. Rakoff has been a judge on the U.S. District Court for the Southern District of New York since 1996. He has also been an Adjunct Professor of Law at Columbia University since 1988. He worked for many years in private practice. From 1973 to 1980, he served as Assistant U.S. Attorney for the Southern District of New York.

Rakoff graduated from Harvard Law School in 1969. He clerked for Third Circuit Judge Abraham Freedman.

Roberts, John

John G. Roberts Jr. has been the Chief Justice of the United States since 2005. He was elevated from the D.C. Circuit, where he had served since 2003. Before that, Roberts was Principal Deputy Solicitor General of the United States from 1989 to 1993. He was assistant counsel to President Reagan from 1982 to 1986 and worked in the U.S. Attorney General's office from 1981 to 1982. He has also practiced law at Hogan & Hartson, now known as Hogan Lovells.

Roberts graduated magna cum laude from Harvard Law School in 1979. He clerked for Second Circuit Judge Henry Friendly and for Supreme Court Justice William Rehnquist.

Scalia, Antonin

Antonin Scalia has been the Senior Associate Justice of the Supreme Court of the United States since 1986. Before that he was a judge on the D.C. Circuit from 1982 to 1984. He also taught at the University of Chicago Law School from 1977 to 1982. Scalia was Assistant Attorney General for the Office of Legal Counsel from 1974 to 1977. He was a Professor of Law at the University of Virginia from 1967 to 1971. From 1961 to 1967 he practiced law at Jones Day in Cleveland.

Scalia graduated magna cum laude from Harvard Law School, where he edited the Law Review.

Scheindlin, Shira

Shira Scheindlin has been a judge on the U.S. District Court for the Southern District of New York since 1994. She was in private practice from 1986 to 1994. She served as a U.S. Magistrate for the Eastern District of New York from 1982 to 1986 and served as Assistant U.S. Attorney for the Eastern District of New York from 1977 to 1981.

Scheindlin graduated from Cornell Law School in 1975 and clerked for Southern District of New York Judge Charles Brieant, Jr.

Schiltz, Patrick

Patrick J. Schiltz has been a judge on the U.S. District Court for the District of Minnesota since 2006. Schiltz was a professor and associate dean at the University of St. Thomas School of Law from 2000 to 2006. He taught law at the University of Notre Dame Law School from 1995 to 2000 and practiced law from 1987 to 1995.

Schiltz graduated magna cum laude from Harvard Law School in 1985. He clerked for Supreme Court Justice Antonin Scalia, accompanying Scalia from the D.C. Circuit to the U.S. Supreme Court.

Stevens, John Paul

John Paul Stevens was an Associate Justice of the U.S. Supreme Court from 1975 until his retirement in 2010. He was a judge on the Seventh Circuit Court of Appeals from 1970 to 1975. After his admission to the Illinois Bar, he practiced antitrust law. Stevens earned the Bronze Star in the U.S. Navy during World War II.

Stevens graduated from Northwestern University Law School in 1947, with the highest grades in the school's history, and he served as editor-in-chief of the Law Review. He clerked for U.S. Supreme Court Justice Wiley Rutledge.

Sumption, Jonathan, Lord Sumption

Lord Sumption has been a Justice of the U.K. Supreme Court since 2012. He had previously been Judge on the Courts of Appeal of Jersey and Guernsey, and in 1992 he was appointed a Deputy High Court Judge. Sumption became Queen's Counselor in 1986. He was made an Officer of the Order of the British Empire in 2002. He is writing a multivolume work on the Hundred Years' War.

Sumption graduated from Magdalen College, Oxford University in 1970, and was called to the Bar from the Inner Temple in 1975.

Thompson, O. Rogeriee

O. Rogeriee Thompson has been a judge on the U.S. Court of Appeals for the First Circuit since 2010. She was an Associate Justice of the Rhode Island Superior Court from 1997 to 2010 and previously served as judge on the Rhode Island District Court. She was in private practice from 1979 to 1988, with a three-year stint as Assistant City Solicitor for the city of Providence. She served as a staff attorney at Rhode Island Legal Services from 1976 to 1979.

Thompson graduated from Boston University School of Law in 1976.

Traynor, Roger

Roger Traynor served as the Chief Justice of the California Supreme Court from 1964 to 1970 and as an Associate Justice from 1940 to 1964. He became a full-time member of the University of California, Berkeley law school faculty in 1930. During the 1930s, he was a consulting tax expert to the State Board of Equalization and helped draft much of the state's modern tax code. During his time on the bench, he authored more than nine hundred decisions. He is perhaps most renowned for creating the area of law now known as products liability. Some of his many awards include the American Bar Association's highest award for jurisprudence, the Whyte School of Law Medallion, and the ACLU Earl Warren Civil Liberties Award. Traynor died in 1983.

Traynor graduated in 1972 from the University of California, Berkeley, with a PhD in political science and a JD. He was editor-in-chief of the law review.

Wald, Patricia

Patricia Wald was a judge on the U.S. Circuit Court of Appeals for the D.C. Circuit from 1979 to 1999 and served as Chief Judge from 1986 to 1991. Before that, Wald was Assistant Attorney General for Legislative Affairs during the Carter administration. She served on the International Criminal Tribunal at The Hague. Wald now sits on the Privacy and Civil Liberties Oversight Board. She has received more than 20 honorary degrees. Wald was named the 2011 Constitutional Champion by the Constitution Project, and received the ABA Medal in 2008. In 2004, she earned the American Lawyer Hall of Fame Lifetime Achievement Award.

Wald graduated with honors from Yale Law School in 1951, where she was case editor of the Law Journal. She clerked for Second Circuit Judge Jerome Frank.

Wood, Diane

Diane Wood has served on the U.S. Court of Appeals for the Seventh Circuit since 1995. Before that, she was a lawyer in the Department of Justice's Antitrust Division. From 1981 to 1992, she taught at the University of Chicago Law School and served several years as Associate Dean as well. Wood was an attorney at Covington & Burling from 1978 to 1980. She also worked briefly for the U.S. Department of State.

Wood graduated with high honors in 1975 from the University of Texas at Austin Law School, where she served on the Texas Law Review. She clerked for Fifth Circuit Judge Irving Goldberg and for Supreme Court Justice Harry Blackmun.

Practice Pointers

Part 1: Setting the Stage

Teaser Openers: Succinct and Unresolved

- A great *Teaser* opening asks a compelling question and leaves the reader wanting to learn more.
- It works best for disputes that are legal at their core and that hinge on facts that can be easily grasped.
- It pairs well with a simple, natural style, and it demands ruthless editing.
- Start with a sentence that frames a legal issue or broad general principle.
- Follow that opening sentence with a couple of sentences either juxtaposing the parties' arguments or presenting the specific factual context.
- Conclude with a final sentence stating the question that the court must resolve.

Trailer Openers: Detailed and Unresolved

- If the narrative speaks for itself, jump right into the tale, keeping details to a minimum.
- If some context would help the reader absorb the facts, start the introduction with an opening line that tells what the case is about, or what it's not about.
- Edit for tone. The point of a *Trailer* opening is to convey open-mindedness and receptivity to all sides' arguments, so resist the temptation to slant the presentation. Strip the introduction of authorial intrusions, especially adverbs, and consider framing the facts in the losing party's favor.
- And finally, edit for style. Replace long words with short ones, and vary sentence length to keep the narrative flowing.

Sound Bite Openers: Succinct and Resolved

- Start with a sentence that frames the legal issue ("This case is about"). For more color, consider styling the opening sentence as a question.
- Add a pair of sentences that either juxtapose both sides' arguments, or provide necessary factual and legal context to explain the court's decision.
- Conclude with a final sentence announcing your decision.
- Edit for tone, seeking a balanced presentation of the facts. Does the losing party get a fair shake?
- Edit for style, cutting unnecessary qualifiers and heavy connecting words that will slow the reader down.

Op-Ed Openers: Detailed and Resolved

- Lead off with a short memorable opening line.
- Narrate the factual and procedural context.

- Introduce the parties and juxtapose their competing legal positions.
- Conclude with a sentence or paragraph summarizing the result and offering at least one reason in support.

Part 2: The Tale

- Subtract all details—proper names and titles, calendar dates, times, street addresses, quantities and weights—that play no role in the analysis.
- When the parties don't provide enough information, make up the deficiency—within reason. Add well-known facts necessary to establish context, but avoid relying on facts that are unsupported or that are likely to be disputed. If you're wondering which side of the line a source falls on, consider how you'd react if a juror wanted to refer to it during deliberations.
- Emphasize the facts that are the most important to your reasoning. Treating them at length, add detailed descriptions, quote testimony, reproduce images, or otherwise give the reader a picture of the evidence. You can also de-emphasize facts by summarizing them in a sentence, using abstract words and conclusions.
- The court can function as a character in the story who expresses a point of view. The court is a teacher, a guide, a resource to the reader. Don't be afraid to inject some personality into your factual account.
- Formatting devices can help the reader process complex facts. Use headings, subheadings, bullet points, and numbered paragraphs to draw the reader's attention to facts, to facilitate comparisons, and to highlight disputes.

Part 3: The Meat

- Remember these six questions to organize your legal analysis:

  1) What logical questions might occur to a reader who is skeptical of your reasoning, and in what order? Answer those questions one at a time with just a sentence or two apiece.

  2) Why should your answers be trusted? Under each answer, list the applicable authorities, facts, and reasons, and then explain the connection between authority and answer in your own words. Quote and copy sparingly at this juncture.

  3) Is your answer to any question likely to be controversial? If so, acknowledge all viable counterarguments ("To be sure," "Although it is true that," and so forth) and explain why they should not prevail.

  4) What natural or logical divisions would make the analysis easier to navigate? Consider breaking down the overall structure by topic, by party, by motion, by claim, by chronology, or by any other principle that bestows a beginning, middle, and end onto the analysis.

  5) Use traditional outline structure (I, II, III; A, B, C), a modified structure, bullet points, headings, or other visual cues to organize your analysis. If you or your court disfavor these devices and prefer either the uninterrupted-essay approach or the continually numbered-paragraphs approach, break up long paragraphs so that the analysis isn't overwhelming.

  6) Finally, add cues to help the reader navigate at the micro level within the sections. Start with a short "umbrella" paragraph previewing the analysis; add a short "umbrella" paragraph at the start of each section; always present old information before new; add transitions within and between paragraphs to show how your points connect to one another; and end each section with a short conclusion.

Try these techniques on your analyses as well:

- When analogizing, home in on key facts that link the cases while avoiding extraneous facts.
- When distinguishing, avoid getting bogged down; focus on the key points of difference, and omit extraneous facts.
- Whether you are analogizing or distinguishing, favor merged snippets and single-sentence quotations in parentheticals over block quotes regurgitated from the case you're analyzing.
- Use parentheticals for apt single-sentence quotations. Otherwise, use them to explain why a case is on point—or not. Begin with a participial phrase describing exactly what the court did and why. Because parentheticals can be hard to read, make sure that yours follow parallel structure.
- If you must use a block quote, don't just dump the quote and run; use the lead-in sentence to tell the reader what the quote has to say about the point you're making, and why the reader should care. Think of it as introducing a stranger to a friend.
- Don't be afraid of the occasional footnote to discuss arguments and authorities that do not warrant treatment in the text but that might still interest the reader. For example, a footnote can be a great place to acknowledge the history of a law, to distinguish a line of cases, or to incorporate a policy argument.

Part 4: Style Must-Haves

Sentence strategies

- As your default style, strive for natural and direct speech. Avoid the common trap of overwritten, overwrought prose.
- Replace cumbersome sentence openers like *Additionally* and *However* with short conjunctions and short, light phrases.

- Try to write one sentence per page that starts and stops on the same line.
- For variety and reader engagement alike, include the occasional question or rhetorical question.
- Check all series and comparisons for parallel form.

Word Strategies

- Replace the common wordy phrases listed in Part 4 with the suggested lighter or shorter alternatives.
- For key passages, replace abstract or trite verbs with "zinger" verbs. Consult my list of 55.
- Use the occasional pair of dashes to highlight a word or phrase that would otherwise go unnoticed.
- For strong comparisons or contrasts, consider using a semicolon.
- Use the occasional colon as a replacement for causal words and phrases like *because* or *due to the fact that*.
- Broaden the array of transition words and phrases that you use to link your points.
- Consider linking the beginning of a new paragraph with something that the reader remembers from the end of the paragraph before.

Part 5: Style Nice-to-Haves

- Although you can be a great opinion writer without ever using a single metaphor, simile, example, analogy, allusion, or rhetorical device, remember that such devices help tap into your readers' collective experience, help make otherwise abstract points stick, and help make judicial writing more like "writing."

- Metaphors and similes work best when they are unexpected and are infused with physicality. Choose your prism from outside the law.

- Examples and analogies should be styled as narratives or hypotheticals. For the former, consider opening with "Imagine," "Take," or "Suppose." For the latter, consider completing an "It's as if . . ." prompt for a particularly potent point.

- Literary and pop-culture references can add flavor as well, but avoid the overused ones, such as an invocation of Orwell's *1984* or a reference to Dickens's *Bleak House*.

- If you're aiming for the record books, play with the tools of classical rhetoric, especially pure repetition, repetition with a twist in word form, and inversion or *chiasmus*.

Part 6: Dissents

When your objection is mainly factual:

- Does the majority gloss over unhelpful facts? Highlight those facts in detail and explain why they unmoor the majority's legal conclusions.

- Does the majority misconstrue the facts that it does emphasize? Draw sharp contrasts between competing characterizations of the same record.

- Does the majority trot out a real-world analogy that has seductive appeal but that otherwise misses the mark? Dismantle the analogy or offer one that's more apt.

When your objection is mainly legal:

- Call out the majority for ignoring or glossing over a key case or line of cases without justifying the departure from stare decisis.

- Show how the majority is exaggerating the importance of authorities or is glossing over key points of difference.
- Place isolated quotations in their broader context.

When your objection is that the majority is elitist or identifies with entrenched institutions:

- Characterize the majority as being out of touch with the views of the citizenry or of failing to defer to democratically elected institutions.
  - o Show how the majority favors the agenda of the intelligentsia, and note how these views contrast with those of ordinary people as expressed through democratic institutions and representatives.
  - o Show how the majority favors the interests of the wealthy and powerful, and address how the rights of ordinary people would fare under the majority's decision.
  - o Show how the majority appears to take sides in a legitimate cultural dispute that should await democratic resolution.

When your objection is that the majority is overtly populist and favors the will of the majority above all else:

- Show how the majority is pandering to the masses and is thus endorsing unworkable legal or policy principles.
  - o Show how popular sentiment has changed over time, and emphasize the court's obligation to provide stable, predictable rules.
  - o Give examples of when the dominant group has sought to suppress the rights of minority groups, and emphasize the court's obligation to protect the less powerful.

Notes

Introduction

1. Michael Kirby, *On the Writing of Judgments*, 22 Australian Journal of Forensic Scientists 104, 104 (1990).

2. *Id.* http://www.michaelkirby.com.au/images/stories/speeches/1980s/vol21/829-Aus_Conf_on_Literature_and_the_Law_-_On_the_Writing_ of_Judgments.pdf. Kirby note___, *On the Writing of Judgments*, slip at 10–11.

3. Lord Denning, The Family Story 216 (1982).

Part 1

1. Richard Posner, Reflections On Judging 256 (2013).

2. Richard A. Posner, *Judges' Writing Styles (And Do They Matter?)*, 62 U. Chi. L. Rev. 1421, 1430 (1995).

3. Posner, *supra* note 1, at 256.

4. William Domnarski, In the Opinion of the Court 108 (1996).

Part 2

1. I first learned of these passages in an article by Australia's Justice Michael Kirby, who himself cites an article from a legal scholar at McGill University named Dennis Klinck.

2. Richard Posner, Reflections on Judging 251 (2013).

3. *Id.*

4. *Id.* at 260–86.

5. FED. R. EVID. 201(b).

6. Baskin v. Bogan, No. 14-2386, slip op. at 9 (7th Cir, Sept. 4, 2014).

7. Adam Liptak, *Seeking Facts, Justices Settle for What Briefs Tell Them*, N.Y. TIMES, Sept. 1, 2014; Allison Orr Larsen, *The Trouble with Amicus Facts*, 100 VA. L. REV. (December 8, 2014), Vol. 100 (2014); William & Mary Law School Research Paper No. 09-273. http://www.virginialaw-review.org/sites/virginialawreview.org/files/Larsen_Book.pdf.

8. Mitchell v. JCG Industries, No. 13-2115, slip op. at 9–10 (7th Cir. Mar. 18, 2014).

9. Gonzalez-Servin v. Ford Motor Co., 662 F.3d 931 (7th Cir. 2011).

10. JEROME FRANK, LAW AND THE MODERN MIND 134–35 (1930), quoted in Aldisert—opinion writing, 3d edition at 133.

11. Patricia M. Wald, *The Rhetoric of Results and the Results of Rhetoric: Judicial Writings*, 62 U. CHI. L. REV. 1371, 1386 (1995).

Part 3

1. Abner Mikva, *Goodbye to Footnotes*, 56 U. COLO. L. REV. 647 (1985).

2. WILLIAM DOMNARSKI, IN THE OPINION OF THE COURT 63 (1996).

Part 4

1. BENJAMIN CARDOZO, LAW AND LITERATURE 9 (1931).

2. Cameron Harvey, *It All Started With Gunner James*, 1 *Denning L.J.* 67, 68 (1986) (quoting LORD DENNING, THE FAMILY STORY (1981)).

3. Jeffrey Rosen, *Strong Opinions*, NEW REPUBLIC, July 28, 2011, *available at* http://www.newrepublic.com/article/politics/magazine/92773/elena-kagan-writings.

4. RICHARD POSNER, REFLECTIONS ON JUDGING 250, 255 (2013).

Part 5

1. See Todd Henderson, *Citing Fiction*, 11 GREEN BAG 2d 171 (2008).

2. WARD FARNSWORTH, CLASSICAL ENGLISH RHETORIC (2011).

Part 6

1. Ruth Bader Ginsburg, *The Role of Dissenting Opinions*, 95 Minn. L. Rev. 1, 3 (2010).

2. *Id.* at 5, *quoting* Antonin Scalia, *Dissents*, 13 OAH Mag. Hist. 18, 22 (1998).

3. Ginsburg, *supra* note 1, at 7.

Table of Cases

23–34 94th St. Grocery v. N.Y. City Bd., 123–24
A(FC) and others (FC) v. Secretary of State for the Home Department, 178, 186, 190, 200, 258, 299–300
Abrams v. United States, 174–75, 190, 239
Albright v. Oliver, 260
Already v. Nike, 176, 256, 262, 265
Alvarez, United States v., 205, 212, 249–50
American Communications Associate v. Douds, 266
Angiodynamics v. Biolitec, 76
Apple v. Motorola, 68–69
Arizona Christian School Tuition Org. v. Winn, 254, 288–89
Arizona Free Enterprise Club v. Bennett, 165, 253, 282–83
Ash v. Tyson, 54–55, 197
Astrue v. Capato, 33–34, 199
Attorney General's Office v. Osborne, 32–33, 184, 188, 189, 203, 207, 210, 216, 229, 230, 304
Awadallah, United States v., 99–100
Bain Peanut v. Pinson, 238
Baltimore & Ohio R.R. v. Goodman, 51–52
Barnes v. Glen Theatre, 261
Belize Social Development v. Government of Belize, 54, 245
Berkovitz v. Arbib & Houlberg, 267
Beswick v. Beswick, 8
Binette, United States v., 52–53
Blueford v. Arkansas, 9–10

Bowen v. Massachusetts, 128–31
Bradley, United States v., 212
Brent, In re, 35–36, 48, 74–75, 117, 122, 171–72, 194–95, 201, 202, 224, 230
Brigham City v. Stuart, 246
Brown v. Allen, 266
Bush v. Gore, 283–84
Cecaj v. Gonzalez, 12–15, 187, 221, 248
Cheney Bros. v. Doris Silk, 20–21, 134–35, 216
Chicago v. Terminiello, 273
Citizens United v. Federal Elections Commission, 278, 287–88, 291
Clark v. Perez, 137–38
Clifford Davis Management v. WEA Records, 8
Cox v. Ergo Versicherung, 111
Coy v. Iowa, 258–59
Cummings v. Granger, 8, 69–72, 198, 202
Cunningham v. Loma Systems, 214
Defore, People v., 265
Doe v. Elmbrook School Dist., 247
Drennan v. Star Paving Co., 8, 50, 113–14
Dumont, United States v., 181
Dunhill v. Burgin, 5, 182, 193, 202–3, 222
Dutton v. Bognor Regis UDC, 8
Earley, In re, 25–26, 111–12, 177, 198, 200, 211
Edwards v. California, 243
Federal Communications Commission (FCC) v. AT&T, 169
Federal Trade Commission v. QT, 73–74, 215, 251–52, 260
Florida v. Harris, 26–27, 179, 184
Florida v. Jardines, 252
Flowers v. Carville, 9
Frank, Jerome, 60
FTC v. QT, 73–74, 215, 251–52, 260
Garcia v. Bloomberg (Occupy Wall Street), 3–5, 121–22
Gatti v. Nat'l Union Fire Ins., 136–37
Green v. The Queen, 18–19, 61–66, 76, 139, 144, 216
Gutman, United States v., 167
Hamilton v. Southland Christian School, 174, 201
Harrison v. United States, 242
Hinz v. Berry, 8

Hubbard v. EPA, 24–25, 52, 127–28, 221–22
Indiana Harbor Belt R.R. v. American Cyanamid, 133–34
In re. *See Name of party*
JCW Investments v. Novelty, 21–23, 67–68, 205, 248
Johnson v. Phelan, 274
Kartinyeri v. Commonwealth, 302–3
Kloeckner v. Solis, 166
Korematsu v. United States, 244, 286–87
Lamb's Chapel v. Center Moriches Union Free School District, 244–45
Lawrence v. Texas, 296–98
Lazarus Estates v. Beasley, 204
League of United Latin Am. Citizens v. Perry, 208
Ledbetter v. Goodyear Tire & Rubber, 271
Lee v. Weisman, 241
Little Rock School Dist. v. North Little Rock School Dist., 19–20, 56, 116–17, 177, 183
Lloyds Bank v. Bundy, 202
Lochner v. New York, 257, 295–96
McFarland v. American Sugar Refining, 204
Mattel v. MCA Records, 15–16, 55, 131–32, 143, 187–88, 217, 248–49
Mayo v. Lane, 245–46
Messerschmidt v. Millender, 138
Miller v. Alabama, 284–85
Morrison v. Olson, 279
Morris, United States v., 45–47
Morse v. Frederick, 266
National Endowment for Arts v. Finley, 261
National Federation of Independent Business v. Sebelius, 276–77
National Labor Relations Board v. Federbush, 193, 242
New State Ice v. Liebmann, 240
Newton v. Walker, 125–26, 151, 178, 190, 200, 210, 213, 216
New York Magazine v. Metropolitan Transit Authority, 28–29, 109–10, 132–33, 201
New York Times v. Sullivan, 16
New York Trust v. Eisner, 238
Nike v. Already, 206
NLRB v. Federbush, 193, 242
Occupy Wall Street (Garcia v. Bloomberg), 3–5, 121–22
Olmstead v. United States, 212

Palsgraf v. Long Island Rail Road, 44–45
Pantechniki v. Albania, 48–49, 217
Parents Involved in Community Schools v. Seattle, 265
Pennsylvania v. Nathan Dunlap, 263
People v. Defore, 265
Petroleo Brasileiro S.A. v. E.N.E. Kos 1, 194, 232
Pineda-Moreno, United States v., 292–93
Prest v. Petrodel Resources, 119, 178, 183, 214
Rancho Viejo v. Norton, 170
Reed v. Massanari, 25
Ritter v. Ross, 255
Rock Island A. & L. R. v. United States, 238
Roe v. Wade, 58
Romer v. Evans, 212, 217, 274–76
Rumsfeld v. Forum for Academic & Inst. Rights, 168–69
R. v. Keegstra, 144–45
Rylands v. Fletcher, 60
Schenck v. United States, 247
Schmeiser v. Monsanto, 100–101, 110, 217
Schwartz v. Warwick-Phila, 17, 196
Schwimmer, United States v., 191
Scialabba v. Cuellar de Osorio, 166, 262
Scott v. Harris, 108, 113–14, 145–47, 187, 195, 205–6, 214
Seaboyer v. H.M. The Queen, 30–31, 112–13, 176, 186, 200, 208,
    211, 228
Sealed Case, In re, 280–81
Seng Tan, United States v., 120, 172–73, 177, 207, 213, 231
Shelby County v. Holder, 259, 264, 305
Shiraz Hookah v. City of Minneapolis, 118–19, 124–25, 223
Sinclair, In re, 106–7, 142–43, 168, 191, 193, 199, 208, 211
Singletary v. Continental Illinois Nat'l Bank & Trust, 243
Siskina, The, 257
Smith v. United States, 6, 256
Snyder v. Phelps, 83–97, 199
Societe Generale v. Geys, 300–301
Southland Christian School v. Hamilton, 181
Sprint Comm. v. APCC Servs, 262
Steffan v. Perry, 137, 149–50
Stenberg v. Carhart, 215

Sykes v. United States, 148–49
Tarpley v. Allen County, 140
Terminiello v. City of Chicago, 294–95, 303–4
Thomas v. Collins, 267
Thomas v. Consolidated Rail Corp., 7
Thornton v. Shoe Lane Parking, 167, 182, 213, 217
Towne v. Eisner, 238
Trimble, United States v., 34–35
Tucker v. Southwestern Energy, 123, 186, 229
United States v. *See Name of opposing party*
University of Notre Dame v. Sebelius, 49
Vandervell's Trusts (No 2), In re, 42–43
Virginia Office for Protection & Advocacy v. Stewart, 240
Virginia, United States v., 27–28, 152
Watts, United States v., 37–39, 105–6, 150–51
Webster v. Reproductive Health Services, 241
West Virginia State Bd. of Education v. Barnette, 239
Whitney v. California, 191
Woman's Choice-East Side Women's Clinic v. Newman, 279–80
Wurridjal v. Commonwealth of Australia, 198, 301–2
Zorach v. Clauson, 191, 204, 207, 266

.

Index

Aldisert, Ruggero, 60
analogies and examples, 121–26,
        154, 247–55, 268, 293*n*,
        296, 298

background facts, 57–59
Berzon, Marsha
    biography of, 310
    legal analysis, 102–4
    openings, 25, 34–35
Blackmum, Harry, 57–58
Brandeis, Louis
    biography of, 310
    dashes, 212
    metaphors, 240
    parallel constructions, 191–92
    voice, 164
    on writing, 307
bulleted or numbered formats,
        5, 73–77, 82, 114–20, 154,
        325, 326

Cardozo, Benjamin
    biography of, 311
    facts, 44–45
    on opinion writing, xxi

rhetorical devices, 265, 267
    on style, 162
    voice, 164
Carnes, Edward
    biography of, 311
    procedural history, 54–55
    sentences, short, 181
    sentences, short openers, 174
clutter, cutting, 44–57
colons and semicolons, 215–19
conversational/impure style,
        14–15, 163–73
cultural and literary references,
        255–64, 268, 285*n*, 329

dashes and hyphens, 14,
        210–15
dates in opinions, 47–50
Denning, Alfred
    biography of, 311
    colons, 218
    dashes, 213
    evocative verbs, 204
    facts, 43, 69–72
    impure/conversational
        style, 167

Denning, Alfred (*Cont'd.*)
  literary and cultural
    references, 257
  openings, 8, 17
  sentences, short, 180, 181
  on style, 162–63
dissents, xxiv, 269–307
  facts, 271–77, 305–6
  law, 277–89, 306
  openings, 18–19, 31
  policy, anti-elitist, 290–98, 306
  policy, anti-populist,
    298–305, 307
  practice pointers,
    305–7, 329–30
distinguishing authorities,
    127–36, 154
double negatives, 300n

Easterbrook, Frank
  biography of, 312
  dashes, 211, 212
  evocative verbs, 208
  examples and analogies,
    247, 251–52
  facts, 73–74
  impure/conversational
    style, 167–68
  legal analysis, 106–7
  literary and cultural
    references, 260
  parallel constructions,
    191, 193
  quoting, 142–43
  semicolons, 215
  sentences, short, 181
examples and analogies, 121–26,
    154, 247–55, 268, 293n,
    296, 298

facts, xxiii–xxiv, 41–77
  background, 57–59
  cutting clutter, 44–57
  emphasizing key, 59–67
  narrative voice, 67–72
  op-ed openers, 34–36
  practice pointers, 77, 325
  visual appeal, 73–77
footnotes, 147–53, 155
formatting devices, 5

Ginsburg, Ruth Bader
  biography of, 312
  dissents, 270–71, 271,
    276–77, 283–84, 304–5
  footnotes, 152
  literary and cultural
    references, 259
  openings, 27–28, 33–34
  on *Roe v. Wade*, 58
Goldgar, Benjamin
  analogizing authorities, 122
  biography of, 312–13
  dashes, 211
  dates in opinions, 48
  facts, 74–75
  impure/conversational
    style, 171–72
  introductions, 111–12
  numbering, 117
  openings, 25–26, 35–36
  paragraph linking, 230–31
  parallel constructions,
    194–95
  sentences, short openers, 177
  transitions, 224

Hale, Brenda
  biography of, 313

openings, 5
parallel constructions, 193
sentences, short, 182
transitions, 222
Hand, Learned
biography of, 313
distinguishing
authorities, 134–35
on judicial responsibility,
xxi–xxii
metaphors, 242
openings, 20–21
parallel constructions, 193
semicolons, 216
headings and subheadings,
82, 108–11
Hoffman, Leonard, Baron
Hoffman
biography of, 314
dissents, 298–300
literary and cultural
references, 258
parallel constructions, 190
questions, 186
sentences, short
openers, 178
Holmes, Oliver Wendell, Jr
biography of, 314
evocative verbs, 204
examples and analogies, 247
facts, 51–52
literary and cultural
references, 257
metaphors, 237–39
parallel constructions,
190, 191
sentences, short
openers, 174–75
hyphens and dashes, 14, 210–15

impure/conversational style,
14–15, 163–73
introductions, 111–14

Jackson, Robert
biography of, 314–15
dissents, 272–73,
286–87, 303–4
evocative verbs, 204, 207
metaphors, 239
parallel constructions, 192
rhetorical devices, 266, 267
similes, 243–44

Kagan, Elena
biography of, 315
dissents, 281–83, 288–89
examples and analogies, 252–55
impure/conversational
style, 165–67
literary and cultural
references, 262
openings, 26–27
sentences, short, 184
sentences, short openers, 179
Kavanaugh, Brett
biography of, 315
dissents, 280–81
procedural history, 54
similes, 245
Kirby, Michael
biography of, 316
dissents, 301–3
facts, 62–63, 64, 65–66, 76
openings, 18–19
on opinion writing, xxii
parentheticals, 139
quoting, 144
semicolons, 217

Kozinski, Alex
  biography of, 316
  colons, 218
  dashes, 212
  distinguishing
    authorities, 131–32
  evocative verbs, 205
  examples and
    analogies, 248–50
  openings, 9, 15–16
  procedural history, 55
  questions, 187–88
  quoting, 143

legal analysis, xxiv, 79–155
  analogizing authorities,
    121–26, 154
  bulleted and numbered
    lists, 114–20
  distinguishing authorities,
    127–36, 154
  footnotes, 147–53, 155
  headings, 108–11
  introductions, 111–14
  paragraphs as
    dialogues, 97–108
  parentheticals, 136–40,
    154–55
  practice pointers, 153–55,
    326–27
  quoting, 140–47, 155
  six steps to shape, 81–97,
    153–54
literary and cultural references,
  255–64, 268, 285n, 329

McHugh, Michael, 61, 63,
  64, 65, 66
McLachlin, Beverley
  biography of, 110, 316–17

colons, 218
dashes, 211
evocative verbs, 208
introductions, 112–13
legal analysis, 100–101
openings, 30–31
paragraph linking, 228
questions, 186
quoting, 144–45
sentences, short openers, 176
Marshall, D.P., Jr.
  analogizing authorities, 123
  biography of, 317
  hyphens, 214
  numbering, 115–17
  openings, 19–20
  paragraph linking, 229
  procedural history, 56
  questions, 186
  sentences, short, 183, 185
  sentences, short openers, 177
Megarry, Robert, Sir, 42–43
metaphors, 237–42, 268, 329
Mikva, Abner, 147–48
  on footnotes
Musmanno, Michael
  biography of, 317
  openings, 17
  parallel constructions,
    195–96

narrative style and voice, 14,
  17, 67–72
numbered or bulleted formats,
  5, 73–77, 82, 114–20, 154,
  325, 326

op-ed openings, 30–39
openings, xxiii, 1–39
  op-ed, 30–39

practice pointers, 11–12, 23,
  29–30, 39, 323–25
sound bite, 24–30
teaser, 3–12
trailer, 12–23
Opinion Writing (Aldisert), 60
outline structure, 82

paragraphs
  best practices, 97
  as dialogues, 97–108
  introduction, 111–14
  linking, 228–32
parallel constructions,
  188–96, 281*n*
parentheticals, 136–40, 154–55
Paulsson, Jan
  biography of, 318
  colons, 219
  dates in opinions, 48–49
  sentences, short, 180
Point Made (Guberman), xxvi, 124
Ponsor, Michael
  biography of, 318
  facts, 52–53, 76
  footnotes, 150–51
  legal analysis, 105–6
  openings, 7, 37–39
  parentheticals, 136–37
Posner, Richard J.
  biography of, 318–19
  dates in opinions, 49
  dissents, 274
  distinguishing
    authorities, 133–34
  examples and analogies, 248
  facts, 45, 46, 58–59,
    67, 68–69
  impure/conversational
    style, 167

literary and cultural
  references, 260
openings, 3, 12–15
questions, 187
similes, 243, 245–46
transitions, 221
voice, 163–64
practice pointers
  dissents, 305–7, 329–30
  examples and analogies,
    268, 329
  facts, 77, 325
  legal analysis, 153–55,
    326–27
  literary and cultural
    references, 268, 329
  metaphors, 268, 329
  openings, op-ed, 39, 324–25
  openings, sound bite,
    29–30, 324
  openings, teaser, 11–12, 323
  openings, trailer, 23, 324
  rhetorical devices, 268, 329
  sentence strategies,
    233, 327–28
  similes, 268, 329
  word strategies, 233, 328
procedural history, 53–56
pronouns, 31

questions, 185–88
quoting, 140–47, 155

Rakoff, Jed
  analogizing authorities,
    121–22, 123–24
  biography of, 319
  openings, 3–5
rhetorical devices, 264–67,
  268, 329

Roberts, John
  biography of, 319
  dissents, 284–85
  evocative verbs, 203,
      206, 208
  impure/conversational
      style, 168–70
  legal analysis, 84–97
  literary and cultural
      references, 256,
      261–62, 262–63
  metaphors, 240
  openings, 9–11, 31–33
  paragraph linking, 230
  parentheticals, 138
  questions, 188
  rhetorical devices,
      264–65, 266
  on role of judge, 270
  sentences, short, 184
  sentences, short
      openers, 176
  similes, 246

Scalia, Antonin
  biography of, 320
  colons, 219
  dashes, 212
  dissents, 271, 274–76,
      279, 280
  evocative verbs, 206
  footnotes, 148–49
  hyphens, 214–15
  legal analysis, 107–8
  literary and cultural refer-
      ences, 256, 258–59, 261
  metaphors, 241
  numbering, 114–15
  openings, 6

  parallel constructions, 195
  questions, 187
  quoting, 145–46
  similes, 244–45
Scheindlin, Shira
  biography of, 320
  distinguishing
      authorities, 132–33
  headings, 109–10
  legal analysis, 98–100
  openings, 28–29
  parentheticals, 137–38
Schiltz, Patrick
  analogizing
      authorities, 124–26
  biography of, 320
  dashes, 210
  footnotes, 151
  hyphens, 213
  numbering, 118–19
  parallel constructions, 190
  semicolons, 216
  sentences, short openers, 178
  transitions, 223
semicolons and colons, 215–19
sentence-level strategies, xxiv,
      157–59, 163–96
  impure/conversational dic-
      tion, 14–15, 163–73
  parallel constructions,
      188–96, 281n
  pithy sentences, 179–85
  practice pointers, 233,
      327–28
  short sentence
      openers, 174–79
  variety in form, 185–88
similes, 243–46, 268, 329
sound-bite openings, 24–30

Stevens, John Paul
  biography of, 321
  dashes, 210
  dissents, 278, 280, 287–88, 304
  evocative verbs, 207
  paragraph linking, 229
  quoting, 146–47
  semicolons, 216
style, xxiv, 162–63, 235–68
  examples and analogies,
    247–55, 268, 293n,
    296, 298
  impure/conversational,
    14–15, 163–73
  literary and cultural
    references, 255–64, 268,
    285n, 329
  metaphors, 237–42, 268, 329
  narrative, 14, 17
  numbered or bulleted
    formats, 5, 73–77, 82,
    114–20, 154, 325, 326
  practice pointers, 233,
    268, 328–29
  rhetorical devices,
    264–67, 268
  similes, 243–46, 268, 329
  See also sentence-level
    strategies; word-level
    strategies
subheadings and headings,
    82, 108–11
Sumption, Jonathan
  biography of, 110–11, 321
  dissents, 300–301
  hyphens, 214
  numbering, 119
  paragraph linking, 232
  parallel constructions, 194

sentences, short, 183
sentences, short openers, 178

teaser openings, 3–12
Thompson, O. Rogeriee
  biography of, 321
  evocative verbs, 207
  hyphens, 213
  impure/conversational
    style, 172–73
  numbering, 120
  paragraph linking, 231
  sentences, short openers, 177
trailer openings, 12–23
transitions, 219–27
Traynor, Roger
  biography of, 322
  dates in opinions, 50
  introductions, 113–14
  openings, 7–8

verbs, evocative and vivid, 14,
    203–9, 289n
visual appeal, 73–77
voice
  impure/conversational
    diction, 14–15, 163–73
  judges role and, xxii
  narrative, 67–72
  passive, 14

Wald, Patricia
  biography of, 322
  distinguishing authorities,
    127–31
  facts, 45–47, 52, 60
  footnotes, 149–50
  openings, 24–25
  parentheticals, 137
  transitions, 221–22

Wood, Diane
  biography of, 323
  dissents, 279–80
  evocative verbs, 205
  examples and analogies, 248
  facts, 67–68
  literary and cultural
    references, 255
  openings, 21–23
  parentheticals, 139–40
word-level strategies, xxiv,
    157–233, 159–61, 196

colons, 218–19
dashes and hyphens,
  210–15
evocative and vivid verbs, 14,
  203–9, 289n
paragraph linking, 228–32
practice pointers, 233, 328
pronouns, 31
semicolons, 215–17
transitions, 219–27
words and phrases to avoid,
  197–203